PIONEERS AND PERSERVERANCE

A HISTORY OF THE ROYAL SCHOOL FOR THE BLIND, LIVERPOOL (1791-1991)

by

Michael W. Royden

A Bicentennial Celebration

First published in 1991 by Countyvise Ltd in conjunction with The Royal
School for the Blind, Liverpool

© Michael W. Royden
ISBN 0 907768 39 3

Laser-printed by Northern Writers Advisory Services, Sale, Cheshire,
M33 4DN
Printed by Birkenhead Press Ltd, Rock Ferry, Birkenhead, L42 3XS.

CONTENTS

List of Illustrations

THE AUTHOR

Michael Royden was born in Liverpool in 1956. Educated at Wade Deacon Grammar School in Widnes, he spent 12 years in commerce before returning to education at the University of Liverpool. There he gained an Honours Degree in Medieval and Modern History, followed by a Post Graduate Certificate in Education at Liverpool Institute of Higher Education.

He has written several articles on local history, including 'The Roydens of Frankby', 'Halewood by the 19th Century', and contributed to the off-beat guide to Liverpool entitled *Liverpool – The Book* (ed. Bernie Carroll). He is a contributor and co-founder of the Knowsley Libraries publication *'The Eye of the Eagle'* and is also a co-founder of Halewood Local History Society, of which he is Chairman. He lectures on aspects of local history, family history, and aerial archaeology. Currently, he teaches in Adult Education, while researching a Master of Philosophy at the University of Liverpool.

He is married and lives in Mossley Hill, Liverpool.

ACKNOWLEDGEMENTS

I have been fortunate to have been taught History by several eminent local historians; the late Maurice Schofield M.A., and Philip Andrews B.A., formerly of Wade Deacon Grammar School in Widnes; Robin Rowe of Liverpool City College (and Widnes Sixth Form College); Paul Booth M.A. and Jennifer Kermode B.A. of the University of Liverpool; and Dorothy O'Hanlon and Janet Hollinshead of Liverpool Institute of Higher Education. To them I owe a great debt of thanks for both stirring my interest, and steering me (hopefully!) in the right direction. I would also like to thank Dr Christopher Allmand and Dr LLoyd Laing, also of the University of Liverpool, for general help and guidance.

Warm thanks are due to my good friend and fellow History graduate Amanda Smigielski B.A., who read through the draft and offered helpful advice and stern criticism.

I am indebted to Susan George of Liverpool Polytechnic, who read the draft on behalf of the School Management Committee. Her constructive criticism and extreme patience were truly appreciated. Mrs George also played a valuable role regarding publication, as did Mr. Allan Gorst, Honorary Treasurer to the School. I am grateful for their keen efforts.

Tom Milburn, the School Bursar, who also read the draft, must also rate a special mention. Over the past two decades he has carefully and painstakingly ensured the continued survival of the School's unique archive, giving up much of his spare time to sift through the books and documents to afford them his methodical touch. Furthermore, inspired by his own researches, he pursued the idea of a commemorative history, which resulted in my appointment. Since then he has given me full support and has consistently given me the benefit of his knowledge of the general history and administrative organisation of the School. His staff in the Administration Office also deserve my thanks.

Initial recommendation to Mr. Milburn came from my (6th) cousin and namesake Michael J. Royden (distant nepotism) to whom I owe a great debt (five pounds at the last count).

Thanks are also due to Stuart Morgan of Northern Public Relations for help with publicity.

Numerous Members of School Staff have given me their time and full co-operation in the preparation of this book. I would especially like to thank Brian Hechle, Ron Delacruz, Christina Wilkinson, and Danny Peacock. I would also like to thank ex-pupil Gillian Wake for inviting me to her home and for her candid openness.

The Headmaster, Derek Marks O.B.E., always greeted me with the utmost warmth and friendliness whenever I visited the School. He and his wife, Lillian, made me feel quite quite at home and were most tolerant of my persistent prying. (Old Macaulay sends his regards.)

My gratitude is also extended to the President of the School, Mr John C. Smyth, who gave me a detailed insight into the post-war period of the School.

I am grateful to Mark Nelson B.A.(Hons.) of the University of Liverpool who gave me valuable assistance during the initial research and indexing of the School Archive.

No preface in a book covering aspects of Merseyside local history would be complete without an acknowledgement to the inimitable Janet Smith, Archivist of the County Museums, and her staff in the Central Local History Library, Liverpool – and this is no exception. All concerned were always most helpful and I would particularly like to thank them for providing facilities to enable me to photograph numerous documents and illustrations, and to permit their reproduction within these pages.

I would like to thank my parents for their love and support, who have always been there when I've needed them (rather than the other way around).

Finally, most of all I would like to thank my wife Margo, who has supported and encouraged me throughout the preparation of this work. She has acted as a sounding board, secretary, life support system and diplomat. She became a word-processor widow in only our first year of marriage, yet only once threatened that she was going back home to her mother's. I owe to her my deepest debt of love and gratitude, and it is to her that this book is affectionately dedicated.

Michael Royden B.A. (Hons.)
10 January 1991

All photographic reproductions of documents are by the Author.
Thanks to Arthur Black for the drawings.

For Margo, with love

With the year
Seasons return, but not to them returns
Day, or the sweet approach of ev'n or morn,
Or sight of vernal bloom, or summer's rose,
Or flocks, or herds, or human face divine;
But cloud instead, and ever-during dark
Surrounds them, from the cheerful ways of men
Cut off; and, for the book of knowledge fair
Presented with an universal blank
Of nature's works, to them expung'd and ras'd
And wisdom at one entrance quite shut out.

Milton
Paradise Lost, Book III

Edward Rushton (1756-1814). Co-founder of the Liverpool School for the Indigent Blind (Elsam, Mann and Cooper).

HIS

Royal Highness

THE

PRINCE OF WALES

VISITED THE

SCHOOL FOR THE BLIND,

ON THE

18TH OF SEPTEMBER, 1806,

WHEN

HE WAS GRACIOUSLY PLEASED TO BECOME THE

PATRON

OF IT,

AND TO PRESENT A DONATION OF

100 GUINEAS.

1
ENLIGHTENMENT AND REVOLUTION

"It was the best of times,it was the worst of times,
it was the age of wisdom, it was the age of foolishness"
(Dickens – *A Tale of Two Cities*)

Liverpool, by the end of the eighteenth century had become a port of international renown, built largely on the profits of the slave trade and ranked after London as Britain's second port. A hundred years earlier the town's position had been rather different. The port of Liverpool at this time was only just rising to greater prominence than ever before and the new age was marked by the completion of the first wet dock in the modern world in 1715. This had effectively removed one of the most notable medieval landmarks in the area – the Pool of Liverpool – and set the impetus for spirited enterprise in a fast growing mercantile area. The building of more docks soon followed, and, together with the buoying of the channel approaches, new roads to Prescot and Warrington, and the first canal in England, (the Sankey Canal, which linked the Mersey to the coalfields of St. Helens), Liverpool was elevated to its new status.

In the town, Church Street and Ranelagh Street were now well built up. Fine houses stood in both Duke Street and Hanover Street, and Mount Pleasant was lined with houses with large gardens. To the north, building had extended as far as the new canal basin, with a much larger mass of housing in the south. However, overcrowding was already becoming a problem. The 1700 population of 5,000 had increased to 25,000 by 1760.

Part of the increase was due to the rise of new industries. Ship building yards lined the north and south shore, rope yards were numerous, as too were the windmills. The watchmaking industry was enjoying a good reputation, while the local potteries were still at their height. (One of the main pottery making areas was Shaws Brow, later renamed William Brown Street.) Communications had been improved to the salt fields of Cheshire, enabling refineries to be situated nearer the coalfields, and of course, to the port of Liverpool, thereby providing further employment for the local inhabitants.

The overriding factor affecting the increase in population was the growth in world wide trade. In 1700 there were around 70 port owned vessels employing about 800 seamen. By 1751 these figures had increased to 220 vessels and 3,319 seamen.[1] Trade was quite diverse in character. The bulk of the Irish trade now moved through Liverpool, due initially to the silting up of the Dee, (although packet boats still sailed to Ireland from Parkgate), and now that Scotland and Wales were also commercially dependant on Liverpool, the town was established as Britain's central port. Liverpool was even beginning to compete with Hull for the Baltic trade.

It was trade with the New World, which brought most prosperity to the expanding port, although trade with the Americas was still fairly small. For Liverpool, the West Indies were far more important. Not only did they supply the main staples of Liverpool trade (sugar, tobacco and cotton), but they were the centre of the lucrative smuggling trade with Spanish Central and South America. At the beginning of the eighteenth century, Bristol had the greatest share of this traffic, but by the mid century Liverpool was well to the fore, bringing in an annual profit of around £250,000.[2] Growing industrialization in Manchester played a significant role too, providing merchants with commodities which were much in demand in Africa, such as coarse woollens and cottons, thus giving the mills greater commercial incentives.

After the 1747 Act of Parliament forbidding foreign vessels to frequent British West Indian ports, large scale smuggling by the Spanish in Jamaican ports was effectively curtailed. The Act inevitably drove traders to seek profitable alternatives, with many Liverpool merchants following the lead of their Bristol counterparts into the slave trade.[3] The sugar and tobacco plantations of the West Indies had for years been worked by the labour of Negro slaves, and by the second half of the century the constant demands of the West Indian owners were met by Liverpool vessels and merchants more than any other.

The last quarter of the eighteenth century, however, saw a remarkable change in public opinion in England with regard to the slave trade. The roots of this could be found in the development of "enlightenment thought" and an increasing awareness of the new concepts concerning the "rights of man".

Enlightenment thought drew its strength and development from a cumulation of a number of interlinking factors; growth in human knowledge, civilisation and rationality; man's increasing control over nature; the progress of trade, production and wealth. It had its foundation essentially in England, John Locke being an early exponent, and sought its illumination from the light of reason; authority and tradition being pushed aside or completely discarded. Individual judgement was to be given full freedom and any theory constructed beyond ordinary experience rejected. Scientific evidence and discovery was given greatest credence over natural superstitions. Great weight to this development in philosophical thought was given by the French "Encyclopedists", such as Diderot, Voltaire, Rousseau and Montesquieu. They foresaw a state of society free from clerical influence, ruled by universal charity, equal rights for all, free from the irrationality which divided men into a hierarchy of higher and lower ranks according to birth or some other irrelevant criterion. Their ultimate goal, however, was self realisation. (Although enlightenment doctrines had very strong roots in England, greater attention is generally focused on France due to the later developments and effects on the Revolution.) The leading exponents were the progressive classes – the mercantile circles, financiers, manufacturers, entrepreneurs and the educated middle class. In England, numerous provincial societies were formed, from which advances came in scientific, industrial and political arenas. The Lunar Society in Birmingham for example, included Josiah Wedgewood the potter, James Watt,inventor of the modern steam engine, and biologist Erasmus Darwin (grandfather of Charles).

Enlightenment was a revolutionary ideology, although until the 1780s much of it was still politically moderate, supporting absolute monarchy – which many thinkers believed rather naively would enlighten itself.

Attitudes towards human affliction began to change in the eighteenth century and this too was mainly due to the development in philosophical thought and progress in medical science. Many afflictions – especially blindness – had for centuries been believed to be the result of divine judgement and punishment of sin – an attitude which appears to have its roots in the ancient East, although in some Eastern countries the blind are believed to be sacred.[4]

It is clear, however, that little relief was provided for the blind, leaving them to fend for themselves, which frequently meant begging in the street.

By the fourth century A.D., Saint Basil is recorded as having established a "hospital" for the blind at Cappadocia which also included the provision of guides,[5] and in seventh century France Saint Bertrand, Bishop of Le Mans, founded an institution for the blind believed to have been sited at Pontlieu in the north west.[6] Legend also suggests that the saintly King Louis IX patronised the L'Hôpital des Quinze-Vingts, an institution built to house his 300 crusaders, who chose to have their eyes put out by the Saracens rather than swear never to bear arms again against the Infidel – although this has been refuted by the researches of Abbé Prompsault. He argues that the institution did exist, although its origin remains a mystery, and that Louis IX merely bought back the plot of land in Paris on which it was built, proved by letters patent of June 1260. King Louis then rebuilt the domicile for the blind and increased the number of pensioners to 300 and gave them an allowance of £30 a year from his privy purse, on condition that this sum was used for making soup for the poor. Begging, however, was encouraged, to help support the home.[7]

In 1329 in London, an asylum was founded by William Elsing, a London mercer. It was known as "Elsing Spittle" or "Spital" and stood near London's Wall, providing shelter for 100 blind men. It was believed to have been confiscated during the Reformation on the grounds that all hospitals erected during the Middle Ages were religious foundations.[8]

For the next 300 years, relief for the blind continued to be sparse, most help coming from monks until the destruction of the monasteries, although in 1601 the Poor Law Act of Queen Elizabeth I made specific provision for relief to be given to the destitute blind, this being the first statute enacting relief on national lines.

There were, nevertheless, attempts to devise a system of raised print to enable the blind to read. The first recorded effort was that of Francisco Lucas of Saragossa in Spain, c.1517, who contrived a set of letters carved on thin tablets of wood.[9]

By the eighteenth century, there was a marked increase in private trust funds and annuities for blind people, the majority of which were set up as a result of bequests in wills. Dorothy Wilson's Charity, founded in 1717 by a bequest for blind persons resident in the city or suburbs of York, was an example of this type of fund.

Yet such charitable acts were very few and far between; the great majority of blind people still being rejected by society and reduced to a life of vagrancy and begging. When they were given work, it was menial. Young blind children were often sold to chimney sweeps to be sent up blocked flues like human brushes. Many adults resorted to travelling with circuses as subjects of ridicule and sick entertainment, amusing customers by fighting in the ring as blind gladiators, for example. Such an incident is known to have taken place a little earlier, in fifteenth century France.

> "In the month of August 1425 under the reign of Charles VII, four blind men, cased in full armour and provided with clubs, were placed in a fenced square of the Hotel d'Arragnac with a large hog, which was to be the prize of whoever should kill it. The struggle having begun, the poor sightless creatures, in endeavouring to hit the animal, struck each other with such violence that but for their armour, they would certainly have killed each other."[10]

Despite the eighteenth century developments already hinted at, little had changed in the public attitude. In September 1771, at the Foire St. Ovide, a traditional fair in Paris, among the sideshows of curiosity and entertainment were a dozen blind men and youths dressed as idiots in silly gowns with frills, dunces, caps on their heads and cut out cardboard spectacles on their noses. There they were paraded as mock musicians, scraping on violins, cellos, and double basses, clearly without skill, producing total distortion to the delight of the abusive audience.[11] A witness to this was Valentin Haüy, an interpreter in the Ministry of Foreign Affairs, who was so moved by the sad sight that he later devoted his attention to the founding of the first school in the world for young blind children.

Later seventeenth and early eighteenth century literature regarding the blind was a mixture of concern for welfare and a search for scientific answers regarding their plight. An early work which called attention to the condition and miseries of the blind was published in Italy in 1646 in the form of a letter to Vincent Armanni, entitled *'Il cieco afflitto e consolato'* (Comfort for the Afflicted Blindman).[12]

In 1689, Locke's *'Essay on Human Understanding'* appeared, which included a discussion on a problem proposed by Molyneux (an academic and member of the Irish Parliament): "if a person blind from birth was suddenly restored to sight, would he be able to distinguish by his eyes alone a globe from a cube, the difference between which he had previously recognised by touch?" Both men determined he would not.

Other scientific works followed. In 1703, Leibniz also concerned himself with the same subject as Locke, and in 1709, Dr. Berkeley, Bishop of Cloine and idealist philosopher, published his *'Theory of Vision'*.

In 1728, Mr Cheselden contributed to Volume 402 of the *'Philosophical Transactions'* a report entitled "an Account of some observations made by a young gentleman who was born blind, or lost his sight so early that he had no remembrance of ever having seen and was couched between 13 and 14 years of age". Cheselden was a celebrated anatomist and had successfully couched for cataracts and restored perfect sight to the young boy. At first the boy was not able to recognise by vision the objects which were most familiar to his touch. It was, in fact, some time before he could discriminate between his long time companions, the family dog and cat. He was observed one day to pass his hand carefully over the cat and then on looking at her steadfastly, said, "So puss, I shall know you another time."[13]

During these early years of the eighteenth century, Nicholas Saunderson was making a name for himself at Cambridge University. Blind from infancy, he made such advances in higher departments of science that he was appointed Lucasian Professor of Mathematics (on the recommendation of the previous occupant of the chair, Sir Isaac Newton). Saunderson was well known for his theories on optics and solar refraction and had gained wide admiration and respect for his work before his death in 1739. Furthermore, he had devoted a great deal of his time to the development of a board, completed by 1720, on which he could work out problems of mathematics and algebra solely by touch.

> "...his fingers ran over his table with surprising despatch; entering the longest calculations, breaking off, and perceiving when he was out, that he easily proved them, and so convenient was the arrangement of the table that his operation did not take him up anything of the time which we should conceive."[14]

Despite the new methods of enquiry promoted by English thinkers, the first true philosophical contribution which attempted to analyse the intellectual and moral condition of the blind came in 1749 from France, in the form of Diderot's *'Lettre sur les Aveugles, à l'usage de ceux qui voient'* ('Letter on the blind, for the use of those who see') which was essentially materialistic and anti-Christian in content.[15] On the look out for philosophical sensations, Diderot had travelled to Puiseaux to visit a blind man by the name of Lenôtre, who had attracted universal attention in almost

6

everything that he did. He was the son of a professor of philosophy in the University of Paris, and had studied chemistry and botany at the Jardin du Roi. In Puiseaux he established a distillery, the products of which he took to Paris once a year to sell. He was accustomed to sleeping during the day and working by night, because at midnight, according to Diderot,

> "...he was free from disturbance himself, and was not troublesome to others. His first care was to put in its place everything that had been displaced during the day; his wife at her getting up, commonly found the house set in rights..."[16]

This Diderot noted was a common attitude towards order and regularity amongst blind persons.

Lenôtre had earned a reputation for his unusual lifestyle and domesticity free from poverty. On the day of his visit, Diderot found him teaching his sighted son to read with the help of raised characters. Lenôtre asked Diderot "an abundance of strange questions".

> "Whether none but those called naturalists saw with a microscope?; and whether astronomers alone saw with a telescope?; whether the machine which magnifies objects be larger than that which lessens them?; whether that which brings them nearer was shorter than that which removes them farther off?..."[17]

He gave unusual answers too.

> "'And what do you take eyes to be?" said Diderot. "They are," says the blind man, "an organ on which the air has the effect which my stick has on my hand."[18]

Diderot continued his report.

> "...one of our company asked the blind man whether he should not be very glad to have eyes? "Were it not for curiosity," said he, "I would full as have long arms. My hands I think, would inform me better of what is doing in the moon, than your eyes or your telescopes. Besides, the eyes sooner cease to see than the hands to touch; that to improve the organ which I have would be as good to give me that which is wanting in me."[19]

His interview with Lenôtre of Puiseaux, together with his account of Saunderson's theories and algebra board, embraced a large part of his Essay. It was received with much enthusiasm in Paris, and marked a significant place in not only the history of literature regarding the blind, but in French philosophy also.

Diderot was also quick to deliver a deserved rebuke to the sluggish indifference of English thinkers who were slow to further their enquiries

A N

E S S A Y

ON

B L I N D N E S S,

In a L E T T E R to a

PERSON OF DISTINCTION;

Reciting the most interesting Particulars relative to
Persons born Blind, and those who have lost their
Sight.

Being an Enquiry into the Nature of their Ideas,
Knowledge of Sounds, Opinions concerning Mor-
ality and Religion, &c.

Interspersed with several Anecdotes of

SANDERSON, MILTON,

A N D O T H E R S.

With Copper-Plates elucidating Dr. SANDERSON's
Method of Working

GEOMETRICAL PROBLEMS.

The THIRD EDITION.

Translated from the French of

M. D I D E R O T,

Physician to His most Christian Majesty,

L O N D O N:

Printed for J. BARKER, No. 7, Little Russell-
Court, Drury-Lane.

(Price 1s. 6d.)

Where may be had that justly admired Poem by Prior,
called HENRY and EMMA;
with a new Frontispiece, price 6d.

The page from Diderot's 'Essay on Blindness' (1749) (translated 1770).

8

into the human condition. His own methods certainly had their roots in England, most notably with Locke, yet Diderot argued, "England is the country of philosophers, virtuosi, and system makers, yet had it not been for Mr. Inchclif[20] we should have known no more of the celebrated Saunderson than what any common man could have told us, as that he knew again such places where he had once been, by the noise which the walls and floor reflected, amongst a hundred other such things all equally common to blind persons." He added, rather sarcastically, "Are Saundersons then so very common in England? Does every town there produce persons, who, without having their sight, read lectures on optics? We are curious of seeing sight given to those who were born blind; but on further consideration, philosophy, I believe, would be found rather a greater gainer by questioning a blind man."[21]

For his trouble, Diderot's well known unorthodox doctrines landed him in the Bastille, where 29 days of his imprisonment were spent in solitary confinement without books or light, a punishment compounded by the fact that he refused to give up the name of his printer. His sentence was, however, cut short, as his services were required in the compilation of the forthcoming Encyclopedia.

In 1763, Dr. Thomas Reid produced his essay entitled 'An Inquiry into the Human Mind', in which he suggested that the blind, if properly instructed, were capable of forming ideas and beliefs about light and colour, except the sensations of light and colour themselves. The object of the work was to refute the opinions previously expressed by Locke regarding the connection he believed to exist between the power and operation of the mind and human knowledge, based on a system of instinctive principles, of which sight was regarded as a necessary instrument. He cited Saunderson's scientific achievements and furthermore, the poetry of a Dr. Blacklock as examples of attainment and "observation" without the benefit of sight.

Thomas Blacklock, blind since only five months old, was born of poor parents in Annan, Dumfrieshire in 1721. Nevertheless, he became a poet, scholar, Doctor of Divinity and a minister of the Scottish Church.[22] (Concerned about the plight of the blind, he drew attention to their situation in an article entry in the Encyclopedia Britannica of 1783.) He had often wished to erect a school to educate children with similar handicaps to his own and this idea became more feasible – and inspired – after he translated into English Valentin Haüy's '*An Essay on the Education of the Blind*' written in 1786. Blacklock, now living in Edinburgh, probably also had access to an article which had appeared a few years earlier in the *Edinburgh Magazine and Review* of September 1774, entitled 'A Letter on the Education of the Blind', by one 'Demodocus'. The introduction stated

> "The following letter...was written at the desire of a gentleman whose curiosity was eagerly turned towards that subject. It was conceived to be satisfactory and valuable; and it is now laid before the Public, from a strong persuasion that it may be of very general advantage."

Blacklock, dutifully inspired, enlisted the help of David Miller as an instructor, who had been blind from birth, but sadly, Thomas Blacklock died in 1791 before his dream could be realised. Miller, however, secured the assistance of Dr. David Johnson, a Leith minister, and through their combined efforts enough money was raised under the banner of the "Society for the Relief of the Indigent Blind", to establish an asylum in Edinburgh, which opened in 1793 with nine pupils. It took the name "Asylum for the Industrious Blind", and as the name suggests, it consisted only of workshops devoted to industrial training, therefore losing the original aims of its founder.[23]

Nevertheless, England and Scotland were moving into industrial times and the belief that it was Christian and moral that the blind should be able to participate in and contribute to that society was becoming more widespread.

It was an achievement to set up an institution for the destitute blind, but to educate them too was still very radical. Free and universal State education proposed by men such as Adam Smith and Thomas Paine was regarded as quite extreme, especially in the aftermath of the French Revolution, although others argued that a State system of education would check the growth of free opinion and perpetuate dogma and tradition. Radical Enlightenment philosophy was not so easy to put into practice.[24]

Meanwhile, a progressive institution had been established in Paris only a few years earlier. Shortly after witnessing the circus spectacle at the Foire St. Ovide, Valentin Haüy came across a small boy begging on the steps of his church at St. Roch, one Sunday after the service. Realising he was blind, and recalling the memory of the poor "musicians", he stood for a moment and watched the urchin with pity. This quickly turned to amazement as he watched the boy run his fingers over the serrations and relief on the coins, obviously trying to deduce their value. Haüy discovered that the young blind boy, whose name was François LeSueur, would, "...at the least acquisition, fly with eagerness to the bosom of his unhappy family, to divide the fruit of his solicitations with the authors of his being, and with his three sisters and two brothers, whereof the last is still on the breast..."[25]

Valentin added to his essay later that, "...it was in the midst of this hard life, as little calculated to inspire as to favour a taste for the sciences, that our first pupil began his education."[26]

Haüy had realised that the blind boy had developed an intelligence by touch – surely there were further possibilities for learning and achievement?

He offered to pay the boy the same amount that he would make in his present situation in exchange for shelter and education. After much persistence and hard work on both parts, the measure of success they achieved prompted Haüy to expand his ideas into the founding of an establishment to give many more children the type of education given to François LeSueur. With the help of his brother, Abbé Haüy (a respected cleric and scientist who founded the study of crystallography) and his wealthy connections, Valentin was able to set up the first school in the world for young blind children, in a house on the Rue Nôtre-Dame des Victoires.

He decided to gather as much information as he could regarding the blind condition and its treatment in the past.

"We had need of encouragement, we confess. Mademoiselle Paradis arrived in this metropolis. She showed us her attempts, and those of M. Weissemburg. We collected those of the blind who lived before our time; we put into execution several of their proceedings; to these we joined the results of our own, and we formed a general plan of the Institution"[27]

Weissemburg, a German, had been blind since the age of seven. He had taught himself to trace signs in relief, such as the maps he had made, with glazed sand for mountains and graded beads for different sized towns. By similar techniques he instructed Maria Theresa von Paradis, a young

Valentin Haüy, founder the National Institution for the Young Blind, Paris, 1785.

Revd. William Shepherd, abolitionist, friend and biographer of Rushton (drawing by J. Dickson).

William Rathbone IV (1757-1809), President of the School 1800.

Edward Rushton.

blind girl from Vienna, who had lost her sight at the age of two. Her parents, being wealthy aristocrats of high rank, spared no expense to give her the best education available for such special needs. With the help of Baron von Kempelen who had devised a mechanical chess player, Weissemburg taught Maria to spell with letters cut out of pasteboard, and to read words pricked upon cards with pins. Baron von Kempelen also made her a press, by which she could print her sentences in ink enabling her to correspond with her teachers and friends. Under the care of Hozeluch she studied piano and organ and became a very accomplished pianist. Her performances at the palace (her godmother being the Empress Maria Theresa, who gave her an annual pension of 200 florins) and in the aristocratic circles of Vienna were received with acclaim. Accompanied by her mother, she then made a grand professional tour through the capitals of Europe with further successes in high society. By 1784 she had reached Paris where she gave brilliant concerts which were witnessed with great enthusiasm by Valentin Haüy, who immediately sought her acquaintance.

Using the information she gave him regarding her own education and the apparatus she had used, together with those works he had collected of earlier writers (most notably Diderot), Haüy began to lay the foundation for a complete system of education for blind children.

His work soon came to the notice of various institutions.

"They demanded of us to see the result of our proceedings; we seized the favourable circumstance of an Academic Assembly, where we were appointed to read a memorial. We took for its subject certain reflections on the education of the blind."[28]

Lesueur was then invited to "perform his exercises in their presence" whereupon he gained their support and benevolence.

The Philanthropic Society who had already begun to try to alleviate suffering among the blind poor, were keen to deliver 12 of their children to the care of Haüy with the assistance of 12 livres per month for each child for a trial period.

Satisfied with the trial, the children were subsequently entrusted, the number now being 14. This was to be the crucial boost of support needed to found the "L'Institution Nationale des Jeunes Aveungles" (National Institution for the Young Blind') in 1785.

Other academic bodies took interest; the Academy of Sciences examined the children and their progress, drawing up reports for wider consultation, and in February of 1786 the Royal Academy of Music performed a concert for the benefit of the school.

"In short,the Lyceum, the Museum, and the Hall of Correspondence disputed among themselves with emulation, the agreeable satisfaction of seeing, in the midst of their academical meetings, young blind children lisp out the first elements of reading, of calculation etc., and in the scenes of learned emulation, where Genius alone had till then found encouragement, beneficence has, for the first time, been seen decreeing a crown."[29]

Into this atmosphere, Haüy finally published his new plan for blind instruction; his *'Essay on the Education of Blind Children'*. Blacklock, in his Encyclopedia article noted (after a lengthy résumé of previous eighteenth century educational theory).

"...a work has lately been published in Paris which supersedes every former attempt to promote or facilitate the improvement of the blind. The invention of a plan so arduous in its appearance and so practicable in its execution, demanded the highest exertions of the noblest genius to produce it and the most strenuous efforts of indefatigable humanity to render it effectual...its object is to teach them by palpable characters impressed on paper, not only the liberal arts and sciences, but likewise the principles of mechanical operation, in such a manner that those who have no genius for literary improvement may yet become respectable, useful, and independent members of society, in the capacity of common artisans. By these tangible signatures they are taught to read, to write, and to print; they are likewise instructed in geometry, in algebra, geography, and, in short, in every branch of natural philosophy... They have been taught to read music with their fingers as others do with their eyes; and though they cannot at once feel the notes and perform them upon an instrument, yet they are capable of acquiring any lesson with as much exactness and rapidity as those who enjoy all the advantages of light." [30]

To press home Haüy's radical methods, the original editions of his paper were printed and bound by his own pupils using the techniques detailed within it. Furthermore, the reviewer stated, "They exhibit at their own academy, every Wednesday and Saturday between one and two o'clock at noon, to crowds of charitable admirers, by whose liberal donations the institution is now chiefly supported."[31]

Valentin Haüy's publication carried with it a dedication to the Monarch, Louis XVI, who invited him to the palace of Versailles during Christmas 1786. He was to bring with him the children of whom he had heard so much, so that he and his wife, Marie Antoinette, could see their skills for themselves. The Palace hospitality extended to eight days from 26 December, during which time the children left a lasting impression upon their Royal hosts. The Queen, in particular, took great delight in testing whether the children actually read their poetry by touch or from memory. The King, for his part, made Valentin Royal Interpreter, Professor of Ancient Inscriptions, Secretary to the King and conferred the Royal title on the Institution. In addition he promised help, which sadly failed to materialise.

By 1787, the *Ancien Régime* had become politically and economically bankrupt. The system established by Louis XIV a century earlier was now inefficient; political authority was exercised by a small group of privileged nobility; the peasantry, as a result of entrenched feudal traditions in land tenure, outdated agricultural methods and uncontrolled inflation, was in a wide state of poverty. Long wars had led to a massive debt, and attempts by ministers such as Calonne and Necker to reform the system provoked strong resistance from the nobility, who persuaded Louis XVI to summon the States General in the belief that they could dominate it and therefore safeguard their rights. The "Third Estate" with its predominant middle class land owners and merchants, influenced too by the ideas of the eighteenth century political philosophers (such as Rousseau and Montesquieu) and the recent American Independence, had no intention of giving up rights to the aristocracy. They declared the States General to be a "National Assembly", and the wheels of the Revolution gathered pace.

"Liberty", however, was not exactly the word Haüy and his pupils would give to their situation during the early years of French revolutionary turmoil. In the atmosphere of the "Great Fever", mob rule and executions, compassion for a small school of blind children was going to be in short supply, especially with their newly acquired Royal title. By 1791, the support for the School from the public and the various institutions had dried up and it collapsed. The children were swiftly removed to an asylum for the deaf and dumb where little tuition was given. A decade later they were condemned by the First Consul – Napoleon Bonaparte – to incarceration in the horrific Quinze-Vingts workhouse.

Valentin Haüy continued to live in France until 1806 when it became apparent that life there was becoming too dangerous for those who were sympathetic to the *Ancien Regime* and who saw Napoleon as a usurper. Napoleon's enemies were being sought out by his murderous band of thugs, the *'Sans Culottes'*, whose victims frequently came from the wealthy ranks, writers, priests and officials of the Church. Haüy's brother,

Abbé René-Just, had been imprisoned, and, in fear of similar treatment, Valentin fled to Prussia, taking with him one of his former pupils, Remi Fournier, who had been in the Quinze-Vingts workhouse.

Knowledge of Valentin's past work had already reached Prussia, to a Doctor Zeune, an advisor to King Frederick. Valentin was summoned to Court and was persuaded to stay in Berlin to establish the first German school for blind children in conjunction with Doctor Zeune.

He stayed there until the end of the year when the advancing army of Napoleon and the crushing Prussian defeat at Jena meant it was time to move on again. Russia was their next destination where they initially stopped overnight at Mittau. By coincidence, the exiled Comte de Provence, who was to be the future Louis XVIII of France, was also staying overnight. Together they talked of the events in Paris, as well as the fate of Haüy's Institution. As a result of this meeting, news reached Czar Alexander about Haüy's presence in Russia and he was again summoned to Court, this time at St. Petersburg, where he was requested to establish a school for blind children, which was to be the first in Russia. Sadly, it was to be another ten years before Valentin Haüy could return home, to a France now ruled by Louis XVIII in place of the deposed Napoleon.

A new school had been set up in Paris, in a house on Rue-St. Victor, which was coincidentally the same building in which Valentin's brother had been imprisoned in 1806. However, Valentin who was now in his 70s, was not invited to run the new school, nor even allowed inside it for that matter. The directorship had been handed over to Doctor Sebastian Guillié, a determined man with ideas of his own.

Valentin Haüy died in 1822, but not before a ten year old boy was admitted to the Institute that he had founded, and where the boy was to spend the rest of his life. The year was 1817, and his name was Louis Braille.

In Liverpool, institutions founded on private charity had an auspicious inauguration in the form of the Bluecoat School (an excellent example of Queen Anne architecture which still stands today in School Lane, and is a Grade One listed building). Established by Bryan Blundell, it was begun in 1708 and completed ten years later. Blundell had been master and

a. The Poor House 1732.

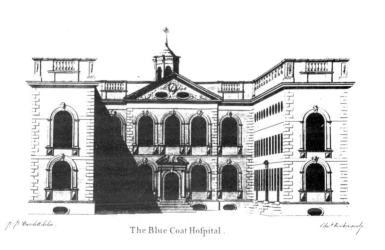

The Blue Coat Hofpital.

B. Bluecoat School and Hospital.

The North Front of the Poor House.

c. Poor House, Brownlow Hill.

The North Front of the Sailors Hospital.

d. Sailor's Hospital.

owner of a vessel employed in transporting paupers, seeking a better life, to the New World. So moved was he by their condition that he resolved to give up his life at sea and devote his time to the running of a new school. (Paradoxically, part of his maritime career was an involvement in the slave trade.)

No such establishment existed for blind children, however, and like most other paupers, they had to rely on handouts from the Overseers of the Poor or resort to begging. At the end of the seventeenth century, the maximum relief allowed to adults was 48 weeks, the amount varying between 6d to 1s a week. In the 1682 Vestry Books for Liverpool Parish Church an entry reads

"lodging for the blind woman ...2s 6d."[32]

Those claiming relief also had the added indignity of having to wear a pewter badge with the town's Arms engraved upon it, or else be denied poor relief.

By 1732, such was the level of tax levied to fund the Poor Relief coffers that it was decided to build a new workhouse to alleviate the burden from the taxpayer and the now hopelessly inadequate original workhouse in Pool Lane, South Castle Street.

The new workhouse was situated behind the Bluecoat School and was in use for 40 years. However, its opening also marked the day that "outdoor" poor relief was to be withheld and only relief to inmates would be granted.

This attempt to cut the poor rate was short lived as the new workhouse became too small to cope with the increasing population. A third and much larger workhouse was completed on Brownlow Hill in 1772. The workhouse also had to cope with the sick and diseased until the 1740s when the council granted a site for an infirmary. It was completed in 1748 and the first patients were admitted in 1749. Again supported by charity, it was an imposing building, with a large courtyard and extensive rear garden. Alongside in 1752, was erected the Seamen's Hospital, for seamen and their families. Every mariner of the port had paid a compulsory contribution of 6d a month towards its support. (Both buildings stood on the site now occupied by St. Georges Hall.)

In 1778 a dispensary was established in North John Street which provided medical advice and medicine to the poor, and was again supported by voluntary subscriptions.

Yet, despite such positive steps made in a Port increasingly influenced by its diverse cultural influx, it was, by the end of the eighteenth century, a town of much pauperism, appalling housing conditions and frequent violence.

In 1792 Erskine, on looking down upon Liverpool for the first time from a local vantage point, had exclaimed that the Port was "...fit to be a proud capital for any empire in the world..." and had "...started up like an enchanted palace, even in the memory of living men."[33] Although rather rhetorical, it was a fair comment regarding the mercantile nature of Liverpool, but the town certainly could not be held up as a model in most other aspects of civilisation. Only a small minority of men had benefited from the great wealth of the port, the majority eking out an existence in sordid conditions and miserable degradation. An American loyalist exile, Samuel Curwen, on visiting Liverpool in 1780 wrote that

"...the streets were long, narrow, crooked and dirty...We scarcely saw a well dressed person...The whole complexion of the place was nautical and so infinitely below all our expectations that nought but the thoughts of the few hours we had to pass here rendered it tolerable..."[34]

In 1795 it was calculated that every seventh house was open for the sale of liquor, supplied by the 37 large breweries of the locality, and rum was imported in large quantities from the West Indies.[35] The streets were frequently scenes of drunkenness, fighting, riots and press-gangs. Local politics were constantly anarchical and corrupt. However, the town's administration of the Poor Law was regarded as being more effective than in any other area of England.

Moves to widen the streets began in 1785 when the Improvement Act for Liverpool resulted in spacious transformations to Castle Street, Dale Street and Water Street, although further opportunity to continue such fine moves was wasted.

A religious revival began in the years after 1780 and saw a period of church building of all denominations. An increase in charitable organisations was a direct result of this, a notable manifestation being the institution of schools for the poor. By 1784, a scheme for the establishment of Sunday Schools was started where children were taught to read and write. This scheme was later modified and carried out on a large scale, forming a basis for popular education in Liverpool.

Although culturally and artistically, Liverpool was still what Ramsay Muir termed a "Philistine town",[36] the period saw the increased attempts by enthusiastic, intelligent men to improve the conditions of all members of society. Most of the credit for this can undoubtedly be centred on the radical liberal factions who, with their frequently unpopular politics, tended to be looked upon with scorn and suspicion by fellow citizens. Vigorous advocates of political and social reform, their opposition to the slave trade, on which the ports' wealth and prosperity was largely based, frequently earned a hostile reception from the mercantile ranks.

Among these reformers were such notable local men as William Rathbone (the fourth, 1758-1809), James Currie (a Scottish doctor, biographer of Burns, author of several political pamphlets and the man largely responsible for the efficient administration of the Poor Law), Doctor Traill (a founder of the Royal Institution), the Reverend William Shepherd (Unitarian minister of Renshaw Street), and a man who is frequently alluded to as being one of Liverpool's greatest citizens, William Roscoe.

Born in 1753, Roscoe was the son of an innkeeper of Mount Pleasant and was articled to a Liverpool solicitor in 1769. A man of high intellect and wide reputation, he was nationally famous for his poetry and verses set to music. At the age of only 19, several years before the abolition movement commenced, he dared to publish his views in verse.[37] Later, in 1787, once the movement had been established, he produced a long work entitled the *Wrongs of Africa*, following it up a year later with *A General View of the African Slave Traffic*. Throughout his life he was to continue this approach and frequently spoke out about the injustices and corruption that he saw around him, especially those in his home town.

In a similar literary exposé, Roscoe was supported by a friend, Edward Rushton, a blind poet and former sailor on slave ships who spoke from personal experience. He wrote his *West Indian Eclogues* in 1787, which although not regarded as great poetry, certainly drove home his hatred of oppression and the love of liberty.

William Roscoe, co-founder of the School and President 1798 (Sir Martin Archer Shee) (courtesy Walker Art Gallery).

Public opinion regarding the slave trade largely began to change in England around this time, especially after the abolition movement had been established in London. Naturally, there was little turn around in Liverpool where the movement was received with much hostility. The Corporation even went to the trouble of paying a Jesuit, Reverend Raymond Harris, £100 for his pamphlet which confirmed the scriptural approval of the slave trade, of which he assured "its conformity with the principles of natural and revealed religion delineated in the sacred writings of the Word of God".[38]

His work did not go unanswered in Liverpool, as a direct attack came from the Revd. Henry Dannett, incumbent of St. Johns,[39] who published a reply in 1788 entitled *A Particular Examination of Mr. Harris's Scriptural Researches on the Licitness of the Slave Trade.*

Although there were only two Liverpool members of the London based abolition movement, William Rathbone and Doctor Jonathan Binns, there were other sympathisers living in the Town now recognised as the centre of the trade, who did not wish to openly declare their beliefs for fear of reprisals. Most of these men were already friends and associates and had come together in the various societies formed in the previous two decades.

In common with other towns in Britain and on the Continent, societies engaged in various collective pursuits were being formed in late eighteenth century Liverpool. One of the earliest was the Academy of Art and Painting formed in 1769 to promote art and design, and within its ranks were many eminent and respected men from local society, such as P.P. Burdett, the engraver; Charles Eyes, town architect; John Baines, Master of the Free Grammar School; Matthew Gregson, antiquary; and the ubiquitous William Roscoe.

Other societies followed, frequently political in nature. The Conversation Club had been formed as early as 1768, meeting at George's Coffee House, and debated such radical topics as voting by ballot. However, it was the French Revolution and the subsequent suppressive policy of Pitt's Government that was to arouse the most widespread debating in Liverpool. Societies were formed with both conservative and radical foundations. In support of the government, for example, were the Association for King and Constitution, which met at The Buck and Vine in Hackins Hey,

A

PARTICULAR EXAMINATION

OF

Mr. HARRIS's SCRIPTURAL RESEARCHES

ON THE

Licitnefs of the Slave Trade.

Ipfe Crudelis judicandus eft, qui Libertati non favet.
Cancel. Fortescue de laudibus legum. Cap. 42.

By HENRY DANNETT, M.A.

MINISTER OF ST. JOHN'S, LIVERPOOL.

LONDON:

PRINTED AND SOLD BY J. PHILLIPS, GEORGE-YARD,
LOMBARD STREET; T. PAYNE, MEWS-GATE;
AND D. PRINCE AND COOKE, OXFORD.
MDCCLXXXVIII.

Title page from Henry Dannett's 'Licitness of the Slave Trade' (1788).

and the Friends to the King and Constitution, which met at The Eagle and Child in Redcross Street.

Far more formidable was the fellowship formed by Dr James Currie and William Roscoe in 1795; the Debating Society, which met weekly in the Long Room, Marble Street, attracting large audiences. Inevitably, it was forced to dissolve itself in 1797, due to its contravention of the Seditious Meetings Act of December 1795.[40]

Other societies were formed with philosophical and literary interests to the fore. One such society, of which we know no name, had a small membership of around a dozen individuals and met weekly, again in a local hostelry, and among its members was the blind poet, Edward Rushton. It was from this small intellectual gathering that in 1790 the idea for a much needed institution was born.

PIONEERS AND PERSEVERANCE

"Our doubts are traitors, and make us lose the good
we oft might gain, by fearing to attempt."

(Shakespeare)

Edward Rushton knew too well the plight of the blind, as he himself had been blinded as a teenager after contracting a disease while away at sea. Living in an age where little was done to alleviate such a handicap, or to bring out latent capabilities, Rushton showed strong character, fearing no-one, while pursuing his progressive ideals and supporting radical causes. Among his intimate friends were many of the respected thinkers of the local societies, such as Roscoe and Currie. He was also a poet and his subjects were frequently the controversial issues of his day.

Rushton was born in John Street, Liverpool on 13 November 1756, the son of Thomas Rushton, a victualler by trade. From the age of six Edward was sent to the Liverpool Free School, where he was educated until he was 11. In similar fashion to many other local boys of his age he was apprenticed to a shipping company with West Indian interests. In young Edward's case it was the firm Messrs. Watt and Gregson.

His youth at sea was full of incidents which must have had considerable effect on his character. At the age of 16, while still an apprentice, during a storm he courageously took the helm of the ship which the captain was considering abandoning, and guided it safely back into Liverpool. This act of bravery was to be endorsed on his indenture of apprenticeship.

In 1773 he became second mate on a slave ship sailing to Guinea. During the passage he formed a friendship with a young Negro boy by the name of Quamina, whom he taught to read. Shortly afterwards, while both were part of the crew of a small boat despatched to the shore, the vessel capsized. Rushton swam towards a small water cask where Quamina was already safely holding on. Quamina, seeing that his friend was too exhausted to reach him, bravely jeopardized his own safety, and pushed the cask towards Rushton, saving his life. Quamina was never seen again.

Later that same year, while on a slaver bound for Dominica, Rushton

a. 'Early in 1790, I regularly attended an association consisting of ten or a dozen individuals for the purpose of weekly discussion.' (Drawing by Arthur C. Black.)

b. Edward Rushton. Bust by John Gibson R.A. (c.1814) (whereabouts unknown).

27

became so sickened with the brutality meted out on the slaves by the captain, that he remonstrated with him forcefully, and was charged with mutiny and threatened with the irons. Almost all of the slaves had fallen victim to contagious ophthalmia[1] which in the appalling conditions had spread like wildfire. Only Rushton took pity on them and tried to bring what relief he could. His actions resulted in his own personal tragedy as he too caught the disease. His left eye was completely destroyed and the right so badly damaged that he became blind.

It is likely that, given the horrendous conditions on slave ships, such a disease was not uncommon. Indeed the great abolitionist, Thomas Clarkson, in his book *The Cries of Africa*, tells a story of a French slaver on which 39 Africans lost their sight and being of no commercial value, were contemptuously tossed overboard.

When Rushton arrived home, his father took him to several of the leading medical men of the day, even the King's oculist, all to no avail. To add to his misfortune he was turned out of the family home, his father now having remarried to a woman who could not tolerate her new step-son's presence. Fortunately, an aunt took him in and Rushton stayed there for seven years. During that time he lived on an allowance of 4s a week given to him by his father. Out of that scanty sum he paid a young boy threepence a week to read to him.

Rushton spent much of his time studying literature, politics and philosophy. He especially loved to read the plays of Shakespeare and the prose and verse of Milton. He may have found additional inspiration in the achievements of the sightless Milton as in 1782 Rushton published his first poem *The Dismembered Empire*, a political work hostile to the American War. Political developments in America continued to interest him throughout his life. In 1797 he wrote to ex-Presid .t George Washington on the subject of Slavery, questioning Washington's blatant hypocrisy in retaining numerous slaves for his own use while fighting England for "Liberty" and "Independence". The letter was returned by Washington without a reply. He wrote in similar fashion to the radical ' 'homas Paine, author of *Rights of Man* and *Common Sense*, questioning the confinement of his libertarian ideals to only the "white slaves" (although Paine had played a role in the abolition of slavery in Pennsylvania in 1780). Paine too turned a deaf ear.[2]

28

'Will Clewline' by Edward Rushton (1806)

Edward Rushton's views on the slave trade were becoming widely known and during the early 1780s he formed his first association with men of similar outlook – William Roscoe, Dr. Currie, William Rathbone and the Unitarian minister William Shepherd.[3]

Around this time, his father, probably trying to make amends for his earlier unkindness, established Edward and his sister in a tavern at 19 Crooked Lane. Rushton was not suited to the work, although he did have the help of his new wife Isabella, and moved on to become editor of the *Liverpool Herald*.[4]

In 1787 he published the first of his poems dealing with his abhorrence of the slave trade; *The West Indian Eclogues* – which was dedicated to Dr. Porteus, the Bishop of Chester, a noted abolitionist. So well known had Rushton's reputation and views become, that when Thomas Clarkson visited Liverpool pursuing his investigations on the Slave Trade, he sought out Rushton and gave him much credit for his contribution to the abolitionist cause.

The following year, his uncompromising attitude led to him leaving his position at the *Herald*. This time Rushton was concerned with the excessive barbarism of the press gang. His partner on the newspaper, worried about a possible backlash resulting from Rushton's allegations, suggested publishing a retraction, but Rushton refused, and resigned his post. His poem *Will Clewline* reflects his views on the brutalism of the press gangs.[5]

A short while later he established himself as a bookseller at 44 Paradise Street, but yet again his outspoken views made him enemies and lost valued custom. It was now the period of Revolution in France and Rushton made no attempt to moderate his radical thoughts. Nevertheless, he refused help from his friends while his business floundered, being quite prepared to accept the consequences of voicing unpopular ideals.

At length his business recovered and he was able to live out his life in relative comfort and give his children a good education.[6]

The name of the literary and philosophical society of which he was a member is not known. Taking his friendship with Roscoe and Currie into account, it may have been a fore-runner of the ill-fated radical Debating Society formed by those two gentlemen in 1795.[7] Whatever the name, it was the birthplace of an idea to provide relief for the indigent blind. Rushton described later how the idea originated.

> "Early in the year 1790, I regularly attended an association consisting of ten or a dozen individuals who assembled weekly for the purpose of weekly discussion; and one evening, the conversation having turned on the recently established Marine Society, it was observed by a member of that body, Captain W. Ward, that the committee for the management of the Marine Fund had declined the acceptance of small donations. It immediately occurred to me that if an institution could be formed, in Liverpool, for the relief of its numerous and indigent blind, the small donations thus declined by the Marine Committee might be brought to flow in a channel, not less benevolent, and prove of essential service in the establishment of a fund for the benefit of that unfortunate description of the community."[8]

Forcibly impressed with the idea, Rushton mentioned the design "on the moment", and soon after produced two letters on the loss of sight. The first of these bemoaned the plight of the blind person[9] (see appendix 2), and the second, according to Rushton, "contained an outline of an institution, by which it was hoped that the pecuniary distress, and consequently the gloom of the sightless, might in some degree, be alleviated". Rushton planned that

> "... an association should be formed consisting entirely of blind persons; that the names of females as well as males, should be registered and that each individual should contribute a small matter weekly, or monthly, with which, and the benefactions of the humane, such a fund might speedily be established, as would afford to each a weekly allowance in cases of sickness, superannuation etc."[10]

Edward Rushton was, however, conscious of the enormity of such a task and the influence in society that would be required to carry it through.

> "This attempt I knew to be singular and that I had no personal influence to recommend it; yet, as the sufferings of the indigent blind were great, and as good might be the result, I was resolved to persevere. There was also another stimulus: The Liverpool Marine Society had originated in a conversation between two individuals at the close of a convivial meeting and the effects of this Society were likely to prove highly beneficial; nor had I forgotten the invigorating remark of Shakespeare – *'Our doubts are traitors and make us lose the good we oft might gain, by fearing to attempt'*."[11]

Encouraged by such reflections, Rushton placed the letters before his associates in the Society, and the idea of "...mitigating the misery of those hitherto neglected unfortunates, was unanimously approved."[12]

They did, nevertheless, sound a note of caution, advising that the letters should not be inserted in the Liverpool papers until the "...sanction or patronage of certain leading characters could be procured".[13] With such advice Rushton "...thought it expedient to acquiesce." He began to develop his plan.

"Among the members of our small but interesting society was a respectable musician of the name Lowe who was himself in a sightless state; pleased with the plan, and having intercourse in the way of his profession with several affluent families, Mr Lowe requested that he might be furnished with copies of the letters, in order to leave them in the hands of a few wealthy individuals, among whom, he was confident he could soon procure patrons for so novel, yet so benevolent, an undertaking. The copies were accordingly made out and Mr Lowe had them in his possession for several months.."[14]

During that time the letters were shown to many "respectable characters" without success. The idea may have foundered there, except that by October 1790 they were shown by Lowe to the Reverend Henry Dannett, the author of the anti-slavery *Licitness of the Slave-Trade*, and incumbent of St. John's. Dannett "...expressed himself warmly of the design..."[15] and enquired after the author of the letters. He then sent Lowe away with a message requesting Rushton's company at breakfast the following morning.

Meanwhile, just a few months previously, Rushton had secured the help of another acquaintance, a blind musician by the name of John Christie of 46 Church Street. Their friendship had been formed some years earlier in what Rushton termed "a fellowship in misfortune" (with respect to their sightless plight), and it was to him that Rushton communicated his idea soon after it was formed. Christie's reaction boosted Rushton's hopes.

"...it was not only warmly approved, but he endeavoured to promote it by showing the copies of my letters whenever he thought they could be communicated with any prospect of success..."[16]

Yet, months passed with no success, even though Lowe had received some "splendid promises".

In the beginning of September 1790, one evening while Rushton and Christie were again discussing how to develop the the idea and gain positive support, Christie hit upon the idea of "...having a place appropriated to the use of the blind, wherein, by gratuitous musical instruction, they might soon be enabled to provide for themselves, which, to a well disposed mind, must ever prove a source of the highest satisfaction..."[17]

Rushton's idea of the institution as a form of charity pension had now been expanded to include a plan to find a suitable place to teach music to the blind so that they could hopefully master an instrument sufficiently well to earn enough money to support themselves. This, they believed, was an ideal solution that would suit all.

On 22 September 1790, a letter was written at Christie's request, expanding these ideas, which was sent to a benevolent friend, Mr Edward Alanson, a Liverpool surgeon, appealing for his help and support (see appendix 3).

Several days later, acting upon advice received from Alanson, several manuscript copies were made of the letter and put into circulation. According to Rushton, "...one was left with Mr Gore and another with Mr Billinge[18] in order to be laid in their respective counties; and before I went to breakfast with Mr Dannett, in consequence of the invitation brought by Mr Lowe, I called upon John Christie, procured a copy of the letter to Mr Alanson, and took it with me."[19] Rushton described the meeting.

"I was received with every mark of attention...my letters and that of John Christie had his decided approbation...he expressed himself pleased with the prospect of something being done for the indigent blind; (Dannett) talked of procuring subscriptions and of preaching a sermon on the occasion by which he hoped to obtain a collection of at least forty pounds, which would serve as a fund to commence with, and he appeared particularly anxious to have a meeting of a few individuals, friendly to the cause, some of whose names were then mentioned, in order to discuss a plan, and frame a few regulations for the government of the future institution. After staying for about two hours, I withdrew, leaving the three letters in the possession of Mr. Dannett, and believing, if a meeting were to take place, that the benevolent business would speedily be carried into execution."[20]

On his way home that morning, Rushton called on John Christie eager to inform him of what had gone on in the meeting with Dannett, and showed much excitement at gaining the support of such an influential figure.

A week or ten days later, both men were invited to dine with Mr Dannett. They were not alone in receiving an invitation. Also present were local philanthropists Richard Carson and William Roscoe; the Reverend John Smyth, incumbent of St. Anne's; and their friend Robert Lowe. Two

a. The meeting at Dannett's house: Richard Carson, John Christie, Revd. John Smyth, Revd. Henry Dannett, Edward Rushton, William Roscoe, Robert Lowe.

'...a sheltering establishment for the indigent blind appeared to be the ardent wish of them all...' (Drawing by Arthur C. Black.)

b. The Golden Lion Inn, Dale Street.

other men were also invited; Mr Alanson the surgeon, who was indisposed, and a Mr Sutton, who, not having made Mr Dannetts acquaintance, thought it to be a mistake and did not attend.

Immediately after dinner, Mr Dannett commenced the business by reading Rushton's two letters, and then those of Christie. After passing the letters around the table it became apparent from the ensuing discussion that "...a sheltering establishment for the indigent blind appeared to be the ardent wish of them all..."[21].

There was, however, difference in opinion as to the scale on which the establishment should commence, and as to the employment which would prove the most suitable. Nevertheless, not a single word was uttered against the idea itself.

The idea contained in John Christie's letter was discussed by name as "Christie's Plan" and the beneficial scheme as "Rushton's Plan". The latter was incorporated at that meeting into the whole design and mentioned in the printed plan, which was soon to be published. "Christie's Plan" was to be the ground work and "...several rules and regulations were committed to writing during the afternoon, and to these Mr Roscoe appeared particularly attentive."[22] It was late in the evening before the company separated and in order that the infant scheme "...might benefit by the observations which had been made during the discussion, it was agreed that the second meeting should not be held 'till after the interval of a week."[23]

Accordingly, on the following Monday (which was most likely 25 October 1790), another meeting was held at the house of Mr Dannett. The regulations drawn up at the first meeting were read and after "...some little alterations and ammendations of little moment..."[24] the documents were left in the hands of Mr Dannett, in order that they could be submitted to the press.

At this point we may become familiar with the dispute that subsequently arose as to who actually founded the School. Such a dispute is not surprising, given the number of gentlemen participating in promoting, discussing and physically working on the idea, all keen to see its fruition. Once the institution was established, much of the initial day to day running was carried out by Dannett, as we shall see. There is no surviving evidence of any further assistance from Rushton, although Christie taught

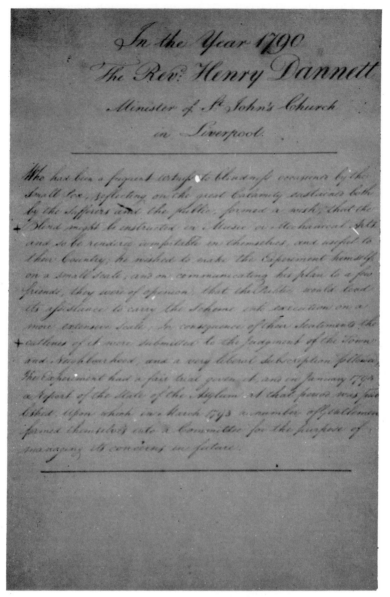

In the Year 1790
The Revᵈ Henry Dannett
Minister of Sᵗ John's Church
in Liverpool

Who had been a frequent witness to blindness occasioned by the Small Pox, reflecting on the great calamity sustained both by the Sufferers and the Public, formed a wish, that the Blind might be instructed in Music or Mechanical Arts, and so be rendered comfortable in themselves, and useful to their Country; he wished to make the Experiment himself on a small Scale; and on communicating his plan to a few friends, they were of opinion, that the Public would lend its assistance to carry the Scheme into execution on a more extensive Scale. In consequence of their Sentiments the outlines of it were submitted to the Judgment of the Town and Neighbourhood, and a very liberal Subscription followed. The Experiment had a fair trial given it, and in January 1792 a Report of the State of the Asylum at that period was published, Upon which in March 1793 a number of Gentlemen formed themselves into a Committee for the purpose of managing its concerns in future.

Management Committee Minute Book, 1793, Henry Dannett's Introduction (Page 1).

music to the inmates for many years. Such initial hard work and commitment may have prompted Dannett to wilfully accept acclaim as the sole founder of the institution. His position in the community was of obvious importance – which may also have affected his relationship with Rushton and Christie, the latter actually being in a subordinate role at the Institution.

Certainly by 1793 Dannett attributed the whole idea to himself, as is witnessed in his copperplate frontispiece of the *Proceedings of the Committee for the Blind Asylum* in March of that year.

"In the year 1790, the Rev. Henry Dannett, minister of St. John's Church in Liverpool, who had been a frequent witness to blindness occasioned by the Smallpox, reflecting on the great calamity sustained both by the sufferers and the public, formed a wish, that the Blind might be instructed in Music or Mechanical Arts and so be rendered comfortable in themselves, and useful to their country; he wished to make the experiment himself on a small scale; and on communicating his plan to a few friends, they were of opinion that the Public would lend its assistance to carry the scheme into execution on a more extensive scale; In consequence of their sentiments the outlines of it were submitted to the judgement of the Town and Neighbourhood, and a very liberal subscription followed..."[25]

It would appear that Dannett allowed those who did not know any better to assume that he was, in fact, the originator of the idea and founder of the Blind Asylum. It would do no harm, he might have thought, and would certainly help his position both in society and in the running of the Institution. However, in 1804 Dannett made a more public claim (although we do not know what form it took) which finally came to Rushton's notice. Rushton's reaction was to draw up a detailed account of the early stages and developments as he could remember them, to 'set the record straight'. He was severely critical of Dannett's claims.

With regard to the letter of Christie's which Rushton took with him to the breakfast meeting, he stated:

"...this I mention the more emphatically because it has been said, nay even sworn, by Mr Dannett that he never saw the letter of John Christie, nor any other document relative to the Institution previously to its being established. Nor is this the only particular in which Mr Dannett has deviated from the truth. He has stated that "Christie and perhaps Rushton made application to him as being a likely person etc.etc". Now Christie and Rushton being entirely unacquainted with Mr Dannett never did apply nor had they ever the least idea of applying to him; on the contrary, the application was made by Mr Dannett to me in consequence of the letters which had fallen into his hands as before related...".

Rushton continued with a scathing rebuke.

"...Mr Dannett has also deposed that in originating the Liverpool Institution for the Blind he had no assistance from any being on earth. Now if this statement be not the result of mental imbecility I will venture to say it is one of the most singular and shameless that ever was made..."

He concluded his transcript,

"...thus in a brief, unvarnished way I have given the origin of the Liverpool Institute for the Blind. If I have stated falsehoods, those falsehoods may readily be refuted by an appeal to living testimony" (Roscoe and Christie for example, were still alive) "...if I have adhered to the truth, the deposition recently made by the Rev. H. Dannett, whether proceeding from forgetfulness or design, must necessarily be erroneous..."

Philosophically he declared,

"...the cause of truth can never be promoted by a warfare of positive assertions..."[26]

Dannett was certainly keen to support his own position, as in October 1805 he requested a signed affidavit from the Committee of the School for the Blind to back up his claims regarding the foundation of the School. In reply, the Committee declared,

"In consequence of a publication by the Rev. H. Dannett, relative to the original project for the establishment of the School in which the affidavit is mentioned to have been left at the School and which Mr. Brand [Superintendent/Governor of the School] says was left with him for the purpose of general inspection, as this Committee are unwilling to interfere themselves or to permit any Servants of the School to be engaged in what appears to them to be a personal difference of opinion between the Rev. H. Dannett and Mr. J. Christie, it is resolved that Mr. Brand be ordered to send to the Rev. H. Dannett the affidavit which he received from him together with a copy of this resolution."[27]

The publication referred to has yet to be traced but may have been made as a form of "signing off" or summary of his life in Liverpool, as in 1804 Dannett had moved to Hopton Wafers in Shropshire.

A study of guide books and history's of Liverpool published in the nineteenth century reveals little consistency regarding the founders; Dannett, Rushton, Christie, and Alanson all being mentioned and rarely at the same time.[28] One even mentions another name so far not considered (which occurs in the same company as Dannett, Rushton and Christie).

"...it is said indeed that the primary idea was suggested to him (Dannett) by Henry Arnold of Ormskirk, a blind lad who was afterwards admitted into the School on 1 August 1791 and quitted it in 1798. In 1797 he was appointed organist at the Parish Church in Halsall.

> He engaged extensively in the manufacture of corn sacks and seamens' hammocks at Ormskirk, supporting his Father and Mother and contributing to educate, support and fix out in life several of his brothers and sisters. He may now be said to be affluent..."[29]

This, however,is the only attribution to Henry Arnold and did not appear until 1825.

Of the references to the Institution in the contemporary guides, no founders' names are mentioned at all in Moss' *Liverpool Guide of 1796*, and in Wallace's *Descriptive History of Liverpool* (1794), he refers to Dannett as the projector of the Institution "...who many months supported this Charity after its establishment and to whom the present success of the plan is principally indebted..."[30]

A further mystery surrounds the suggestion that the idea for a benevolent institution was first published in a local paper in July 1775. This is mentioned in Troughton's *History of Liverpool* in 1810 (p. 155), but gives no detail as to where or by whom it was written. The guide book *Streets of Liverpool* suggests it was written by an anonymous writer in *Williamson's Liverpool Advertiser*.

Despite a search of the existing copies of the local press for that period, no such trace can be found, nor in any other form of publication. It may be possible that the 'Letter on the Education of the Blind' by 'Demodocus', published in the *Edinburgh Magazine* in November 1774, had reached Liverpool. It must remain a mystery.

It is certain, nevertheless, that the founding of the Institution cannot be attributed to one man alone. Rushton had the idea for a benevolent fund, which came from his discussions in the philosophical society; Christie, who had the idea for a kind of institution where the inmates could be taught music, therefore having a chance to make life more tolerable and to be able to support themselves; and Robert Lowe, who spent much time and effort circulating the letters. Roscoe, Smyth, and Carson played their part at the meetings, and Dannett brought together these men who were likely to make a significant contribution, and also put his name to the public announcements to give them credence. Alanson too played a small role in an advisory capacity. In addition, most of the group were known to continue their support during the early years of its establishment, though Rushton appears to be a notable exception – (in his incapacitated state and lack of musical talent this is not surprising). We do not know if he had any later involvement – his name is not mentioned in any of the School Committee notes or reports.

The original founders therefore, are these eight men who all played a significant role in the early pioneering days of the School. Rushton may have had the original idea of wanting to help alleviate the plight of the blind in some way, but Christie's expansion of this plan was closer to the actual manifestation of the Institution.

Meanwhile, we must put this dispute to rest and return to look at the consequences of that second meeting at Dannett's house. The documents left with Reverend Dannett were drawn up into an official announcement as *A Plan for Affording Relief to the Indigent Blind* and this was inserted in *Williamson's Liverpool Advertiser* on Monday 22 November 1790 (see appendix 4).

The *Plan* contains much of the flavour of Christie's letter – certainly the opening paragraph, and the idea that the blind should not be burdensome to their friends, family or community, and would benefit from the instruction of music.

The following week, the Reverend Dannett drew up *Some Particulars Relative to a Plan, etc.* as an addendum to the published *Plan*. This was dated 1 December 1790 and appeared in the form of a printed circular combining both the *Plan* itself and the *Particulars* (see appendix 5).

The complete plan was ambitious from the very beginning. Not only did they intend to teach a member of the blind person's family to write and read music so as to help in the pupil's studies, but they also hoped to be so successful in their overall achievements as to be a model for other towns to follow suit and care for their blind in a similar manner.

On 29 December 1790, the Reverend Dannett submitted a further announcement to *Williamson's Advertiser*, which was published a few days later on 3 January 1791 (see appendix 6). This was to be the final notice to the public, prior to the intended opening of the school in the second week of January, and advised how to subscribe to the charity, what would be taught, and brief answers to the main criticisms already voiced.

Unlike Paris, this institution was planned to cater, where possible, for blind persons of almost any age – the first institution of its kind in the

a. Following the meeting at Dannett's house the Plan is announced.

'Williamson's Advertiser' Monday 22 November 1790.

b. The opening of the School is announced.

'Williamson's Advertiser' 3 January 1791.

world. With the school due to open on 10 January 1791, the plan had finally reached fruition.

THE WHISTLING OF A NAME

'a plan so novel in its kind
must in its infancy be extremely imperfect'

Reverend H. Dannett

For the first two years the School had very mixed fortunes. A problem that soon became evident was the unsuitability of the buildings used by the School.

Situated in 6 Commutation Row opposite the potteries of Shaws Brow,[1] two houses which had recently been erected, were rented by the Charity for the sole use of the School. Dannett looked upon them from the beginning as being temporary, and found that for the purposes of his "experiment" they were "...much too small; incapable of accommodating the present number without injury to their health."[2]

The School was beset with teething troubles, most of which were related to running costs. Teachers, who were difficult to come by, were engaged on high salaries; on average at a guinea a week, and the School found it difficult to sell enough goods produced by the pupils to pay for teachers' wages, let alone for the blind themselves. Of course, many of those under initial instruction could not be expected to produce saleable goods for some time, but meanwhile, they still had to be fed, and even receive a wage, which would be paid at a higher rate if they were married with a family.

In the first two years the number of blind persons engaged at the School fluctuated between 25 and 52, who earned weekly from three to 6s each. Of the original 52 enrolled at the School, 16 were employed making whips, 15 blind women spun and reeled linen yarn, while one nearly blind woman warped and wove it; another, totally blind from infancy, cut the cloth into shirts and sheets before making them up; four blind girls and a boy were learning the harpsichord; two made woollen mops; eight elderly blind people picked oakum for ships' caulking and six made baskets and hampers, also covering bottles with wicker for exportation.

During that time some had learnt their trades and had returned home to put them into practice, hoping to lead a more independent life and earn

a. Commutation Row (centre). Two houses at No.6 were rented as a school. The first purpose-built school was to open in 1800 on the site now occupied by the Odeon Cinema, London Road (right).

b. 'Views from the Commutation Row School', Lime Street 1797 (William Herdman).

c. 'Shaws Brow, Looking West (1845) (William Herdman).

their own living. Those who remained were thought by Dannett to be happy and contented, remarking "...their works prove, that when they have an opportunity of being instructed, they are capable of becoming good mechanics, and consequently useful members of society."[3]

He was quite scathing of those who had fallen by the wayside.

"...the rest, who have left the Asylum, have either been dismissed for misconduct, or been blind minstrels, who, long inured to habits of idleness and dissipation, have soon become disgusted with useful industry and returned to their strolling occupations; fortunately for the morals of the sober and the diligent whom they left behind them..."[4]

The music taught at the School was not for "minstrels" and for this reason instruction on the violin was not given. To be a fiddler on the streets or in the alehouses for example, was to be no more than a common vagrant and beggar. The aim of the School was to produce 'respectable' musicians who could be employed as church organists or music teachers. Therefore, it must have been disappointing for Dannett and Christie to be restricted to a limit of only six music pupils at a time, due to the shortage of suitable teachers.

Certain trades proved to be a failure, both in the teaching and the learning and were abandoned, incurring further costs, due to the expense of necessary machinery and materials. The manufacture of whips was by far the most costly, but to Dannett's despair (as he believed it to be potentially the most lucrative of their trades) support could not be found for the business and after two years it was still running at a loss. The engagement of a permanent teacher in this post was a continuous problem. Dannett reported,

"Whether it may be advisable to continue this part of the Asylum business, must be left to the discernment and better judgement of those who may succeed to the management of the Charity. If it should ever experience the encouragement which it merits, it will be found highly profitable to the Asylum; and an employment helpful to the blind, requiring almost constant walking and manual exercise. Some thousand grosses of whips are exported annually from this kingdom, which the Asylum might afford better and cheaper than the whip makers. Should it appear ineligible, the sail cloth manufactory might be substituted in its place; it would employ all the women in spinning the hemp to much greater advantage than line spinning and some of the men in weaving the yarn in Gorton's patent loom, which is worked by swivels, and is admirably calculated for the use of the blind; this branch would find in Liverpool a constant and never failing market for all they could manufacture. The basket manufactory, though less profitable, is in one respect, more useful. Blind men who come from a distance may be taught in the course of

Cranes map of Liverpool 1797 (extract)

Commutation Row in centre to the left of the Infirmary

Commutation Row   London Road site soon to be utilised for the new school building.

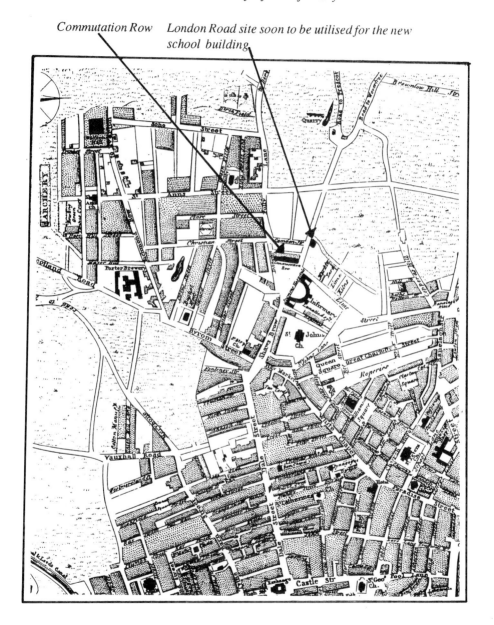

two or three years to make good baskets and hampers, and may then return to their friends to gain a few shillings weekly, by following their employment at home."[5]

There was now a waiting list of blind persons from all over the country wanting to attend or live at the Asylum, and Dannett was resolved on the plan of a purpose built school. Subscriptions were already being made in Blackburn, Preston, Rochdale and Bury towards the cost of such a building, which, it was intended, would contain workshops, ware-rooms, sales-shops and other facilities deemed beneficial to the inhabitants.

Dannett was not content with Liverpool's pioneering work existing in isolation. After only a few months' experience he declared,

"There is great reason that a neighbouring town which enjoys peculiar advantages in her manufactures, for giving employment to the Indigent Blind; and it is expected that the town alluded to and Liverpool will divide the blind Poor of the county of Lancaster..."

Not content with that he continued,

"...it is much to be wished that these institutions may become general. Almost every shire in the kingdom has one or two capital towns, which may easily discover local and peculiar branches of manufacture, to employ all the blind of each county; indeed, basket making, mop making, spinning of yarn, knitting, music,etc., may suit every county. And thus, a class of our fellow citizens, who have hitherto been only burdensome to their friends, and unhappy because unemployed, may be rendered useful members of Society, and made happy in themselves by being relieved from extreme poverty, and (what is worse than poverty) that languor and tedium vitae, which must, at most hours, infest minds that are vacant, or employed only in brooding over their misfortunes."[6]

The town alluded to above was most certainly Manchester, but Dannett's dream regarding that town was not to be realised in his lifetime. Although Manchester was still the next town in the county to erect a blind asylum, it was not to be until 1837, almost half a century later. Henshaw's Blind Asylum, as it was originally known, was founded in a building erected by public subscription in Old Trafford. It would probably have been built much earlier if not for a dispute over a Will. In 1810, Thomas Henshaw, an Oldham merchant, bequeathed a sum of £20,000 for the purpose of establishing an Asylum for the Indigent Blind. This Will, however, was contested by his relatives, and 25 years were to pass before the Court of Chancery finally gave a verdict in accordance with the terms of the Will, which provided that none of the money should be spent on building. (In 1823, before the matter had been resolved, the Executors of the Will enquired if the Liverpool School would accept the £20,000 should it

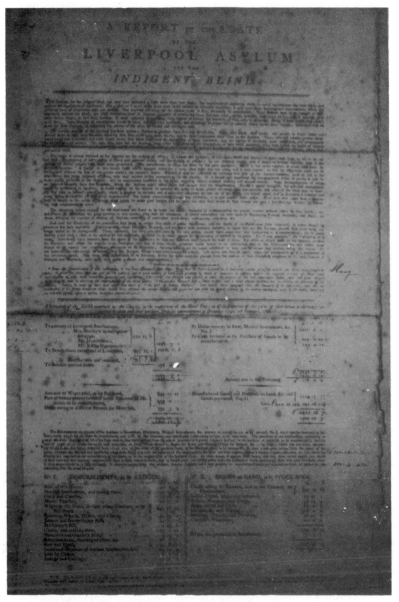

The first management report of the School (1791-2) – published on Dannett's resignation, February 1793.

be procured.) Poor public response to appeals for land and suitable buildings had also delayed matters, but when the Asylum eventually opened, interest had swollen the endowment fund to £50,000. Fifty years later, the Asylum possessed investments valued at £70,000 and the property at £23,000. It was amongst the wealthiest institutions in the land.

Unfortunately, when the foundation deed was drawn up there was no provision for education. The Asylum provided only residential facilities and vocational training, which hampered effective utilisation of its wealth.

We have already heard in the first chapter how the Edinburgh Institution was founded in 1793, and in that same year the great port of Bristol was also to have a school. (A charity pension had previously been instituted there in January 1784, following a bequest of £3,000 by a John Merlott. John Merlott's Charity was to provide pensions for blind persons over fifty years of age.)

Nine years later, two members of the Society of Friends, Messrs. Bath and Fox, founded their School for the Blind in Callow Hill Street, Bristol. The first trades attempted were plaiting whips and spinning flax. Stay lace manufacture was later tried for a short time, and was soon followed by basket-making. The school began with four boys and two girls, who, after initial training, were later given employment. To begin with they attended daily, but in 1803 accommodation was provided, firstly for resident girls and then later for boys. Forty years later it had grown to such a size that it was necessary to move to another site, in Lower Queens Road, where almost 100 pupils were catered for.

The only other institution to lay claim to birth in the eighteenth century was the School for the Indigent Blind in St. George's Fields, Southwark in London, which was founded in 1799. Its inception was owed to the efforts of four men; William Houlston, Samuel Bosanquet, James Ware and Thomas Boddington. Fifteen blind persons were to be educated, maintained and instructed in a trade. The site of the first school was soon taken over for the building of the Bethlehem Hospital, the school moving to a site opposite St. George's Circus. By 1827 there were 110 resident boys and girls who could stay for a maximum of six years. In 1901 the site was purchased by the Baker Street and Waterloo Railway, and new school premises were opened the following year at Leatherhead.

On the Continent numerous schools had sprung up from the beginning of the century; that of Vienna in 1804, founded by Dr. Klein, who was its director for around 50 years; Steglitz near Berlin in 1806, after initial preparation by Haüy on his way to Russia (where he also founded St. Petersburg School in 1807); Dresden, also established in 1807; and in 1808, three institutions – those of Amsterdam (by an association of Freemasons), Prague (by a charitable society) and Stockholm. In 1809 Dr. Hirzel organised the school at Zurich and two years later, Copenhagen was established by the "Society of the Chain", a body similar to that of the Freemasons. Two institutions were founded in Dublin, the Protestant Richmond Institution in 1810 and the Catholic Molyneux Asylum in 1815.

In the early nineteenth century, few schools were to open in Britain. Norwich was the first, in 1805, followed by the Jewish School in London in 1819. An Asylum was founded in Glasgow in 1826, and the Institution for the Deaf and Blind in Belfast in 1831. Two years later, the Yorkshire School for the Blind was opened in York.

In fact, it was the 1840s before Dannett's hopes began to be realised. Institutions were founded at Manchester, Exeter, Newcastle, Brighton, Aberdeen, Nottingham, Birmingham, Bath, Leicester, Sheffield, Devonport and Plymouth all within twenty years. In Liverpool a second School, that of the Catholic Blind Asylum, was opened in Islington in 1841. This was the first school in England for handicapped children to be established by a religious organisation.

Despite the high aims and ideals shown by Henry Dannett, the reputation and image of both himself and the School, after almost only two years had become tarnished in late 1792. Whilst still in its experimental stages it was rocked by the revelation of a scandal. Malicious rumours spread around the town that certain blind women had been confined due to pregnancy and that there were irregularities in the payment of wages. To such an institution, dependant largely on the confidence and the goodwill of the local people, these were devastating circumstances. Desperate to reassert its position and role in the community,the School publicly presented two affidavits in the local press. On 27th December 1792 *Gore's Advertiser* ran the following:

49

The scandalous reports so industriously spread respecting the Asylum for the Blind in Liverpool having been so far credited as materially to injure the interest of the Charity, it becomes necessary in justice to the Institution and to the public to prevent the further circulation of such cruel aspersions, which it is hoped will be effectually done by the publication of the following affidavits. Such persons as may yet entertain any doubts on this subject may have them cleared up by a personal enquiry at the Asylum; and it were much to be wished that those, who have been most forward in propagating so wicked a slander, had been at the trouble of taking this measure before they had indulged themselves in an attack on an Institution which depends entirely on public opinion for support. A report of the state of the Charity will be published with all possible expedition.

Liverpool to wit,

Thomas Howard of Liverpool, Book-keeper, maketh oath that he hath paid and kept the accounts of weekly wages to the women and girls a the Blind Asylum for the space of 17 months last past, and upwards, and hath, during all that time frequently attended the Asylum and been conversant with the regulations and conduct of the houses. And this deponent further saith that none of the said women have, during the time afsd. been confined by child-bearing, or are they, or any of them likely to be confined, to the knowledge or belief of this deponent, but that the reports propagated respecting the same are totally *false and groundless* as this deponent is well convinced, this deponent having regularly paid them their weekly wages, as appears by the accounts which may now be seen in his possession.

Sworn the 19th day of Dec. 1792 before John Blackburne

Thomas Howard

Liverpool to wit,

John Christie of Liverpool, Music-master, maketh oath that he hath attended the Blind Asylum, in Liverpool, for the space of 20 months last past and upwards, and hath instructed the persons admitted there in music. And this deponent saith that the conduct of the women and girls under this deponents case, hath during that time been regular and orderly, and that none of them hath, during the time afsd. been prevented from attending by child-bearing, as this deponent is fully convinced, from the regularity of their attendance, nor doth this deponent know or believe that any of them are likely to be so confined, but that the reports spread to the injury of the Charity in this respect are, as this deponent believes, perfectly *false unfounded and malicious*.

Sworn the 19th day of Dec. 1792 before John Blackburne

John Christie

In the February following Reverend Dannett published his promised report on the state of the Charity (the contents of which, specifically regarding the operation of the School, we have already referred to). Despite the Charity making a loss of £300 in the first two years Dannett praised the pupils saying that "...they have earned nearly two thirds of their own

50

and their teachers' wages – And there is little reason to doubt, but in future years (should the public deem the institution worth continuing) they will gain the whole; even if their wages should be a little increased".[7]

In his introduction to the Report Dannett philosophically declared, "...A Plan so novel in its kind must in its infancy be extremely imperfect; it will want those furnishings and improvements which the polishing hand of Experience only can bestow..."

He continued,

"...Since the commencement of this institution, it has been discovered that Mons. Huay (sic) had in Paris a school on a somewhat similar plan, in which the blind were taught to spin; to print for their own use and for the public; and to read authors of their own printing by means of characters in relievo, which the exquisite delicacy of their touch enabled them to trace with wonderful accuracy and expedition. This school was founded and carried on under the auspices of the late unfortunate Louis, who took great delight in visiting it, and in observing the improvements of its blind pupils. This amiable Monarch had a heart to feel, and a hand always stretched out to relieve, the distresses of his subjects. Indeed, he seems to have had about him much of the "milk of human kindness". One would have imagined that the humanity of his character, and the remembrance of his former beneficent deeds, would have softened the savage breasts, and preserved him from the brutal violence of his lawless murderers, who, by his death, have cast an indelible infamy upon a nation, heretofore deemed civilized!"

Written very shortly after the execution of 21 January, Dannett's emotional reaction to Louis' death clearly shows the abhorrent feeling towards the events taking place in France.

Regarding the comments contained in the Report on the Paris Institution, it seems news had finally reached Liverpool a surprising seven years after it had opened.

Dannett, however, was now at the end of his tether after a difficult and demanding two years where he had played a major role in establishing the School and taking on the responsibility of its management, only to see the reputation of the School and himself destroyed by unfounded, malicious rumours. In frustration and despair he concluded his final report.

"...And now the Conductor of the Institution begs leave to resign this child of public beneficence into the hands of its Parent;- a little improved, he hopes, though its education has been expensive. The calumnies, which have been invented, and circulated with malicious industry, to injure him and the Asylum, prevent him from being any longer useful in management. Those calumnies, had they extended only to his own person, should have

AT A MEETING OF THE FRIENDS

OF THE

INSTITUTION FOR THE BENEFIT

OF THE

INDIGENT BLIND,

HELD AT

THE GOLDEN-LION, DALE-STREET,

PURSUANT TO THE REQUEST CONTAINED IN THE REPORT OF THE STATE OF
THE ASYLUM, LATELY PUBLISHED,

RESOLVED,

THAT it appears to the gentlemen present at this meeting, that the institution has been attended with a success equal-to the most sanguine expectations of its friends, and that it merits the warmest support of the public :

THAT the thanks of this meeting be given to the Reverend Henry Dannett, for his great exertions to establish this charity, and his unwearied attention to its interests :

THAT Mr. Dannett having resigned the sole management of it, this meeting is of opinion that it should be conducted by a committee to be chosen by the subscribers :

THAT another meeting of the friends of the institution be held on *Saturday* the 16th of *March* instant, at eleven o'clock in the forenoon, at the *Golden-Lion* (at which they are earnestly requested to attend) where a plan for the future management of the charity will be submitted to their consideration, and a committee chosen to carry it into immediate effect.

JOHN SPARLING.

March 1st 1793.

52

passed over him unregarded, as a summer-cloud; for he hopes that he is not such a slave to the opinion of the multitude, as either to be much depressed by its censure, or elevated by its praise. The *'aura popularis'*, the 'whistling of a name', have never, for a moment, been the object of his ambition; he does not therefore much lament the want of them. But when an attack made on his character involves the character, and affects the interests of an institution very dear to him, which promised much benefit to an unfortunate class of his fellow creatures, and which must depend for its support and continuance principally on its reputation; the consequences are no longer indifferent to him, and he cannot help sensibly feeling the wound. He has, however, the consolation to believe that the Asylum, though it may have drooped for a while, will revive and flourish again, when the management of it is transferred to less obnoxious hands. May those who follow him in its direction, derive the most heart-felt pleasure from the exercise of their benevolent attentions to it; and, instead of Obloquy and Reproach, meet only with public gratitude and encouragement."

Mr Dannett duly resigned his position on the publication of his Report in February 1793. The subscribers of the School were quick to act in this moment of crisis. A meeting was called on 1 March 1793 at the Golden Lion in Castle Street, where it was resolved that the School was a success, despite the gossip-mongering, and that it should certainly be continued.

Thanks were given to the Reverend Henry Dannett 'for his great exertions to establish this Charity, and his unwearied attention to its interests',[8] and it was decided to elect a committee-run administration for the future management of the School. To arrange this, a further meeting was called for on 16 March at the same venue.

At that General Meeting a plan was presented proposing how the School should be run in the future; this was streamlined by those present into what they believed was a workable format, and as a consequence, the first Management Committee was elected, which comprised:

John Sparling Esq. President
Revd. Henry Dannett M.A. Vice-President
William Cubbin Esq. Treasurer
Committee

Revd. J. Smith B.D.	:	Mr E. Alanson
Revd. T. Bold M.A.	:	Mr H. Parke
Revd. J. Yates M.A.	:	John Lyon M.D.
Revd. C. Winstanly M.A.	:	Joseph Brandreth M.D.
Mr Pudsey Dawson	:	Johnathan Binns M.D.
Mr Robert Ward	:	Mr Waterworth
Mr Denny	:	Mr Noble
Mr Sause	:	Mr Owen

auditors
Mr Humble   Mr Daggers

There were several well known names elected which undoubtedly went a long way to reassert the respected position of the School. The new regulations called for four clergymen to serve on the Committee and this was duly attended to, with the election of the Reverends Joseph Smyth of St. Thomas', Thomas Bold of St. Catherine's (formerly the seceders' temple in Temple Street), John Yates, the Unitarian Minister of Paradise Street Chapel and Charles Winstanly of Trinity.

It was also felt beneficial to have medical gentlemen involved in the close government of the School. The surgeon Edward Alanson, who had been involved in the founding of the School, was an obvious candidate. Dr Jonathan Binns too, a colleague of Roscoe and Currie and outspoken abolitionist, was a respected choice. Dr Joseph Brandreth and the surgeon Henry "Harry" Parke were frequently alluded to as physicians of considerable celebrity. Dr John Lyon was also elected – he was well known to many of this group of eminent men, especially those who were members of the local debating societies and the local Lyceum Club (which housed the first lending library in Britain), where philosophical and intellectual exchange were the norm.

The Presidency was given to John Sparling, who, ironically, considering the background of this peer group, had come to his present rank in society as a result of profits made from his involvement (mainly in the 1760s) in the "African Trade".

Born in Bolton-le-Sands in 1731, John Sparling was the son of a yeoman. Little is known of his early life, which was probably spent at sea, but by 1759 had become a merchant in Liverpool. In partnership with William Bolden and Samuel Shaw (a notable slave-trader), he held considerable investments in shipping and was quite prosperous by the 1760s. It is likely too that some of his vessels were involved in privateering. However, after the War of Independence, Sparling concentrated most of his efforts on direct trade with Virginia.[9]

In 1793, almost the entire north district of Everton was owned by Sparling, as was the Petton estate in Shropshire. His Everton estate was known as St. Domingo,[10] where in that same year, his new home, the magnificent classical mansion St. Domingo House, was erected. By 1785 he was sufficiently prominent in local affairs to be appointed Sheriff of the County of Lancaster and in 1790 elected Mayor of Liverpool.

John Sparling 1731-1800 (by Romney). First President of the Blind Asylum.

St. Domingo House, Everton, residence of John Sparling.

In these his later years, he was said to be "one of the last of the old school of Liverpool Merchants". When he attended the "Change he was dressed with precision and care, generally wearing a gold laced waistcoat, as was the mode of his day, and a three cornered or cocked hat. He was one of those wealthy and upright traders of Britain, of the eighteenth century, whose attire and conduct were on a par, so far as plainness, precision, regularity and substantial worth will suffer the comparison to be carried."[11] Such was the first President of the Blind Asylum.

A brief analysis of the the new plan for the government of the Blind Asylum reveals that it was much more workman-like and less idealistic than that drawn up in 1790. This was, perhaps, inevitable considering the make up of the new Committee and the problems of the previous two years.

At the meeting of 16 March, it was resolved to make immediate application for support in the form of annual subscriptions and contributions towards the cost of erecting a new building. The plans and resolutions made by the new administration were to be inserted in the Star, and the Liverpool, Manchester, and Chester newspapers for the public's attention.

Sir ;

THE Governors of the BLIND ASYLUM
having well considered the impoverished state of its
finances, are unanimously of opinion that this institution can no longer be conducted without the aid
of an *annual* Subscription.   Trusting however, that
the liberality of a generous Public will not allow a
scheme so useful to a very distrest portion of their
fellow-creatures and to Society to be abandoned,
and the Blind to be reduced to a vagrant and mendi-
cant life, they take the liberty of soliciting your beneficence towards the maintenance of this charity.

They will depute two Members of their Committee who will call upon you within a few days in
behalf of these *poor* and *blind* objects of your
compassion.

> *By order of the Committee.*

BLIND ASYLUM.
August 6th, 1793.

Appeal Notice 1793.

57

On 6 August, the Committee issued a printed circular which was aimed at promoting the cause for annual subscription, informing the receiver of the pamphlet that the School "will depute two members of the Committee who will call upon you within a few days in behalf of these *poor* and *blind* objects of your compassion."[12]

In the first year of this new government it was further decided that a pension scheme be established and that "...each blind person who shall be admitted to the benefit of this Institution, shall pay two-pence weekly out of his or her wages, to create a separate fund of money, which shall be placed out at interest, as a means of support when they are past labour, or when they are disabled from work; of which disability a certificate must be produced signed by a majority of the medical gentlemen of the Infirmary or Dispensary;"[13] Although the final regulation may have been difficult to comply with in practice, the governors were obviously looking forward with admirable concern towards any potential helplessness, and attempting, in tandem with technical instruction, to provide some sort of security throughout life for those in their charge.

In 1793, the Committee issued a full list (probably written and compiled by Dannett) of all those who had been admitted to the School since its inception. Forty-six men and women were listed, 27 of whom had left. Regarding the 19 still at the Asylum (the lowest number since the school opened), reports of their trades learnt, progress, wages, and character were given.

All were reported to be "decent", also "sober" in the case of the men; and 'regular' in the case of women. None of the men, except for a young ten year old, were learning music when the list was issued (although previous pupils had done so before they left); four made whips; the others baskets, bears and line; their wages averaging four shillings per week. All the women were trained and employed in spinning flax, earning three shillings per week, except for three women who also learned music, their wages being reduced to 1/6d per week.

There were numerous reasons stated for the first departures. Five, much to the gratification of the School, were able to return home, sufficiently trained to support themselves in their respective trades. Eight had left due to varying extremes of idleness, drunkenness, and tendency towards "minstrel behaviour". James Boucher, for example, who was an Ir-

58

AT A GENERAL MEETING OF THE SUBSCRIBERS AND FRIENDS TO THE ASYLUM IN LIVERPOOL,

FOR THE BENEFIT OF THE

INDIGENT BLIND,

HOLDEN AT THE GOLDEN LION, IN DALE STREET, ON TUESDAY THE 14th OF JANUARY, 1794.

PURSUANT TO PUBLIC ADVERTISEMENT.

THE accounts for the year 1793, were exhibited and approved. And it was ordered, that a report of the situation of the charity be published as speedily as possible.

It was also ordered, that an additional number of blind persons be admitted into the Asylum; so that the whole number does not (for the present) exceed forty, and that the committee be requested to publish the terms of admission, and the mode of application.

That in pursuance of a recommendation of the committee (now approved) the annual meeting of the subscribers and friends to the Asylum, be hereafter held on the second Tuesday in January, instead of the first, which is the day on which the members of the marine society annually meet.

That the thanks of this meeting be given to the president and other officers for the last year, for the great attention which they have paid to the interests of the Asylum.

That the vice president be requested to accept the thanks of the meeting, and that letters be written to Mr. Medley, Mr. M'Donald, Mr. Bruce, Mr. Price, and Mr. Pennington, expressive of the same, for their sermons and collections for the benefit of this institution, and also to Mr. Yates, and Mr. Joseph Smyth, for their warm recommendations of this charity from their pulpits.

That a letter of thanks be also written to Mr. Clement Noble, jun. for his assistance in arranging the accounts of the charity, and that he be requested to accept a whip, manufactured by the blind, as a token of the services he has thereby rendered them.

And it appearing to the gentlemen now assembled, that this institution (being in its infancy) it would be beneficial to the Asylum, if the officers of the last year could be prevailed on to continue their services for another year, and the president, vice president, treasurer, and several of the committee, having, at the earnest request of this meeting, consented to do so: the following officers were elected for the year 1794.

JOHN SPARLING, Esq. PRESIDENT.

REV. HENRY DANNETT, VICE PRESIDENT.   WILLIAM CUBBIN, Esq. TREASURER.

COMMITTEE.

REV. J. SMYTH,	Mr. DENNY,
T. BOLD,	Mr. NOBLE,
J. YATES,	Mr. J. SUTTON,
C. WINSTANLEY,	Mr. VENABLES,
Dr. BRANDRETH,	Mr. NELSON,
Dr. LYON,	Mr. RIGMAIDEN,
Mr. ALANSON,	Mr. DAGGERS,
Mr. PARKE,	Mr. J. LIGHTBODY, jun.

AUDITORS.

MR. PUDSEY DAWSON,   Mr. HUMBLE.

VISITORS.

Mr. BOLDEN   Mr. REES,
Mr. ALLAN PEARSON,   Mr. ROBERT WARD.

And it was ordered, That the committees (which are holden on the first Tuesday in each month) should be open to the subscribers and other friends of the charity.

J. SPARLING, CHAIRMAN.

The COMMITTEE of the SUBSCRIBERS to the ASYLUM in LIVERPOOL, for the benefit of the

INDIGENT BLIND,

DO HEREBY GIVE NOTICE,

THAT in consequence of the resolution of the general meeting of the subscribers held at the Golden Lion in Dale-street, on Tuesday the 14th inst. twenty more blind persons will immediately be admitted into the Asylum; and such persons as mean to recommend candidates for admission are requested to consider the following report of the nature and design of the institution, and to observe, that no application can be attended to, unless accompanied with answers to the subjoined queries, addressed, post paid, to Mr. John Graystock, at the Asylum, Liverpool, and signed respectively by a medical gentleman, and a clergyman of the parish where the person applying resides.

The advantages of this charity are, that during their continuance at the Asylum, the blind will be instructed in some useful art or trade, to which their genius appears best adapted, and by which they will be enabled to earn something at their own homes towards their subsistence, and pass their time with comfort to themselves.

Those who learn any mechanical art or trade, will be continued in the Asylum three or four years; at the expiration of which period, it is supposed they will be able to gain their own livelihood; when they must leave it, to afford an opportunity for others to receive the same instruction.

Every such person will be allowed, towards his or her support, a weekly sum not less than 1s. 6d. nor more than 5s. (except in extraordinary cases, to be judged of by the committee) such weekly allowance to be encreased by the committee, from time to time, according to each person's attention and ability; and to every married person, an additional weekly sum of six-pence will be paid.

Annual Report for 1793 (January 1794)

59

ishman and "strolling fiddler", was dismissed for "idleness and corrupting the well disposed, and because he would follow his minstrel employment". Bartholomew McGennis, also Irish, was "sometime in the Asylum, but chose to stroll about with his bag-pipes, rather than work regularly at the Asylum". Perhaps the greatest offender in the Committee's eyes was Thomas Garrett of Liverpool, a whipmaker who "was not content with his wages without going out at night to ale-houses to play on his fiddle. He was the most impudent fellow that came to the Asylum, and would have corrupted the rest and made them discontented". At the other extreme, George Hughes, also of Liverpool, "thought he could earn more by entertaining passengers in the Eastham boat; this is the most decent man of the blind minstrel tribe".

Of the remainder, three had died, three were unable to learn a trade, one was removed by her mother, one became incapacitated and one found other employment. Two women were dismissed for misconduct and imprudence – no other details were given: we can only surmise the possible links with the recent troubles.

A music pupil was also sent home, until the Asylum could afford to pay for his tuition, and one youth, Henry Arnold, was returned home to Ormskirk until his Parish Overseer of the Poor paid the arrears of the agreed support due to the School.

Indications of Surgeon Parke's skill were also evident within the list; Henry Derbyshire of Liverpool, "a very old man, gained for some time 1s. 6d weekly by picking oakum; he recovered the sight of one eye by the skill of Mr Parke".

At the General Meeting of 1794 in the following year, it was decided to admit 20 more pupils up to a total of 40, and terms of application and admission were published. Those learning mechanical arts or trades would be allowed to stay three or four years after which they were expected to leave and support themselves by the trade they had learned. Wages were to be not less than 1s. 6d per week up to a maximum of 5s. which would be reviewed according to "attention and ability". An additional weekly sum of 6d was to be paid to married persons.

The teaching of music was revised – only six pupils at any one time would be instructed, and the only instrument taught was the harpsichord,

LIVERPOOL ASYLUM

FOR THE BENEFIT OF THE

INDIGENT BLIND.

At a meeting of the committee of the subscribers to the Asylum in Liverpool for the benefit of the INDIGENT BLIND, holden Tuesday the 21st January, 1794,

IT WAS ORDERED,

" THAT such persons as mean to recommend candidates for admission are re-
" quested to observe, that no application can be attended to, unless accompanied
" with answers to the subjoined queries, addressed POST PAID to Mr. JOHN
" GRAYSTOCK, at the ASYLUM, LIVERPOOL, and signed respectively by a medi-
" cal gentleman, and a clergyman of the parish where the person resides."

QUERIES

TO BE ANSWERED BY A MEDICAL GENTLEMAN.

What is the nature and supposed cause of the applicant's blindness?

Is it total?

Is it deemed incurable?

QUERIES

TO BE ANSWERED BY A CLERGYMAN.

What is the name of the blind person?

What the age?

How long has he or she been blind?

What is the place or parish where the party was born?

What is the party's present place of residence?

To what place or parish does the party now belong?

How long has he or she resided there?

Has the person ever followed any trade, occupation, or employment, and what?

How is the person at present supported?

Is the party married?

If married, what is his or her family?

Hath the party any estate, annuity, salary, pension, or income for life or otherwise,
and what is the amount thereof?

If any, how doth it arise?

Did the party ever receive alms, or relief from any parish as a pauper; and if any,
from what place or parish?

Are the blind person's parents living or dead?

If living, what are their names, residence, and condition or circumstances, and
also what family have they?

Has the blind person been a common beggar, wandering minstrel, or played upon
any instrument at ale-houses, within two years before application for admission: such persons being entirely excluded?

Does the party bear a character of regularity, decency, and sobriety?

J. M'CREERY, PRINTER.

*Compulsory questionnaire to be completed before entry to the school
could be considered (1794).*

61

to give the pupils the opportunity to become organists. Such pupils could continue at the Asylum for four to eight years, and on leaving, if suitably qualified, were given five guineas towards the purchase of an instrument.

Most of the pupils admitted were already receiving support in one form or another, either from friends and relatives or from the Parish Overseers if they were destitute. It was expected that such pupils were only to be admitted if this upkeep was continued and paid into the Charity funds.

Despite the Committee's intention to increase funds further by collecting annual subscriptions from August 1793, their plans were hit by the outbreak of war with France – the result of which was a financial crisis and an inevitable acute shortage of cash. Fearing for the future, men hoarded their money; merchants were unable to obtain payments from abroad, or to continue credits to the clients at home; there was a run on the banks, and many businesses that were far from insolvent crashed due the lack of hard currency.

The government met the situation by issuing exchequer bills to merchants and normal dealing was gradually restored. Most merchants, however, now proceeded with understandable caution.

In Liverpool, one of the four banks in the town had to close its doors and the others might have followed suit but for the prompt action of the principal merchants who announced their confidence in the banks and their readiness to accept the private notes which the banks had been permitted to use. In fact, the public meeting held by the merchants to consider this state of affairs was held on 23 March, only a week after the General Meeting of the Blind School Subscribers, which goes some way to reflect the mood of the men at that earlier meeting, especially the likes of John Sparling.

So then, to return to the General Meeting of the following year where the subscribers heard the Report for 1793; on the intended plans for annual subscriptions, the Committee declared

"This resolution would have been followed up by an immediate collection,but unforseen events prevented it. Unfortunately for this, as well as other charitable institutions, severe distresses happened in the commercial world, which, in some degree, extended to many generous individuals; so that it appeared to the Committee an unfavourable season for soliciting that benevolence, which the inhabitants of Liverpool are at all times, so willing to show to any scheme that promises the comfort or the alleviation of the misery of their fellow creatures. Add to this that many gentlemen, well wishers to the Charity, had concerns of their own and their friends to attend to, which of necessity demanded their principal care and diverted their minds from remoter objects.[14]

Unfortunately, the check on commerce in the town also affected the sale of stock produced at the Asylum. This inevitably had repercussions on the Charity's ability to pay the wages of its teachers and pupils. Unwilling to see the effort of all concerned collapse, Henry Dannett advanced the necessary sums himself.

By the time of the Meeting in January 1794, the commercial world had reasserted its position, subscriptions increased and the auditors who had now arranged the accounts into a satisfactory order, reported that the Charity was no longer in the Red. Sadly, they also reported that out of £453 received from Liverpool subscribers, £359 had been lodged in the bank that had gone under, and was lost.

Nevertheless, the School and Charity were now on a more even keel, and as experience was gained, the running of the School over the next few years became more efficient, thanks to the concerted efforts of its governors. Numbers at the School increased within a year to 33 and by 1798 had risen further to 54, reinforcing the urgent need for new facilities.

It was to those ends that the governors began to concern themselves with growing commitment.

4
PRAGMATISM AND PATRONAGE

"Less of an Asylum...

...more approaching to a School"

In 1776 William Moss compiled his first edition of a visitor's guide book to Liverpool, and in his introduction remarked that

> "Wealth being the result of Commerce, the flourishing state of the town has enabled it to make efforts for its internal improvement, and which it has recently done in a manner not a little extraordinary; this, with the pleasant and salubrious situation of the town, the convenience of sea bathing, its amusements and the lively cheerful air which regularly pervades it, have of late years made it the resort also of Strangers of all descriptions, for the purposes of health and amusement..."[1]

Yet, a survey made in the town only a few years earlier, gave a quite different picture. Of the 8,148 inhabited houses of the town, 1,728 contained inhabited cellars, and in these appalling conditions dwelt 6,780 people, almost four to every cellar and almost ten per cent of the towns' total population.[2] Inevitably, poor health and disease were common. Outbreaks of smallpox were frequent and remarks made on the Blind Asylum concluded that "...most of these unfortunate objects have lost their sight by smallpox. It is to be lamented that so great a majority of the poor still retain their prejudices against inoculation. A plan of general inoculation was formed here some years ago, and every persuasive means made use of to induce the lower ranks to accept it; but to so little effect that at last, after a trial of two or three years, it was given up."[3]

The plan of inoculation was not that of Edward Jenner – his first experiments in vaccination were not made until 1796 and his results not published until two years later. It is possible that the inoculations were a continuation of the plan introduced by Lady Mary Wortley Montague in 1717. (Her husband was British ambassador to Turkey and it was from there that the Eastern practice of inoculation was introduced to England.)

The necessity for such a measure may be judged when it is realised that one in every twelve of the deaths in London during the eighteenth century was due to smallpox.[4]

Conditions such as those in London also began to occur in Liverpool which resulted in similar pioneering actions taken regarding inoculation.

The problems of unhealthy overcrowding were not lost on the governors of the Blind Asylum, who reported in 1796, "...the houses at present engaged as temporary workshops are much too small for the number already admitted, and are consequently found to be prejudicial to the health of the blind."[5]

The move to raise funds to erect a new building had now begun in earnest, and by the end of 1796, £538 had been received into the building fund. This was in addition to the annual funds raised for the running of the Charity. The Committee were keen to remind the public that the Asylum was nowhere near the estimated target of self sufficiency based on profits from the products of the trades pursued within the Institution. This was especially due to the "...unproductive employment of the musical pupils, the great expense of Teachers, Overseers and unavoidable waste of materials in every kind of article which the Blind are taught to manufacture... By these statements...," the Committee declared, "...it is presumed the public will be convinced that the Charity is not possessed of any foundation sufficient to secure its permanency, independent of the continued contributions of its friends and supporters. One heavy expense, it is hoped, will shortly be removed by the erection of a commodious building better adapted to the designs of the institution; to promote which desirable object; and for which specific purpose, *unsolicited* contributions have for some time vested in the hands of trustees; additional aid has been promised to forward the design, and such a plan is now in agitation, as will probably be carried into effect within no very distant period."[6]

The help of the Church was secured that same year, following an approach to the Right Reverend the Lord Bishop of Chester, under whose control Liverpool lay, for permission to raise funds through the Diocese of Chester. Pamphlet circulars were despatched to clergy throughout the diocese, requesting "...the favour of a sermon from you at your own church for the benefit of the Institution, and for specific purpose of enabling the Committee to erect a commodious building for the Blind to work in...".[7]

A Sunday in Lent was to be the desired day for the sermon and the Committee also enclosed copies of the Annual Reports to be distributed

PRESUMING upon your good disposition to promote the works of charity, the Committee who have the management of the ASYLUM FOR THE INDIGENT BLIND in this town, have taken the liberty to request the favour of a Sermon from you at your own church, for the benefit of that Institution, and for the specific purpose of enabling the Committee to erect a commodious Building for the Blind to work in. The houses at present engaged as temporary workshops are much too small for the number already admitted, and are consequently found to be prejudicial to the health of the Blind. As the Charity is not of a local nature, but is open to objects from any part of the kingdom, it is hoped your congregation will not think it unreasonable that they should be solicited to contribute their assistance towards rendering this unfortunate and helpless class of their fellow creatures more comfortable and more happy. Your Diocesan has been consulted upon the propriety of the application, which the Committee now venture to make, and from the annexed letter, addressed to the Rev. John Smyth, Vice President, you will perceive how far it meets with his concurrence and good wishes

The Committee have inclosed a few Reports of the State of the Asylum, which will supersede the necessity of their entering into a particular explanation of the nature of the Charity ; and which you are requested to distribute amongst such of your parishioners, as, in your opinion, are most likely to encourage and promote so benevolent an Institution. Of the time most proper for preaching the Sermon, the Committee think you are the best judge, and therefore they have only further to desire that you will preach, or cause it to be preached, on some Sunday in the month of January ; or as much earlier as may suit your own convenience ; and that you will, (after deducting postage, and any other expenses) remit, either in cash or bills, the amount of the contributions you may collect, to *Edward Houghton, Esq.* Treasurer to the Asylum for the Blind, in Liverpool, in order that the Committee may be enabled to ascertain as soon as possible, how far they are justified in making the necessary preparations, for the intended Building, and to what extent.

I have the honor to be,

Reverend Sir,

Your obedient humble Servant,

GEORGE VENABLES, President.

Liverpool, 13th December, 1796.

Committee Appeal Notice addressed to clergy, requesting they preach a sermon on behalf of the school.

among those parishioners, whom, it was felt, would most likely promote the cause.

The plan proved most successful. In its first year, £656 towards the building fund was raised by the church collections alone, which enabled the Committee to reach a position where they could begin to look for a plot for their desired purpose.

At the top of Shaws Brow, between Islington and the Infirmary, where today stands the Museum of Labour History, a small plot of land lay vacant. This, the Committee felt, was an ideal position for the new school, being opposite the Commutation Row houses, and close to the Infirmary and parish church of St. John. Little upheaval would be necessary, and those in lodgings would have no need to move.

On 2 February 1796, a monthly meeting of the Committee was held in the Asylum music room, with the governors of the Infirmary and local inhabitants of Islington also in attendance. They had been called together "...for the purpose of taking into consideration the propriety of applying to the Liverpool Corporation for the grant of a plot of land lying between the Infirmary and Islington..."[8] It was decided the matter be adjourned until Dr. Currie had collected the opinions of his colleagues at the Infirmary.

A second meeting was held the following week with the same persons in attendance, when a letter from the Infirmary was read, giving no objection to the proposal. It was signed by seven governors, four of whom, Brandreth, Parke, Lyon and Brown, were also on the Asylum Committee.[9] A petition was subsequently lodged with the Corporation requesting the grant of the required land.

The Committee were clearly keen to proceed in an organised and open manner by consulting with the local residents and the adjacent Infirmary (despite the existing connections between the two institutions). Even so, the locals were quite unhappy with the proposals. While the Committee's application was under consideration, a counter petition objecting to the plan was drawn up by the Islington residents and presented to the Council.

On 16 August that same year, the President, on behalf of the Committee, wrote to the Mayor, declaring "...anxious to relieve the Gentlemen of

Council from the unpleasant dilemma into which they have been reduced by the opposition, which some of the inhabitants of Islington Brow have made to the petition lately presented to them by the Corporation, we beg leave to withdraw the same..."[10]

So, as a result of such early examples of open consultations, petitions and people power, the respectable objectives of the Asylum governors had returned to square one.

It took the Committee only until the following May to seek out an alternative piece of land, again close to Commutation Row, and to commence negotiations. Situated in Prescot Lane, opposite Camden Street (see map of 1797 – the site today is bordered by Hotham Street and Pudsey Street and is occupied by the Odeon Cinema Complex), the plot was owned by John Leigh, a local attorney, member of the Town Council and neighbour of Mr. Parke. According to Picton, Leigh had "...probably a greater amount of foresight than any other man of his day. Acting on these convictions he invested all the funds at his command in the purchase of lands around Liverpool. This he did to such an extent as to seriously embarrass himself during his own lifetime and to entail large burdens on his successors' (although many years later his family were to benefit greatly from land sales enforced by the Railways Act).[11]

On 6 June the Committee discussed Mr. Leigh's letter asking £500 for the plot – a sale possibly forced due to his financial embarrassment. Four days later, Leigh accepted the Committee's reduced offer of £450.

The Committee wasted no time; on the same day that their offer was accepted they requested that "...several professional gentlemen prepare Ground Plans and Elevations for the intended building and to be submitted by the 16th June...".[12]

Three sets of plans were received and on 18 July those submitted by John Foster & Son were accepted, and the following advert placed in *Gores Advertiser*.

"Any person willing to contract for erecting a building in Prescot Lane opposite Camden Street in Liverpool intended for the Blind Asylum and for providing materials and finishing the same may send in proposals in writing on or before Tuesday the first day of August next to the President and Committee at the Asylum where the Plans and Elevations of the intended building with particular descriptions, in the meantime, may be seen by applying to John Graystock, Clerk to the Asylum."

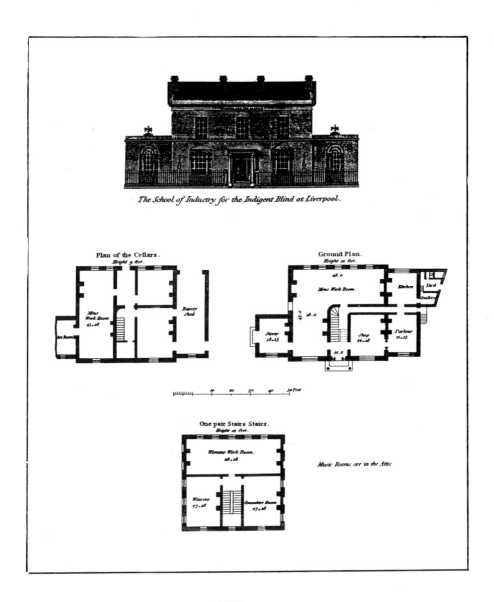

The School of Industry for the Indigent Blind at Liverpool.

Plan of the Cellars.
Height 9 feet.

Ground Plan.
Height 11 feet.

One pair Stairs Stairs.
Height 11 feet.

Music Rooms are in the Attic

Plans of the New School (completed 1800).

No records exist regarding replies to the advert, but what is certain is that the building fund was still inadequate. On 10 January 1798 the Annual Report for the previous year was presented to the Committee, which stated that a building plan had been selected and

"...appears to comprehend the various requisites of the Institution and to combine them with that plainness and simplicity so peculiarly proper in a building intended for charitable purposes. In order however, to execute this plan an additional sum of £1500 will, on the lowest calculation, be necessary..."[13]

The tender was re-advertised in April 1798 following concerted efforts to raise funds, which included further appeals to local and distant clergy, plus house to house collections arranged by the Committee, who were each allocated an area in the Town.

On the 16th April, a Select Committee was formed to supervise the Building operations, which included William Roscoe (the new President of the Asylum), William Rathbone (the merchant and slave abolitionist), and Messrs. Hope and Bird, whose own plans for the new building had been rejected in favour of Fosters.

By 1 May 1798 several proposals had been considered. The Committee declared, "that of John Foster & Son specifying a much earlier time than any of the others, and being on the whole thought the most eligible, Mr Roscoe and Mr Roe are appointed to agree with J. Foster & Son at a sum not Exceeding £2170 without Pallisades".[14]

John Foster jnr, the architect of the Building, was elected to the Committee that same year. He was the son of John Foster, the Secretary and General Surveyor of the Docks. Together they designed and carried out the works of the Princes Dock, and later, Foster Junior was to become Architect and Surveyor to the Corporation, designing some of the best known buildings in the town, notably the 5th Custom & Excise Building (which was damaged beyond repair during the Second World War). The Asylum Building was one of his earliest designs.

Among his colleagues on the Committee for 1798 were the aforementioned Roscoe and Rathbone, William Hope (merchant, after whom Hope Street is named), Matthew Gregson (the antiquarian), Joseph Cazneau, (merchant, who also gave his name to the street), and Samuel Stainforth, son of the Mayor of that year, who became Mayor himself in 1812 (he was known locally as "Sulky Sam" due to his forbidding appearance).

70

John Foster Jnr. (1787-1846), corporation surveyor, architect of the first school building, extension and chapel.

The Asylum benefited greatly from such powerful and influential men managing its affairs, especially when it came to fund raising, men that were also wise enough to tread warily to keep public opinion with them, as in the matter of the Islington land dispute.

A man hitherto unmentioned had served on the Committee each year since its inception, and continued to do so until his death in 1816. He was Pudsey Dawson, and became so well known for his tireless work on behalf of the School, that later historians mistakenly believed he was the founder.

Pudsey was born in 1752. His father was a Doctor at St. George's Hospital in London and a descendant of the Pudseys of Bolton Hall in Craven, Yorkshire. Pudsey settled in Liverpool in 1776 as a result of his mercantile interests. He lived with his family in 35 Rodney Street, and of his 12 children, three were killed in the Napoleonic campaigns.

The sacrifice of his three sons in the French campaign was not an isolated loss of Liverpool men. The fact that his sons particularly were looked upon as heroes, reflected the growing patriotism that was sweeping through the Town in the late 1790s.

For the townsfolk the war had begun with a sense of remoteness, and the manifest air of apathy frequently resulted in the presence of the press gang. But now, in 1798, invasion from France appeared imminent, and the coming rebellion in Ireland was showing its first symptoms. In the previous year seven companies of Liverpool yeomanry were raised, and a year later a further 2,000 volunteers were mustered on the Mosslake Fields[15] as the two battalions of the Royal Liverpool Regiment of Volunteers. One of the battalions was commanded by Pudsey Dawson, now with the rank of Colonel (he was to be Mayor the following year). His battalions remained in arms until the 1802 Peace of Amiens.

Meanwhile, the Committee were still intent on pushing through their building project as quickly as possible and were becoming especially concerned about the living conditions of their charges. In October 1798 it was reported that,

"...the great inconveniences sustained by the persons employed in this Asylum, as well from the difficulty of finding suitable places of residence sufficiently near the Asylum as from the unhealthiness of the situation where many of them live, and the injury arising

Residence of Pudsey Dawson, 35 Rodney Street, reputed to be the first house built on Rodney Street.

Pudsey Dawson (1752-1816) (committee member 1793-1814).

73

from their being exposed to improper society – having been under consideration it is recommended to the Committee to think seriously of some plan for obviating these inconveniences, and to endeavour to have such plan digested for the consideration of the approaching annual meeting."[16]

Foster was swiftly requested to prepare a plan for suitable dwelling houses on the west side of the land behind the new building and "... to consider how far the east front of such houses could be made subservient to the intended plan for a covered yard for spinning".[17]

Much has been said regarding the officialdom surrounding the School but how did this affect the pupils on a personal basis? Regular personal contact with the pupils by the Committee was uncommon, except by those who were elected as Visitors for the year. Regarding authority, the daily lives of the pupils were more concerned with their teachers, local clergy and, above all, the Clerk of the Asylum, John Graystock, who was effectively a headmaster, and his wife, who was matron.

Matters of great concern were still referred to the Committee, such as decisions regarding new admissions and serious misbehaviour, where occasionally those concerned were required to appear before them.

At the same time that the Committee were debating the living conditions, they were also called upon to deal with complaints that had been received regarding the "very rude and unbecoming behaviour of Turner, Rothwell, Newton and Handford [pupils, boys, aged between 11 and 14] during their attendance in Church". Having been "...repeatedly reproved for it, they were brought up again and informed that if a similar complaint was brought forward in future, the delinquents would certainly receive corporal punishment and be exposed on the following Sunday in Church, with a label denoting their crime and punishment".[18]

Graystock himself was ordered to appear before the Committee on 16 August 1799. It was reported that

"...It appears evident, as well from his own confession, as from the testimony of others, that the conduct of Mr. Graystock towards Margaret Wilding [a 22 year old blind woman] hath been very censurable, it is the unanimous conclusion of this meeting that he be dismissed from his office as Clerk to the Institution and that he be desired to settle his accounts with as little delay as possible...it is also concluded that Mrs Graystock be permitted to remain for the present if she shall be so incline, and that when she leaves, the Treasurer be directed to make her a present of Twenty Guineas in consideration of the respect which the Committee feel for her character and the service which she hath uniformly rendered the Institution."[19]

As to the actual nature of the offence no further details are known, but such incidents were isolated, and must be afforded fair perspective. Matters such as this stand out in period reports, proving to be attractive for anecdotal and social interest, as in 1798 and 1799 the Committee were spending most of their time and energy on the completion of the new building. There is no doubt though that Graystock had brought shame to his wife and family, and the extract certainly reflects the sympathy the Committee felt for his poor wife.

Regarding the new building, Foster was experiencing early unionism and strike action by his workers in August 1799, and in exasperation he declared, "If the different workmen can only be kept to their work, without again breaking off on account of wages, the building may be completed in three months". Yet, four months later in December, work was still incomplete; "...the workmen employed on the new building having applied for and appearing to be deserving of some pecuniary compensation as an encouragement to them to get forward with more expedition, Mr. Leicester and Mr. Roe [of the Building Committee] are authorised to do what they think needful herein and repay them".[20]

With the completion of the new School imminent, a decision was needed as to the future of the Commutation Row houses. Initially, it was felt that they could be used as rooms to board pupils of the School, "so bringing them more immediately under the eye of the Governor, particularly during the hours when they are not at work."[21] However, this idea was dismissed once further land alongside the new building became available. This gave the Committee a wider scope for expansion; much greater than the previously requested plans from Foster for small dwellings. The Committee reported,

"...after maturely discussing the board and lodging of such pupils of each sex as may be the most likely to be injured in their health or morals by being placed in promiscuous boarding-houses, it is concluded that it is more eligible to erect houses on the ground concluded to be purchased, adjoining the present building, rather than to occupy the two houses in Commutation Row."[22]

The land behind the new building was shortly purchased from Thomas Rylands for £300.

Foster was again requested to draw up plans, this time to include the land lately purchased. He was asked to pay due regard to certain requirements, such as, there was to be only one point of access, and "the houses for each sex to be kept completely distinct, and that there be distinct portions of land each for the purpose of exercise and recreation". Each house was to be of a size to "lodge around eight pupils and the beds be large enough for only one person". Regarding sanitation, an ample water supply was to be provided to each house and "special attention be given to ventilation". Finally, the buildings were to be so constructed as to allow future enlargement, should the need arise.[23]

In the meantime, the new School had opened on 1 March with a total of 68 pupils, an increase of 23 on the previous year. The building contained separate work rooms for men and women, storerooms, a small ropery, and a shop, which sold products of the School to the public. There was also a committee room where future meetings would be held, apartments for the Governor and music rooms in the attic. There was to be a change of name too; it was now to be known as the Liverpool School for the Indigent Blind; this the Committee believed, would avoid any misconception that boarders were accepted.

Yet another plot of land was acquired by the School in 1798, but buildings were not to be planned for this site. The land, which was in Formby, was offered to the School by the Reverend Mr. Formby for the purpose of a willow plantation. The Committee, who had had great difficulty in obtaining suitable material for School stocks, immediately grasped the opportunity and set a plantation management plan in motion. "Three Cheshire acres" (approximately six to eight acres) were leased from the Reverend Mr Formby, trees were purchased, and 100 tons of manure were delivered to the site.

A deputation of Committee members travelled to Formby in March 1799 to check on progress. With them was an experienced basket maker, "...a person very well acquainted with the manner of making Plantations of Willows". On their return they had "...satisfaction to report that every method which had been previously adopted has met with his full approbation and he has also favoured us with some very useful hints".[24]

The main problem that had faced those entrusted with the setting up of the plantation was the immense workload of planting the trees before the end of spring. Thirty Formby men were recruited but this was found still insufficient. The expense of the project was beginning to rise closer to a

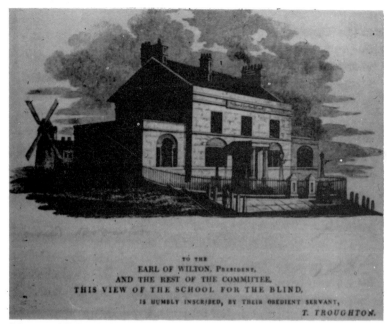

TO THE
EARL OF WILTON, President,
AND THE REST OF THE COMMITTEE,
THIS VIEW OF THE SCHOOL FOR THE BLIND,
IS HUMBLY INSCRIBED, BY THEIR OBEDIENT SERVANT,
T. TROUGHTON.

*Liverpool School of Industry for the Indigent Blind (1805)
(T. Troughton).*

*William Herdman's 1824 painting of the School. Based on Troughton's
Sketch of 1805.*

level that would defeat the object of the whole exercise, when, "...one of the workmen invented an ingenious implement to be added to a common plow by means of which they were enabled to make Furrows in the earth a foot and a half deep which so much expedited their progress that they have been enabled to completely finish the business in a much shorter time than could reasonably have been expected".[25] By May 1799, the plantation of 60,000 willows was complete, and a rent free lease, from the Reverend Formby, was taken for a minimum of 14 years.

In 1800, John Sparling, the first President of the School, died. In his last years he had not forgotten the School, and left a generous legacy of £100 for the Charity. His Will also contained binding clauses to prevent his heirs from disposing of his beloved St. Domingo Estate; it took ten years and an Act of Parliament to finally to liberate his family from its demands. He was buried in a tomb he had had constructed in Walton Churchyard, which was visible from the mansion, no doubt intending to remind those residing at St. Domingo for generations to come of who created their delightful residence. Later, in the mid-nineteenth century, the House became a Roman Catholic college, but not before it had played a more unusual role for a short time after Sparling's death.

The Estate was inherited by his son, William Sparling, a lieutenant in the 10th Regiment of Dragoons, who became rather infamous as the result of a duel in which he killed Edward Grayson, the shipbuilder.

William had been calling on Anne Renshaw, daughter of the Rector of Liverpool, and Committee member of the School for the Blind. An anonymous letter was sent to William regarding the character of the young lady and her family. On the basis of the letter's contents he broke off the engagement by way of a letter to her Father, causing his daughter much distress. Despite not having met young Sparling, Grayson, who was Anne's Uncle, took it upon himself to publicly brand him a scoundrel and villain. Sparling, who had been abroad since the parting, wrote to Grayson on his return, and after hostile exchanges, which lasted from October 1803 until February the following year, a challenge was finally sent to the aggrieved uncle and the parties met at dawn on Sunday 24 February 1804, opposite the Toxteth Chapel in the Dingle. From there they moved down to Knott's Hole, a secluded dell near the river where the duel took place.

Two shots rang out but only one met its target, and Grayson fell from a

Left: William Sparling (1777-1870) (son of John Sparling).

Below: Knott's Hole, Dingle (scene of the Sparling – Grayson duel).

79

wound in his right thigh. Dr McCartney (his Second) and Harry Parke, the surgeon in attendance, rushed to his aid and carried him to his post-chaise. He was hurriedly taken to his house, where he died a week later from his wounds. (Mr Parke, of course, was the Surgeon to the Blind School, and still serving on the Committee.)

There followed, on 4 April 1804, a trial at Lancaster, where it took the jury 20 minutes to acquit Sparling and his Second, Captain Colquit R.N., of the charge of wilful murder.[27] It was still the period where gentlemen could settle their differences according to that traditional code of honour without recrimination. Despite the infamy and scandal surrounding the duel at Knott's Hole, the Town had not yet seen the back of this "honourable" method of settling a gentleman's quarrel. Sparling never returned to St. Domingo, and on taking up residence at his family's other estate at Petton in Shropshire, he quickly adapted to his new role as local squire.

A few months earlier, matters of national security were again at the forefront of people's minds, especially those whose livelihoods depended on foreign trade and calm waters. The Peace of Amiens had proved to be no more than an armed truce, and by May 1803 hostilities with France broke out once more. Parliament addressed the Crown with assurances of support, and again Liverpool men rallied to the cause. John Bolton, one of the wealthiest and public spirited of Liverpool merchants (who had previously served as the second President of the Blind Asylum), made an offer to raise and equip a regiment of 600 men at his own expense – the number later being increased to 800.

Volunteer forces were now raised in the town on a larger scale than ever before, such was the growing fear of invasion and the naval threat to shipping in the area. At a review in 1804, 180 officers and 3,686 men paraded, which included a regiment of artillery from among the boatmen on the River.[28]

In September 1803, Prince William (afterwards Duke) of Gloucester was appointed Commander of the district's forces and on being despatched to Liverpool, took up residence at St. Domingo House. Old Sparling would never have dreamed that despite his Will, St. Domingo would benefit Liverpool Society with an impromptu royal court.

While still in command of his regiment, Colonel John Bolton experienced the most tragic incident of his life. Early in 1804, he had been instrumental in securing the post of Customs Jerker for a friend, a Major Brooks. (Brooks had caused mischief in the affair of 1804 when he reported Grayson's allegations to Sparling.) Later Brooks requested an increase in pay which was referred for approval to the West India Association, of which Bolton was President. The appeal was turned down. According to Brooks, Bolton had dismissed his claim asserting that "£700 a year was quite enough for a young, unmarried man".

The grudge now borne against Bolton led Brooks to pursue his former friend with unremitting malice. Finally, a meeting was arranged between the men at Millar's Dam on Aigburth Road on 20 December 1804. Yet, even before they reached the ground, the authorities, who had been tipped off, arrested both of them, and as a consequence they were bound over to keep the peace for 12 months.

For the next year, Brooks kept up his insulting behaviour. On the very day that their bond expired, he sought out Bolton, and on accosting him in Castle Street, insulted him to such an extent that Bolton had no option but to issue a challenge.

Both men were again arrested before any meeting could take place but were only detained a few hours. On his release, Brooks sent a friend to Bolton with a challenge to appear that afternoon, 20 December 1805, in a field on Fairclough Lane, then in the rural outskirts of the town (and now on a spot which lies beneath the Royal Liverpool Hospital).

In addition to their Seconds, the surgeon to the Blind School, Harry Parke, was again in attendance, having been picked up by Bolton's carriage as it passed his door on the corner of Newington-bridge.

It was such a cold, dark dreary, December evening that the pistols had to loaded by candlelight. The Major fired first without hitting his target. Colonel Bolton returned the shot which hit Brooks in the eye and killed him on the spot. Bolton fled into hiding until after the inquest, which found him guilty of wilful murder, but did not find just cause to prosecute, as public opinion was entirely in his favour.[29]

In the announcement of Brooke's death in the local paper, much was said of his character and temperament, but no reference whatsoever was made as to how he met his end. Despite the outcome, such methods of set-

John Bolton (second President of the Blind Asylum).

tling arguments had finally had their day and this was to be the last known duel in Liverpool.

On 18 September 1806, Royalty once again came to Liverpool, which was to prove of great benefit to the School. The town was honoured by a visit from the Prince of Wales (later George IV) and the Duke of Clarence (later William IV), where the guests were entertained by the Earl of Derby at Knowsley Hall. The Royal brothers toured the streets of Liverpool and were driven round the arcades in a carriage – a feat, according to Picton writing in 1875, " never performed before or since". Later in the evening, a magnificent banquet was given in their honour at the Town Hall, with Prince William (their cousin), the Earls of Derby and Sefton, and the Mayor, Henry Clay, among the dignitaries present.

Before the banquet though, a special call was in order. The Prince of Wales and his entourage paid a visit to the School for the Blind, an indication of the standing and respect the School had now achieved, both locally and nationally (the visit was, no doubt, encouraged by Lord Derby who had been President of the School during the previous year).

There the Prince minutely examined all the manufactures, of which he declared himself "highly gratified", and expressed similar satisfaction at the appearance of the pupils in general. The Royal party then ascended into the music room, where they heard the Hallelujah Chorus performed by the School choir. The Prince was strongly affected and expressed his "sympathy and approbation".

Pudsey Dawson was not a man to let such an opportunity slip by, and swiftly brought to the Princes attention the fact that the School was still in its infancy and was "very far from a state of perfection". Furthermore, the "fostering care of Royal Patronage might be the means of increasing its growth and extending the blessing which it already bestows to the blind".

To Pudsey's delight, and to the pleasure of his associates gathered around him, the Prince replied that it was "...exactly what he wished, that he was delighted with it having been solicited, and he accepted it with the greatest pleasure". His Royal Highness promptly ordered ten guineas to be distributed among the pupils and 100 guineas to be paid for the benefit of the Institution.[31] Thus, the School secured its Royal Patronage which has continued unbroken to the present day.

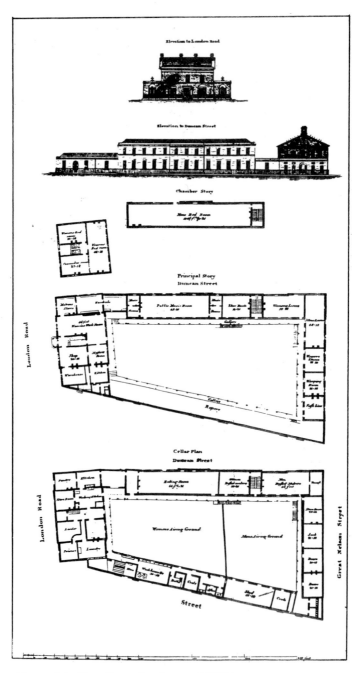

Plans of the New Extension (opened 1812).

84

The 100 guineas was a great boost to the Charity, which was still pre-occupied with raising funds for the extension to the new building. After numerous submissions and rejections, Foster's plans were adopted by the Committee in April 1806, although over the next few months he was to be frequently requested to redraw certain details to comply with fresh requirements of a Building Committee intent on producing the best facilities for the money available and to make full use of the new land at their disposal.

The additional buildings were to be quite extensive and were to accommodate the entire block of land at the rear of the School, reaching back to a path shortly to become Great Nelson Street. The principal stack of buildings to the front of Duncan Street (later renamed Hotham Street) were three storeys high, intended for a refectory, dormitories, music-rooms and work-rooms. Facing Great Nelson Street (now Lord Nelson Street), the two storey section contained work and store rooms; and the section of the building bordering the path later to be known as Pudsey Street was to be used as a ropery with washouses and baths in the cellar. Around the internal perimeter of the new extension was a first floor gallery supported by stone pillars and cast iron arches. Iron pallisades were to surround the whole building and were also to form a division between males and females in the courtyard.

Foster's estimate for the work, again in the stipulated character of a "perfectly plain manner", amounted to £7,021 10s 0d. This was far in excess of funds available, but to the credit of the Committee, taking the urgency of the project into account, it was resolved on 16 April 1807, to proceed with the building in stages, the cost of which was not to exceed the current level of the building fund. Work on the principal building, estimated at a cost of £2683 was given the immediate go ahead.

Over the next five years, as and when funds would allow, Foster was requested to proceed stage by stage until on 30 December 1812, 53 males and 18 females were at last admitted into the new buildings.

The completion of the School as a self-contained residential, technical institution, together with its Royal Patronage, moved the School into a new epoch.

In the eyes of the managers of the School, yet another goal had been

Sketch of the planned extension (1810) (Troughton)

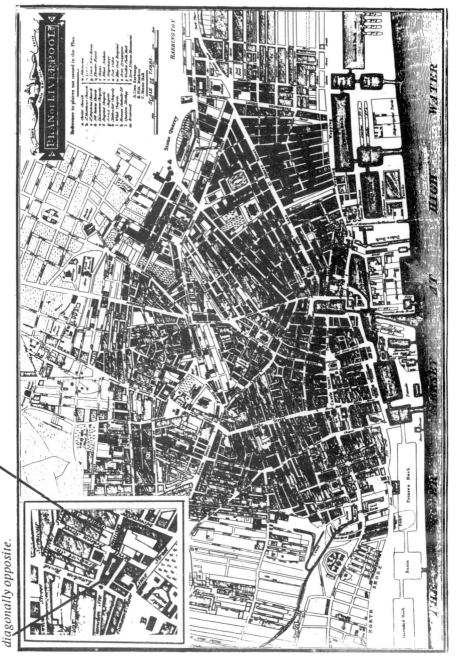

London Road School with New Extension occupying full plot reaching to Great Nelson Street. The bare plot soon to be used for the Chapel lies diagonally opposite.

Thomas Kaye: A CORRECT PLAN OF THE TOWN OF LIVERPOOL engraved by Gregory 1810

achieved. Their dream of expanding the Asylum involved more than just bricks and mortar. As the plans for these additional buildings were put into operation, they had declared

"Increased experience has enabled us to improve the nature of the establishment under our care, and we have continued during each successive year to render it less of an *Asylum*, where the ease and comfort of the blind were principally considered, and more approaching to a *School*, where they should be instructed in some useful art or trade, by which they might be enabled to procure for themselves a comfortable livelihood."[32]

There can be no doubt that in the treatment of the pupils it was quite clear how the "principal considerations" had begun to shift.

5
REGULATION, ROUTINE AND RELIGION
– A New Order

"The object of Punishment is, prevention from evil;
it never can be made impulsive to good"

Horace Mann
Lecture and Reports on Education (1845)

"It seems expedient that Mr. Brand [the new Superintendent, appointed
1805] should have the power of punishing the disobedient pupils by
solitary confinement or detaining them at work for three hours beyond
the usual time of quitting their labour"

(Committee Resolution, 23 Oct. 1805.)

After the rhetoric and eulogising by the promoters and overseers of the
Institution, certain realities of daily life behind the doors of the School at
first glance come as quite a shock. Yet, punishments meted out at the
School do not seem to be any more harsh than in other schools during the
period, for the handicapped or otherwise. (Even at Eton, discipline was
often very harsh. John Keate, headmaster from 1809 to 1834 won himself
a reputation as a flogger. One day in 1832, at the age of 60, he beat no less
than 80 boys.)

Solitary confinement was common in numerous schools and in the
Blind School its most severe form was known as the "Black Hole" – the
French *"Cachot"*, confinement in the dark, a rather ironic punishment. A
diet of bread and water usually accompanied this sentence, as did a flogging. Such treatment was known too at other establishments, such as
Rowland Hill's private school in Birmingham, which was actually regarded as progressive and ahead of its time in the early 1800s. Dickens'
terrible picture of Dotheboys Hall in *Nicholas Nickleby*, with the brutal
Whackford Squeers as its master, is no doubt, a caricature, but most likely
one founded on reality.

Excesses on the part of the pupils were considered as being caused by
little provision made for their free time, which resulted in many schools
working their pupils very hard for long hours.

We have already witnessed the desire of the Committee for boarded accommodation at the School to allow for maximum supervision and control.

Furthermore, masters could not always be relied upon, or even be expected to help with discipline. In 1815, for example, two masters, Robert Styles and Edward Baker, were found guilty of misconduct on the premises. On imposing a deduction from their wages for three months, the Committee also resolved that they should be "severely reprimanded; and that if in future they be found drunk in the School or countenance that dangerous vice; or allow any of the money paid in rewards to the pupils be expended in liquor, that they be immediately dismissed".[1] This invariably left the Superintendent of the Liverpool School alone in managing upwards of 75 pupils, many of whom were middle aged adults. Under such conditions, he may have had to resort to a rule of terror. This does not necessarily imply harsh treatment, but a rule where fear determines behaviour and control.

A glance again at Dannett's initial plans for his pupils and the treatment given to them during the early years does contrast with the order of the early 1800s. (An extract from the Rules may be consulted in the appendices.) The rules drawn up by the Committee during this period were not unduly harsh, but certainly curtailed freedom, especially with the imposition of a 12 hour day during winter. During Joseph Brand's governorship a stricter regime was undoubtedly enforced.

Moral codes were to be strictly adhered to. Understandably, relationships of an amorous nature between pupils, and pupils and servants, were common, and always took place under clandestine circumstances.

If such relations were discovered, various steps were taken. In January 1800 George Eaton and Elizabeth Jones, both minors, were found to be in each other's company. George "...declared his determined resolution to be married to Elizabeth Jones...", but, the Committee reported, "...although much influence and advice has been used to dissuade them from such a step he be sent home to his own parish."[2] A few days later, Elizabeth "disgraced herself" and was dismissed.

In contrast to these events, the Committee, in the same week were distributing 15 guineas amongst the pupils – a gift which had become an annual New Year custom.

In the following year, the School had extreme problems with Joshua Sutcliffe, a basket maker, who had entered the School from Leeds a year earlier. Regarding his case it was reported that,

"...having been addicted to fornication and appearing not likely to be reclaimed, though much exertion had been made for that purpose, it is ordered that he be discharged from the Institution and that this take place as soon as he can be delivered to his friends."[3]

Joshua was an active 13 year old.

Poor Henry Gatley, a 21 year old, was taken home in 1803 by his father for three months, to "...wean him from a connection which he was inadvisably forming with one of the servant girls...".[4] He returned after the required period, where he continued at the School for another two years, after which he qualified to teach music. He left in 1805, with great credit despite his earlier problems, to become organist at St. Matthews (which faced Commutation Row). In addition, the Committee lent Henry a harpsichord in reward for his good conduct.

Amorous relationships continued to undermine the discipline and the moral spirit expected by the Governors. In 1805, the Committee made official application to the local clergy not to perform marriage services either by banns or licence, involving pupils of the School without their written consent. This applied to pupils of all ages. The punishment for "clandestine courtship" or "illicit marriage" was to be instant dismissal, as was the withholding of information or being an accessory to the offence.

These measures had been drawn by the Committee in consequence of the recent "clandestine marriage" between pupils John Davies (aged 20) and Elizabeth Barrow (aged 19). The Governors were furious and mounted an immediate investigation. Both were dismissed, John on 5 January, and Elizabeth "was sent to the parish of her husband [which was Shenstone, Staffordshire] on 25 January":[5]

In the self-reassurance that, in the end, they had not abandoned their former charges without hope, the Committee reported that John had acquired "...sufficient knowledge of basket-making to be able to maintain himself" and that Elizabeth "...had learnt to spin, make baskets, list shoes, and window-line, by which she may contribute considerably towards her maintenance".[6]

The Committee were not finished with the matter, however. Frances Babb, in consequence of her duplicity respecting the marriage of her friend, was also dismissed. Yet, in her case, the Committee relented the following week, after she had written expressing her penitence for her past conduct, promising in future to strictly observe the laws of the Institution. Nevertheless, she was only allowed back on condition that she made a declaration of her penitence to Mr. Blundell (the School Chaplain and Secretary), in the presence of all the females in the Charity. This she did, and continued at the School until 1810 when, on qualifying in numerous trades and wishing to leave, the Committee, in consequence of her "industry and uniform good conduct" presented her with six guineas.

To be fair, the Committee was not unduly harsh; after all, discipline had to be maintained in a mixed school of this nature, with as little upset in daily routine as possible, and routine was important for the efficient running of the establishment. Furthermore, the Governors were prepared to show their support for those who did abide by the set parameters, evidence of their desire to see pupils lead as normal and integrated a life as possible. At the very same meeting held to deal with Davies and Barrow, the Committee resolved that "Joseph Ackers, being about to make a proper connection in marriage, and with a woman enjoying the advantage of sight, and in other respects eligible, has the approbation of the Committee so to do".[7]

For those who had spent their time well at the School, observing its rules, showing good character and improving their skills in their trades, the Governors were anxious to reward their endeavours when the time came for them to leave and attempt to support themselves.

Musical pupils who had shown good aptitude or had reached a sufficient standard to teach music or become church organists, were invariably given a harpsichord on loan, together with a few guineas to help them become established.

Those who had learnt trades were given between two and eight guineas, tools for the job, and an initial supply of necessary materials before their return to the outside world. Sadly, not all succeeded, and occasionally pupils were re-admitted under the pretence of learning another trade, although this was rare.

Pupils occasionally absconded, but again, this was rare, especially when punishment was a good flogging and a term in solitary on bread and water. Fourteen year old Benjamin Williams of Brilley in Hertfordshire twice absconded within his first two months at the School. He had been taken from his parents, who were "strolling beggars", and placed in the School by a benevolent lady from Worcester. Sadly, he could not adjust to the sudden change and one January morning in 1805, he was spotted on the road to Ormskirk. Suspecting he had run away, the Superintendent ordered a constable to be sent after him. Young Ben was taken at Ormskirk and placed in the House of Correction on being returned to Liverpool. There he was to wait until the parish officers of Brilley sent for him. He never returned to the School.

Solitary confinement was also administered to pupils guilty of theft, Mary Hughes, for example, receiving one month's punishment in 1813, although in 1803 John Lawrence, a 22 year old from Middlesex, was dismissed after only nine months at the School for stealing a leg of pork. Yet, compassion was continuously in evidence. When it was found that a top-coat belonging to 17 year old Thomas Parkin had been stolen from him, on its discovery at a Norris' Old Hall Street Pawn Shop, Mr Brand ordered it to be redeemed at a cost of 6s, which would have been more than a week's wages to young Thomas.[8]

In October 1809, William Watt made a desperate appeal for help to the Committee. Sixty-three year old William was one of Dannett's original admissions and still at the School, although he lived at home with his wife and family. He was received by the Committee in quite a distressed state "owing to his inability from his wages to support those who are dependent upon him". Full of sympathy for his case, the Committee awarded him five guineas "as a reward for the constant attention which he has paid to the improvement of the pupils".[9]

This was a further example of the concern shown by the Governors for the pupils in their care. Although discipline and regulation was strict and punishment severe during this early period in the Schools' history, the Committee, especially through their Visitors, were continuously monitoring conditions, making reports, and trying to improve the existence of those within, wherever they were able. Of course, some of these improvements we have already considered, especially regarding the buildings and facilities, but on a more personal basis, pupils' diet for example, came under scrutiny in 1801.

Dr Bostock and Mr Blundell, in their role as Visitor and Chaplain, were becoming increasingly concerned as to the appearance and eating habits of the pupils, so much so that ten guineas were given to Revd. Blundell to "relieve the immediate wants of such of the pupils as are most in need".[10] Two weeks went by, after which it was decided that the kitchen be converted to more public use and that the School should provide "a good substantial and nutritive dinner for such of the pupils of both sexes who may be deemed not likely to expend their weekly allowance to the best advantage in this respect". A sub-committee was briefed to put the resolution into practice and to monitor the situation.

Health and sanitary conditions were much improved too when in 1804 a piped water supply was finally installed by the Corporation Water Works. Although the general health of the pupils was seemingly closely monitored, the affliction that had tragically put them there in the first place was not to ignored or forsaken. Operations were carried out during the early years, usually relating to cataracts, by medical gentlemen on the Committee. Dr John Lyon, for example, was thanked by the Committee in 1802 "for his great and kind attention to the pupils, particularly evinced in a successful operation lately performed on the eyes of one of them who was born blind".[11] Details regarding the operations are frustratingly scanty.

By 1809, it was decided that a Medical Committee be formed to examine the pupils and to give their opinion if there was the future possibility of operations being performed on any of the pupils eyes and to what advantage. Most of the Committee men seconded we have already met; Physicians being Doctors Joseph Brandreth, John Rutter, John Bostock, and Robert Lewin, and Surgeons John Lyon, Joseph Brandreth (son of the Doctor), Richard Forshaw and Harry Park. A few months later, one of the co-founders of the School, Edward Alanson, was added to the team. It was resolved on 18 February 1809 that the surgeons examine the eyes of the pupils and to report back to the Medical Committee with the names of those, who in their opinion, were proper subjects for surgery.

The week after that report was made, it was decided to obtain written

a. Edward Alanson 1747-1823, co-founder of the School and Management Committee Member.

b. Henry Parke 1745-1831, surgeon to the School and Management Committee Member.

c. Joseph Brandreth 1746-1815, Management Commitee Member 1793-1815.

d. Dr. John Rutter, Management Committee Meber, 1799-1803, 1810-30.

consent from the friends of those pupils whose condition could be operated upon with a reasonable chance of success. Eight of those pupils had cataracts, including Henry Gatley, although the friends of two of those pupils refused permission to operate. Eight were suffering from opacity of the cornea, and of the operations considered here, two were for artificial pupils.

Sixteen with palsy of the optic nerve were thought to have a chance of successful treatment and were to be tried with either glasses or electricity. Of the remaining pupils, 34 men and 18 women, all were sadly deemed incurable.

The precise method of this early medical use of electricity is not recorded, although it is quite likely that it was used to stimulate the muscles of the eye. For this purpose Mr Brandreth, who was also a surgeon at the Infirmary, presented the School with an "electrical machine" in March 1809.

Just a few days earlier on 19 February, he had performed the first of the planned operations, when he had couched the right eye of George Flint. Again, to our frustration, no further details are recorded, nor of any other of the operations which took place, although later documents refer to them as "successful". George was still at the School, however, until 1814 when he left to become organist at Worksop, but this too is rather inconclusive as almost a third of the pupils were recorded as "partially sighted". (In the School's definition, the partially sighted had lost their sight "to all useful purpose".)

By September 1810, the efforts of the Medical Committee were regarded as being of "valuable benefit" to the School, and a resolution was passed to formerly institute the medical board as a permanent fixture. Fourteen gentlemen were appointed, and to them "was entrusted the entire care and management of all circumstances relative to the medical and surgical attendance of the pupils".[12] In addition, two local apothecaries were appointed to the School, as was a House Physician in June 1816, to care for the general health of the pupils.

The pupils were sometimes vulnerable to "medical men" from outside who wished to promote new methods or use them as guinea pigs for "quack" ideas. The Medical Board were fully aware of this threat to their pupils' health and safety, and laid down strict regulations to ensure adequate protection.

In 1812, the Committee received a request from a man named Williams, an itinerant oculist who had lately arrived in the Town, for permission to undertake treatment of some of the pupils of the School.

The Committee were extremely suspicious of his credentials and being sceptical of his intentions, resolved that Mr. Brand be ordered to prevent the pupils, as far as possible, from placing themselves under the care of Mr. Williams.

The Committee offered to "avail themselves of the proffered assistance of any able, intelligent and experienced Oculists (who may bring with them testimonials of their abilities from respectable practitioners) in endeavouring to restore the sight of any of the pupils of the School",[13] but, they added, all details of the proposed treatment must be made known to them [the Committee] first, to secure official permission. With a note of complete dismissal they concluded, "...nor can they [the Committee] give their sanction to the employment, in this Institution, of an itinerant, of whom they have no knowledge, but from his own advertisements."

In the early nineteenth century, no legislation existed to restrict the practice of medicine and surgery to properly qualified persons, nor was there a regulating body consisting of those who had qualified, for the supervision of their own profession. Therefore, the reputation and status of qualified men were frequently undermined by the numerous itinerents or self styled physicians who carried on flourishing businesses in many districts. In the Liverpool directory for 1800, for example, there are listed 12 "physicians" and 39 "surgeons" alone. It is hardly surprising to find that the School's Medical Committee, in addition to protecting the pupils, were also concerned with their own standing and ultimately, their livelihoods.

The small group of medical gentlemen serving on the Committee during the first 25 years or so of the School's history, however, were all highly qualified men with excellent credentials. It is no exaggeration to say that they were some of the most eminent men in Liverpool's history, let alone that of the Blind School. In all progressive movements for the benefit of the Town, their names appear time and time again, either as

a. The Infirmary (centre) and the Hospital for Decayed Sailors (wings).

b. The Dispensary (1798).

c. Lunatic Asylum, Lime Street, 1821 (St. John's Church where Henry Dannett was the incumbent is on the right).

d. The Medical Institution.

benefactors or members of Council. The Infirmary, the Dispensary, the Lunatic Asylum, the Lyceum and the Athenaeum all bear evidence of their involvement. Their professional reputation went before them too. Harry Park, for example, was nationally respected for his brilliant pioneering work on diseases of the joints and he was well known locally for the number of midwifery cases he attended. (One of which, in 1809, was the birth of William Ewart Gladstone.) Together with Alanson, his partner in his practice (who was well known for his book on amputation) and John Lyon, he founded the Liverpool Medical Library in 1779, which later evolved with the Medical Society into the Medical Institution, founded by John Rutter in 1837. Rutter, who was appointed first physician to the Town, was also the first President of the Lyceum, President of the Medical Society, and founded the Athenaeum. According to Bickerton, "of the many eminent citizens of Liverpool, it would be difficult to find a man who has left a more permanent mark."[14]

The School's health and administration were undoubtedly in the hands of the best Liverpool had to offer.

In 1812, alterations were made to the building to allow for operations to be performed on the premises, and facilities created to allow for recuperation. The Committee were determined to have the School in a healthy state for the opening of the extension buildings (December 1812) and commissioned a report on the conditions of the dormitories. On discovering that there was a shortage of beds and linen, Matthew Gregson[15] was requested "to provide everything necessary and proper for the accommodation of 75 pupils". Mr Gregson "invented" new bedsteads, "composed of cast irons and wood, easy to take down and refix, without hammer or other tool, so that if infested with vermin they could easily be cleaned and put together again".[16] The pupils were, as far as possible, "made instrumental in supplying the wants of the School",[17] weaving sufficient sheets and bedclothes themselves, together with the basket makers, who bottomed the beds. One stool was judged necessary to each bed and in the centre of each room hung a Liverpool Patent Lamp.

The pupils were now in the middle of a thorough health campaign at the hands of their Governors. A new diet was introduced by Doctors Rutter and Lewin, which was to be strictly adhered to:

Breakfast

Frℴm 1 October to 1 April
Thickmeal made of oatmeal boiled with water and with the addition of salt and cans of butter-milk.

From 1 April to 1 October
Milk thickened with oatmeal with bread in it.

Supper

From 1 October to 1 April
Milk thickened with oatmeal and bread as above.

From 1 April to 1 October
Thickmeal as above and buttermilk
No dry bread at breakfast or supper[18]

The men, "for the sake of cleanliness", were ordered to have their hair closely cut, which was to be carried out by John Graystock, son of the former superintendent, who had been employed to shave the pupils daily since his arrival with his parents in 1793. Females were requested to have their hair frequently well combed or suffer the same fate. Pupils were to be allowed out of the building under supervision on one afternoon per week for two hours "for the purposes of health and exercise". (Later it was ordered that they should walk out every fine morning between 6 and 7 o'clock "to receive the benefit of more air".) All these measures were being taken to bring the School up to a new standard to match the other changes already introduced by the Medical Committee. In addition, a complete revision of the Institutions Rules and Regulations were timed to coincide with the opening of the School's new extension in 1812. The School was now moving into a new and positive phase.

It was clearly set out too, just what was expected of the Superintendent. Aside from the predictable expectations of his character, his behaviour to the pupils was to be "as mild and humane as possible, consistent with the proper exercise of his authority". He was appointed to "enforce strict attention to the rules, to preserve order and harmony amongst the pupils and to maintain over them a firm and steady authority, but tempered with mildness and gentleness of manner". He was allowed discretion regarding the enforcement of detention after hours, but the infliction of corporal punishment and solitary confinement were strictly forbidden without prior authority from the Committee. This, of course, had the benefit of preventing extreme temper or provocation from determining spontaneous disciplinary measures. (It is unlikely that this rule would have been abused, as Visitors did attend and inspect the School on a regular basis.)

Discipline in such cases therefore, was decided after careful consideration by the Committee, and the Dickensian image of pupils being ruthlessly flogged by a wicked governor is somewhat eradicated. Yet, by 1814, it would seem that a number of pupils had had enough of their confined lifestyle and were rebelling.

One June morning it was discovered that the locks on the men's bedroom door had been broken, although it would appear from the records that this was not the first time. Further investigation revealed that a panel on the door at the bottom of the yard, which led out into the street, had also been broken. This was a period that the pupils normally looked forward to, as they were to receive rewards for their recent endeavours, enabling them to make the most of the imminent summer holiday. However, it was resolved that "Mr Blundell be requested not to give the Rewards he was about to distribute as usual, and that the men and boys are not to have any holiday until it is discovered who have been guilty of such riotous proceedings".[19]

If this was not enough, the Superintendent came into the dining room to find that 19 pupils had taken as much as they could stand of Dr Rutter's nutritious diet, or at least the form it had taken in the kitchen, and steadfastly refused to eat their dinner, complaining that "it was not wholesome food". Their claims were given a measure of credence by the troubled Joseph Brand, who decided that the proof of the pudding was in the eating of it and... called in the Visitors to do just that. To the dismay of the rebels, the Visitors, "who had more than once tasted it, declared it to be good". For the next fortnight the unfortunate 19, who had no doubt voiced the opinion of many more not daring to object, faced nothing but broth for breakfast, dinner and supper, with the servants under strict orders not to interfere with the arrangement.[20]

The Medical Committee was again required to uphold their practices and protect their pupils from outside interference in the summer of 1818. A London surgeon, Sir William Adams, wrote to the School expressing a wish to examine the pupils, with a view to performing operations on those he felt may benefit. It would appear that he had come into contact with some of the pupils some six years earlier and was familiar with their condition. The protective Committee forcefully responded with a note of indignation:

"...there exists an officiating Medical Board connected with this Institution, who have on all occasions gratuitously, and most skilfully, attended to all the diseases of the eye and that those cases alluded to in Sir William Adams' letter as having come under his observation six years ago, were selected and *successfully* [Committee's italics] operated upon, and that this Committee, feeling that they should not faithfully discharge their duty to the public and this Institution if they did not attend to every communication for the benefit of its objects, return to Sir William Adams their thanks for the offer of his services, but they do not feel justified in holding out to Sir William Adams the prospect of pecuniary remuneration, but should Sir William Adams' professional avocations call him into this neighbourhood, the Committee would be happy to avail themselves of his services in co-operation with their Medical Board."[21]

Following their decision, the Committee issued a notice to the School informing them of their objection to "the removal of any of the pupils to London for the purpose of having operations performed upon them there, or to any operation being performed upon any of the pupils, but with the concurrence and in the presence of the Medical Board".

Even in Liverpool, the Medical Board were not alone in trying to cure blindness. On 20 June 1820 a meeting of gentlemen, with William Rathbone[22] in the Chair, was held at the King's Arms. (It was originally requested that the meeting be held at the School for the Blind, but this was turned down by the Committee.) There it was unanimously resolved that "an institution for the relief of the poor, afflicted with diseases of the eye, be established in this town and recommended to the support of the public".[23] The Liverpool Institute for Curing Diseases of the Eye was established at 30 Basnett Street which remained open until 1834. A second eye hospital, the Liverpool Ophthalmic Infirmary, was established by Thomas Christian at 29 Slater Street in August 1820. In 1841 it was amalgamated with the Ear Institution and, after a few moves of home, came to the Myrtle Street Building where it stayed for many years.

In 1838, Robert Hibbert Taylor privately opened his Dispensary for the Diseases of the Eye. Between 1838-1846 Taylor reported that over 10,000 new cases had passed through his hands – even though he was only open for consultation for three days a week between 1 and 2 o'clock in the afternoon. It was not until 1871 that one of the best known of Liverpool's hospitals, St. Paul's Eye Hospital was founded, on a private charity by George Edward Walker, after he had taken over three rooms at 6 St. Paul's Square.

To return to 1815, the Committee, keen to maintain the depth of knowledge and experience within their ranks, took up William Rathbone's suggestion to Pudsey Dawson; that if an efficient person for the Committee was required they need look no further than Dr. Traill. Apart from the eminent professional qualifications of Dr. Thomas Traill he was already well known to the School due to his donations of large sums raised at his "Chemical Lectures" in the Lyceum. According to Picton, he was a man of "rare attainments, and of eminent activity in the employment of them. During his residence in Liverpool he was one of the foremost in aiding every project for the promotion of education, literature and science".[24]

It would seem to have been perfect timing to introduce such a man to the workings of the Institution as sadly, a few months later in April 1816, Pudsey Dawson died. The School went into a period of mourning with no strangers or visitors being permitted to enter the buildings until after his internment in St. George's Church. His funeral took place on 25 April, which was attended by the whole School. The Committee met in the Mayors[25] apartments in the Town Hall, at a quarter past eight that morning, before the sombre procession moved along Castle Street to the Church. (The Victoria Monument now occupies the former site of St. Georges.)

It was decided too that some form of memorial in his name should be placed in a suitable part of the School "in order to mark the high sense entertained by the members of the Institution of the zeal and indefatigable attention to its interest evinced by the late Mr Dawson".[26] The Committee decided on a design made by the sculptor Solomon Gibson, of "Charity [*Pilgrim's Progress*] leading Blind Children to the Tomb of their Patron". The cost was 120 guineas and it was to be inscribed with the following.

TO PUDSEY DAWSON
In grateful recollection of the unwearied care with which he watched over the interests of
this Institution during upwards of Twenty-five Years, this Monument was Erected
MDCCCXVII

A niche facing the principal entrance to the Music Room was to be its resting place.

This was not to be the end of the Dawson connection, as Pudsey's son Richard was immediately elected to the Committee.

104

Such ceremony was in stark contrast to the passing of the two central founders of the School, John Christie and Edward Rushton. Christie, who had been ill for sometime, died in 1811 in Knowsley, to where he had retired from his home in Church Lane. He had actually left the School in 1798, although at the request of the Committee he continued to teach pupils at Church Lane. He finally retired in 1802 on an annuity of 20 guineas, awarded by the Committee until his death "in consideration of the advantages which the Charity received from his attention to its interests.[27]

Rushton died of paralysis at his Paradise Street home on 22 November 1814, and was buried in St. James' Churchyard, without even a recorded acknowledgement at the School, although, to be fair, it was now a generation later and he does not seem to have had any contact with the School during that time. In 1807 his sight was partially restored by the skill of a Manchester oculist, Benjamin Gibson, enabling him to see his wife and children for the first time.[28]

The attendance of the whole School to Pudsey's funeral was not just to pay their respects to their tireless benefactor, but also to mark the occasion with a fitting display for which they had now become renowned – their choral singing.

Religion played an important role in School life. All pupils were expected to attend Church at least once on Sunday, either at the Established church or dissenters' chapels. No one was exempt from this and attendance cards had to be signed by the clergy, which then had to be produced in School on their return. Those who failed to attend or misbehaved during service were severely reprimanded (as we have already witnessed in chapter four). Special periods during the week were reserved for the memorising of Manns' Catechisms, which were to be repeated on Sunday evenings in School. Those who failed were again punished. To encourage obedient learning, Mr Blundell purchased a supply of walking canes at a cost of £14, which were issued to those who were attentive to their studies.

Back in 1805, it had been decided that all pupils, musical or otherwise, were to devote one hour between one and two o'clock on Mondays, Wednesdays and Fridays, to the practising and singing of hymns and choral pieces. During those hours the doors of the School were thrown open to the public, who were actively encouraged to come in and listen, to be entertained, and, of course, to hopefully make a donation to the Charity.

The reputation of the pupils' singing spread in quite a short time and invitations came from churches from all over the locality requesting them to sing at Sunday services. For their efforts they usually received remuneration from the churchwardens, although, after 1813, this was to be paid direct to Mr Brand, owing to "mischief resulting from the misapplication of the money". By 1818 their singing had become so popular that it was decided there was a need for a suitable building where they could be heard to full advantage. This, of course, would provide a facility to further exploit a source of regular income. The School was to have a Chapel.

6
THE CHAPEL

"Thus saith the Lord of Hosts. Consider your ways;
go up to the mountains, and bring wood, and build
the house, and I will take pleasure in it;
and I will be glorified, saith the Lord"

Haggai I: v7,8.

In 1811, John Foster, physically and mentally drained from his recent labours on the School Building programme, decided to travel to Greece with a companion, Professor Cockerell of London, to seek both respite and fresh inspiration for his work. So enthralled was he with the specimens of architecture observed during his vacation that he decided to stay in Greece for some time, studying and making drawings of the classical buildings, which he would use as a basis for much of his later work.

Not long after his return to England, he again received a request from the School to submit plans for another building project; this was his chance to utilise his new ideas. The Committee was anxious to capitalise on the popularity of the concerts and Sunday performances of the pupils. It was quite obvious that here was a latent asset which, if correctly managed, could provide the School with a handsome income. This would go some way towards alleviating the burden of continual fund-raising to maintain, or more accurately, ensure the existence of the Charity. Spiritual care, of course, was of no less importance, and it was also felt that the School would benefit from having its own place of worship attached to the Institution. Glasgow and London had their own, so why not Liverpool?

The President of the School for 1818 just happened to be the Lord Bishop of Chester, Dr Law. Whether by coincidence or design no record exists, nevertheless the Committee gave him only two months in office before writing to him on 19 May 1818 on the matter of what they saw as the urgent need for a suitable building to cater for matters spiritual and financial.

The wily Committee-men used a further lever to solicit a positive reply to their requests. It was assessed that if a chapel was erected, this would free the Music Room for re-use; and as there were now 107 pupils in the School, with many more on a waiting list, this room could easily be converted into a new dormitory enabling the acceptance of new admissions. The Committee, of course, placed greatest emphasis on the religious benefits to be gained by all concerned, but although this was no doubt quite sincere, the pecuniary advantages were uppermost in their minds.

Initial funding was again to be secured through public appeal and subscription, which had proved so successful in the past. Once the chapel was opened, the Committee proposed that collections would be made on the doors, in the example already set at the Magdalen Asylum and the Foundling Hospital in London. In fact, this plan had already been successfully adopted at the School in consequence of the extreme public pressure for admittance to Sunday evening service. This source of revenue, plus that which would be collected from pew rents, would provide a handsome income for the Charity.

Three days after receiving the request, the Bishop replied, expressing full support for the proposals. He raised the question of consecration. This issue was to prove a little awkward for the Committee. A short time before the Chapel plans were mooted, Parliament passed an Act granting provision for the expansion of the Established Church and the building of churches. The Committee, wishing to take advantage of this funding, indicated their intentions to the Bishop, only to be advised that the grant applied only to consecrated churches. Holding out little hope under the present legislation for the School to have the Chapel consecrated, the Bishop was of the opinion that it should be licensed. This he would readily grant, although it was "an exception to the general rule". (Consecration would only be granted where the population was large enough to demand it, and in the Chapel's case the Bishop did not believe it to be so.)

Such matters were too involved to be discussed speedily by letter and the Bishop arranged a meeting at the School for 3 July. He did, however, at the request of the School, send a letter to His Royal Highness, the Prince of Wales, to receive his approval of the scheme in his capacity as Patron.

In the meantime, the Committee busied themselves with the drawing up of the finer points of the proposals and the purchase of the necessary land. The estimated cost of the Chapel was to be between £5–6,000, but to enable the building to be commenced as soon as possible, part of the cost, amounting to £3,000, was raised by a loan in the form of £100 shares, each bearing interest of five per cent per annum. Five Committee men were appointed as Trustees to secure the loans and look after the affairs of the Chapel, which included the election of the minister.

On 8 June, the Bishop again contacted the School enclosing the letter he had received from the Prince Regent regarding the Chapel, who was "pleased highly to approve the same and to subscribe 100 guineas towards its construction".[1] The Prince had, in fact, reinforced his ties with the School the previous year, when on 8 April 1817 he recommended to the Committee the admission of a 15 year old blind boy by the name of William Fitzgerald. William was from Hampton, Middlesex and totally blind from measles. The Mayor, John Wright, who was the Chairman for that year reported that "...in a personal interview, I communicated to His Royal Highness the Prince Regent the offer of this Committee to receive the boy recommended by him free of every expense, to which His Royal Highness replied that he felt himself very much obliged by it and that 'it was like the people of Liverpool to do so'...".[2]

When news of the School's intentions became public knowledge, donations began to pour into the Fund, the largest of which came from John Horrocks, a local merchant of Bold Street and a noted philanthropist. He enclosed the sum of £500, requesting that his name should not appear in the newspapers or in the books at the Public News Rooms as, he declared, "this has been productive of many applications from those unknown to me personally or otherwise, and attended with trouble in detecting impositions...you cannot conceive the applications I have from quarters where I never set foot, nor don't know a creature breathing in them...."[3] I am sure no objection to the publication of his benevolent deed could be raised today, despite the potential drawbacks.

August 1818 was a busy month for the Committee, as its plans began to come together and gather pace. Architects drawings had been submitted and required careful consideration; letters were sent to the clergy of the diocese requesting sermons to be preached in aid of the Fund; the Archbishop of York was also contacted for similar purpose. A petition was lodged with the Common Council of Liverpool, "...praying for a grant of the Reversion of the Land for the site of the intended Chapel",[4] and it was decided that the laying of the foundation stone should be celebrated by a

Foster's drawing of the intended Chapel (1818).

Chapel Interior.

special ceremony and a procession through the town. Not unexpectedly, the Lord Bishop of Chester was requested to lay the stone and preach a sermon to mark the occasion.

The plot of land in question was purchased from Mr Watkinson on 1 September 1818 at 9/- per square yard and was situated at the south east corner of the School on the corner of Great Nelson Street and Duncan Street (see Kaye's map of 1810).

But what of the Chapel itself? Two sets of plans had been received, but those of Messrs. Rickman and Aiken, although thought to be "handsome and highly creditable to the taste of those gentlemen", were rejected. The contract, inevitably, was awarded to the ubiquitous John Foster, whose Greek excursion had proved to be a most worthwhile experience. His designs were entirely influenced by the classical Grecian architecture which he had carefully studied, and specifically, his portico intended for the Chapel entrance was copied from the Temple of Zeus Panhellenius on the Island of Aegina. The Doric pediment, which was to face the west front of the building, was to be supported by six fluted columns, with an architrave resting upon pilasters. This character of classical Grecian, which in 1819 was believed to be one of the purest copies in England, was preserved throughout the building, with further decoration on the five windows of the south side. The contract was signed a few days later, on 11 September, with a promise by Foster that the building would be ready exactly a year to the day.

The laying of the foundation stone was arranged for 6 October, and to publicise the event the local press carried a detailed announcement advising the route to be taken, the arrangements regarding the services, and information on how to secure tickets. Leaving nothing to chance, there was also advice regarding which way the horses' heads should be facing for the correct parking of carriages.

During September the School was a flurry of activity, with frequent Committee meetings organising final arrangements, keen to insure against last minute hitches, especially as there were to be so many dignitaries present. The tickets had been printed, 3,000 in all; Mr Foster was requested to organise the police and erect a shed capable of holding 100 guests at the ground; and the Mayor had made the Town Hall available for the reception of the Bishop. Members of the Committee had been detailed

Chapel for the Blind.

THE COMMITTEE have to announce that the PROCESSION for laying the FOUNDATION STONE upon TUESDAY *the 6th October*, will leave the TOWN-HALL at a Quarter before Eleven o'Clock *precisely*, through *Castle-street* and *Lord-street* to ST. PETER'S CHURCH; and after divine Service move forward by *Church-street, Bold street, Leece-street, Rodney-street, Clarence-street, Russel-street, Gloucester-street*, to *Duncan-street*, where such arrangements have been made for the preservation of the ground (the several approaches to which being likewise protected by the Police) as will ensure to those in the Procession the fullest opportunity of witnessing the Ceremony.

The PROCESSION will return by *Great Nelson-street, Lime-street, Queen-square, Williamson-square, Tarleton-street, Church-street, Lord-street,* and *Castle-street,* to the TOWN-HALL.

The *Western* Doors of the Church will be open for admission to the *Gallery*, and the *South-east* Door to the *Seats erected over the Altar*, at half-past Ten o'Clock; the *Body of the Church* being reserved until after the accommodation of those accompanying the LORD BISHOP from the TOWN-HALL.

The COMMITTEE beg leave respectfully to communicate, that Children under 14 years cannot be admitted.

CARRIAGES will range along *Dale-street*, with the horses' heads towards *Water-street*, set down and take up at ST. PETER'S CHURCH, with the horses' heads towards *Bold-street*.

Applications for TICKETS to be made at the SCHOOL for the BLIND, between the hours of one and three on the preceding *Friday, Saturday,* and *Monday,* when the COMMITTEE will attend, and where particulars of the ARRANGEMENT of the PROCESSION may be obtained.

Laying of the Chapel foundation stone. 'Gore's General Advertiser'
Thursday, 1 October 1818.

specific positions on the day, both at St. Peters and the Chapel ground, to receive guests and act as their ushers.

The Ladies were also to assist. Their station was to be at the doors of the Church, where they would receive donations after the service. In this capacity the Countess of Sefton was assisted by Lady Barton, the Hon. Mrs Hopwood the Mayoress, Mrs Blackburne, Mrs Patten-Bold, Mrs Admiral Murray, and Mrs Littledale. (Apart from the last two ladies, whose husbands were Committee-men, their husbands were all former Presidents of the School.)

The Freemasons were invited to take part in the procession too, and were to be led by their Grandmaster. The order of this impressive procession was printed onto leaflets and distributed throughout the town. The School wanted this to be a day for everyone to remember and, of course, give their new plans and the Building Fund excellent publicity.

When the great day arrived, the ceremony was carried out, according to the newspapers, "...in the presence of a more numerous and respectable assemblage of the town and neighbourhood than we ever recollect to have witnessed upon a similar occasion..."[5]

At 11 o'clock the procession set off from the Town Hall, led by the Trumpeters on horseback, looking a quite magnificent spectacle. Upon arrival at St. Peters Church,[6] "...not withstanding the immense concourse of people that was assembled, not the slightest confusion or inconvenience was experienced; indeed, the particular arrangements of the Committee, which had been previously published, were so distinct in directing the public...that although the Church was crowded in every part, there appeared comfortable room for almost every individual of the congregation."[7]

The prayers were read in a "very impressive manner" by the School Chaplain, the Revd. Mr Blundell, and the music selected for the occasion was "executed by the pupils in a style of excellence which might vie with the most scientific performance". The sermon more than matched the occasion; observers noted

"...the force and eloquence of his Lordship's appeal to the minds and to the hearts of his audience was most happily demonstrated in the effect produced upon the congregation; the collection at the doors amounted to £495 18s 6d; being a sum larger than was ever be-

ORDER OF THE PROCESSION

TO LAY

THE FOUNDATION STONE,

OF

THE CHAPEL,

TO BE ATTACHED TO THE SCHOOL FOR THE BLIND,

ON TUESDAY, THE 6th OF OCTOBER,

BY THE PRESIDENT,

THE RIGHT REV.

THE LORD BISHOP OF CHESTER.

Trumpeters;

The Masters, Past-Masters, Wardens, and Brethren of
the Freemasons' Lodge, in Masonic Order;

THE SUPERINTENDENT & MATRON OF THE INSTITUTION;

THE PUPILS OF THE SCHOOL,

Attended by their Masters;

THE COMMITTEE;

THE ARCHITECT;

The Churchwardens, preceded by the Parish Police;

THE MAYOR & BAILIFFS;

THE MEMBERS OF THE COMMON COUNCIL;

The Bishop;

THE CLERGY, IN LINES OF THREE;

OFFICERS IN THE NAVY;

OFFICERS IN THE ARMY;

GENTLEMEN, IN LINES OF FOUR;

THE CARRIAGES.

To PUDSEY DAWSON,
In grateful recollection of the unwearied care
with which he watched over the interests of
this Institution during upwards of Twenty-five
Years, this Monument was Erected,
MDCCCXVI.

MONUMENT to the MEMORY of PUDSEY DAWSON, Esq.
Erected in the Church of the School for the Blind.

fore obtained upon any occasion for any charitable object whatever, in Liverpool, or indeed perhaps we may add, in any other town in the kingdom; and this sum is the more to be appreciated, as coming from those who had for the most part previously contributed to the object for which it was solicited."[8]

After the service, the procession again formed outside and moved off along the planned course, heading for Bold Street before swinging around the elevated route around the town, by way of Rodney Street and Clarence Street, eventually descending Gloucester Street to arrive at the Ground where the stone was to be laid. The whole of the route was lined with throngs of people, thousands turning out to witness the event to see the marvellous procession slowly make its way through the town.

On the arrival of the procession at the Chapel Ground, once all the guests had been accommodated, those members of the public who had crowded around the site were allowed into the Ground to witness the ceremony.

The proceedings began with coins being deposited on the ground with the foundation stone laid over them, while the Deputy Provincial Grandmaster of the Masons briefly acted as Master of Ceremonies. Following this, John Foster, as Architect, stepped up and presented a drawing of the building, which was received with cheers and applause.

After the Bishop had offered a "most devout and pathetic prayer, suitable to the occasion", the Vice-President, Admiral Murray, approached the Bishop and presented him with a silver trowel upon which was an inscription to mark the event.

Suddenly, there was a flourish of trumpets and the whole of the pupils struck up with the 100th Psalm, in which they were joined by a great part of the crowd gathered, estimated to be over 10,000 strong.

Once the proceedings had come to a close, the procession again led off and returned with the Mayor to the Town Hall. The appearance of the procession had been one of great splendour, especially with numerous freemasons present, their various orders and emblems giving much colour to the occasion. The clergy were most impressive in their attendance, and together with the principal gentlemen of the town the event was very spectacular. Indeed, the local press were moved to assert that, "there was never a more pleasing, respectable or more gratifying procession in Liverpool than the one which we have the satisfaction to record."[9]

Surely, the most moving part of the occasion must have been the role played by the pupils themselves, in whose name the day was planned and executed, most especially their performance around the bare waste-land which would soon house their talents to a more refined effect.

Before the Chapel was completed, however, there were still various problems to keep the School busy. Within weeks of commencing work on the site it was felt that there would be an added advantage in the construction of a subterranean passage between the School and the Chapel. Without delay a planning application was lodged with the Council. After an initial refusal, the Committee eventually secured the necessary permission following a little gentle persuasion and an appeal to their compassion. The obvious purpose for such a construction no doubt suggests to the reader the need to protect pupils from the busy traffic expected at the Chapel before and after services. True, an important benefit, and one that was swiftly pointed out to the Council when they turned down the application. Yet, the Committee had another reason. If members of the public could be encouraged to enter and leave the Chapel by way of the tunnel, they could not avoid passing the donation boxes in the entrance hall of the School and most importantly, the School Shop, where the products of the pupils' efforts were on sale, awaiting patrons sympathetic or otherwise.

In February 1819, letters were sent to "both Universities for a lecturer to the New Church", and by August the School had appointed as Chaplain the Revd. Edward Hull M.A. of St. Johns, Cambridge, who hailed from Whalfield, near Hadleigh in Suffolk.

Foster was true to his word and the Chapel was ready in time for an opening service on 6 October 1819, exactly a year after the laying of the foundation stone.

Although the opening did not have the pomp and ceremony of the preceding year, the occasion was still graced by the same Ladies looking after the collection plates, the Mayor and Common Council, plus 2,000 invited guests. The Bishop of Chester again led the ceremony and officially opened the Chapel.[10]

Foster's design, now a reality, was hailed the work of a genius, a permanent mark of distinguished pre-eminence. The Doric portico was ap-

The Chapel on its original site, 1829 (Harwood). Now occupied by Lime Street Station.

proached by a handsome flight of steps in imitation of the prototype, and once inside, the character of the exterior was found to be manifest throughout the building. In later years, many works of art were to grace the interior, the earliest of which was a painting by James Hilton which hung over the altar, of "Christ Restoring Sight to the Blind", for which he received the prize from the British Institution. A contemporary text eloquently describes the character;

> "The countenance of the Saviour beams with benignity, dignity and grace; one hand is employed miraculously opening the sightless eyeball to the orb of the day; the other, uplifted to Him from whom cometh every good and perfect gift. The countenance of the recipient displays faith and hope. Another supplicant, in the foreground, groping in the darkness, amidst the blaze of day, is seeking a similar blessing. Nor must an interesting female figure be suffered to be passed unnoticed; sweetly expressive of hope, of filial love, and of astonishment. The composition is grand, the colouring chaste, the draperies bold; the whole does honour to the British School. The artist, evidently, has had in view the cartoons of Raphael : his genius could not have enkindled at a purer flame."[11]

Once the picture had received its prize, it was bought by a Mr Clarke who offered it for public sale. It was purchased by Henry Wilson who presented it to the Committee for the benefit of the Institution.

At the east end of the Chapel was sited the monument to Pudsey Dawson, having been removed from its former position in the School. A fine toned organ built by Gray of London had also been erected at the east end, which had proved to be a more more laborious installation than had originally been planned. Foster's genius was not without flaws, as the organ – which had been constructed according to the measurements shown on the Chapel plans, was found to be 13 inches too tall when the day came to move it into the building. The ceiling had been built too low. Foster was immediately called in to liaise with the organ builder, making swift alterations to allow sufficient space for the Instrument.

Finally, stoves had been installed (as well as gaslighting) which, "on Mr Sylvester's improved plan, by ingenious contrivance, withdraws the impure air, and substitutes warm or cold air, as the season may require."[12]

The appointment of the new Chaplain began a rift which although unforseen in the initial projections for the Chapel, was to grow wider throughout the 1820s. The Chaplain had been appointed by the Trustees of the Chapel, but as the Chapel was licensed and not consecrated as was originally planned, the Committee still had the power to engage or dismiss clergy. At this early stage, eager to see the Chapel completed and performing its desired role in the community, both the Committee and Trustees were working to the same ends in full co-operation. But, as the administrative demands lessened and settled down into a routine operation, albeit a new one, both parties felt that decisions regarding the up-keep of the Chapel and disposal of its income to be their ultimate responsibility. Any resolution passed by the Trustees, for example, the Committee felt obliged to ratify.

By the late 1820s, this dispute had quite clearly got out of hand and consequently, a sub-committee was commissioned in 1828 to report on the future running of the Chapel. At this stage, the role of the Trustees had finally come to an end, as the purpose for which they were appointed – to secure loans for the building fund and to regulate repayments – was now void, as all outstanding debts had now been cleared. It was obvious that something needed to be done quickly to ensure that such a dispute or conflict of interests never rose again to the detriment of the practical business of running the Institution and Chapel.

The Sub-Committee reported their findings on 22 December 1828, stating that future government should be placed upon a permanent and legalised basis. Immediate measures should be adopted, it continued, for procuring an Act of Legislature, whereby the affairs and estate of the School and Chapel may be legally regulated. The Committee appeared to have been entirely influenced by the operation of both the London and Glasgow Asylums, which by this time, were both conducted under separate Acts of Parliament.

There was also the problem regarding the lease-hold of the Chapel land. Reversion would not be granted by the Council unless the Chapel was on consecrated ground and already the value of the lease-hold interest had diminished due to the death of one of the Trustees.

It was also discovered, to the Committee's alarm, that in a recent case in Doctors' Commons regarding a licensed chapel in Bath, it was found that consecration was necessary to sanction the legal appropriation of alms or collections in their chapel for use of charity. In the eyes of the Sub-Committee there was no doubting the way forward.

The Committee moved very quickly, anxious to protect the future operation of the Institution, and by February 1829 three members were ready to travel to London to assist their solicitor in the progress of the Bill. The Vice-Presid :nt forwarded the draft to William Huskisson (M.P. for the borough), who was requested to present it and give it his full support. Further support also came from Bamber Gascoyne M.P., Lord Skelmersdale, and the Bishop of London.

By 24 February 1829, the Bill had been read in the Commons for a second time, whereupon a petition was presented against it, signed by 27 subscribers to the Institution and around 20 donors to the Chapel Building Fund. The petitioners were heard by Counsel and after two days investigation the Bill was carried by a unanimous vote.

At the same stage in the Lords, the petition was again presented, signed by only one person, William Dixon, a former Trustee, which gives us some idea as to the quarter from where the opposition was coming from, although the exact nature of the objection is unknown. After a day's hearing, the Bill was unanimously adopted without amendment. It received Royal Assent on 13 April 1829 and became law.

A Common Seal of the Charity, engraved by Warwick of London, was exhibited and adopted on 4 August, and later that year on 1 November, the final act in the new legislation took place when the Bishop of Chester performed the ceremony of the consecration of the Chapel.

Within a few months the first Royal Patron of the School, King George IV, had died. The Chapel was placed into mourning, the interior being draped in black and an address soliciting patronage despatched to the new King, William IV (who had been at his brothers side when they had visited the School as Princes in 1806). A reply was received on 5 October 1830 from Sir Robert Peel acknowledging the request, informing the School that the King would be pleased to become Patron.

By 1830 the School was now firmly established, with a national reputation, extensive buildings and facilities and a Chapel which was patronised by the highest ranks of local society, bringing the Charity added bonuses to the benefit of the pupils. All this, together with the new legislation laid down for the future regulation of the Charity, ensured that the School settled down into a routine which, the governors felt, would re-

ANNO DECIMO

GEORGII IV. REGIS.

❋❋

Cap. xv.

An Act for establishing and governing an Institution in *Liverpool*, called " The School for the Indigent Blind at *Liverpool;*" for incorporating the Subscribers thereto ; and also for regulating and supporting a Chapel attached to the said Institution. [13th *April* 1829.]

WHEREAS since the Year One thousand seven hundred and ninety-one an Institution or Asylum has been established in the Town of *Liverpool,* by certain charitable Individuals residing in the said Town and Neighbourhood, for the Relief of the indigent Blind, in which upwards of One hundred blind Persons are at present instructed and employed in several useful Trades and Manufactures, and thereby relieved from much of the Distress and Misery caused by their Affliction, and are taught Habits of Regularity and Industry, as well as the Means of providing for their own Support : And whereas the Mayor, Bailiffs, and Burgesses of the Town of *Liverpool* have granted and conveyed the Scite of the House, Workshops, and other Buildings in which the said Institution is conducted, to certain Trustees, for the Use and Benefit of the said Charity, and which Scite is situate on the South Side of *London Road* and West Side of *Duncan Street* in *Liverpool* aforesaid : And whereas since the Establishment of the said Institution a Chapel hath been erected near to the same, upon a Piece of Land situate in *Duncan Street* in *Liverpool* aforesaid, held for the Residue of certain Terms of Three Lives and Twenty-one Years, created by certain Leases granted by the said Mayor, Bailiffs, and Burgesses, and which

[*Local*]　　　　4 *N*　　　　Chapel

Act of Incorporation 1829.

121

quire their administration to be much more restrained. Their role as a catalytic force pushing through change and pioneering improvements had effectively slowed down to assume a more monitorial role. Improvements, where required, would be piecemeal. There was certainly no need, in their eyes, for new building projects in the foreseeable future. Yet, within a few years the School was to suffer major upheaval, the cause of which had been described in 1831 as

"...the locomotive engines, as they reached Wavertree Lane, began to rush forward at a rapid rate, which was gradually increased, until, entering the Olive Mount excavation, the flying machines burst into the awful chasm at the speed of 24 miles per hour..."[13]

The Liverpool terminus for the new "flying" engines had opened in Lime Street, near the School in 1835, but once the need for expansion became obvious, nothing was going to stand in their way.

School Seal.

122

7
PLEASANT SURROUNDINGS AND AN UNENVIABLE POSITION

"...It won't be pleasant if in future ages,
Some bookworms deeply pouring over its pages,
Should cry "Good Lord! in those degenerate times!
Plain honesty was held the worst of crimes"..."

Anon., *The Porcupine*, 1869

The continuing success of the Liverpool to Manchester Railway, which had opened in 1830, undoubtedly hung on the construction of a terminus near to the town centre of Liverpool. In the earliest days of the Railway, journeys ended either at Edge Hill, or at Crown Street, which was still a mile or so short of the town, the descent from Brownlow Hill proving to be a problem for the engineers.

By 1836, steep tunnels had been bored through the sandstone rib that runs across Liverpool from Everton to St. James' Mount, and Lime Street Station was opened on 15 August. Locomotives, however, were not to be used for another 34 years, the coaches being hauled up to Edge Hill by an endless rope attached to a stationary engine.

The Railway Mania that followed the construction of this pioneering line was to have a substantial effect on the School.

In the mid-1840s, as a result of the Bank Charter Act, railway shares came on to the floor of the Stock Exchange for the first time. Hundreds of Acts of Parliament were issued, authorising over a £100,000,000 of expenditure in railway construction. Expansion of Lime Street Station was inevitable.

As early as July 1846, plans were discussed with a view to enlarging the station. Acts of Parliament ensuring compulsory purchase were all too easily obtained in the maniacal forties, and any buildings in the way of the railway would be swiftly gobbled up. There would be little mercy for the School. The Chapel lay within the block of land intended to accommodate the new enterprise and although the site of the School itself does not appear to have been a direct problem to the railway planners, it was in-

123

cluded in the expansion scheme, later to be used as a goods yard and for the stabling of horses.

Plans detailing the Railway Company's proposals, which stipulated the removal of the School and Chapel, were laid before the Committee on 7 July 1846. A few days later, the Committee agreed "that it would be for the interests of the Institution to comply with the request on the part of the Grand Junction Railway Directors so far as to confer with them on the disposal of their present property".[1] A sub-committee was appointed to negotiate with the Railway directors and it would appear that an extended form of compensation was mooted at a very early stage, as only three weeks later, Mr Elmes, architect for the London and North Western Railway, came before the Committee to receive their suggestions prior to designing a plan for a new church and school.

Life carried on as normal in the School; their main concern was the scarcity of potatoes. Mr Lucy, the Superintendent, on mentioning the difficulty to the Committee, was authorised to "make the Scouse with meat, rice, carrots, turnips, onions, peppers, etc, which has been much approved at the Infirmary and that the pupils be allowed a piece of bread with it."[2]

Little did they realise how that shortage of potatoes would soon effect the town; the result of which would be a massive influx of starving, penniless immigrants from Ireland, devastated by famine.

Life for Mr and Mrs Lucy sadly, did not carry on as normal, for in April 1847, as Superintendent and Matron, the Committee felt that the demands being made on them in their "advanced age and infirm state of health" were becoming too much for them to cope with. In consideration of their "long, faithful and valuable services and the high character which they have bourne" they were awarded a pension at £150 a year. They had served the School for 32 years.

By January 1847 L.N.W.R. finally confirmed their intentions, informing the Committee of their application for an Act to authorise the purchase of the Chapel, but by April terms were being negotiated for the purchase of the School plot too. If the Institution was to lose the Chapel land, which now seemed inevitable, there was no point in holding onto the School plot if a sale could be negotiated enabling a new beginning elsewhere, in, as a member of the sub-committee suggested, "more pleasant surroundings".

On 6 April, the Chaplain was authorised to conclude an agreement with L.N.W.R. to build a School and Chapel on Railway Company land on the corner of Hope Street and Hardman Street, "for a sum of money not exceeding the sum which the Railway Company will be willing to give in addition to the site of the intended buildings".[3] This was by no means a popular decision with all the members of the Committee, however, as it was voted through on a majority of only nine to six. New school plans were adopted a few weeks later, and over the ensuing months negotiations continued, especially with regard to the Act of Parliament, to ensure that the interests of the School were fully protected.

Terms regarding the Chapel transactions were finally laid down and agreed in July 1849. The Railway Company gave to the School their land in Hope Street and Hardman Street amounting to 4670 square yards, plus £2,000, in exchange for the removal of the Chapel and conveyance of the site. Negotiations regarding the School land continued for a little longer, until the Committee finally agreed to the Railway's offer of £9,500 in August 1849.

Fresh plans for the School were necessary, due to an ambitious and commendable decision by the Committee, which earned them great respect among their contemporaries concerned with conservation. It was decided to remove the Chapel and re-erect it on the corner site of Hardman Street and Hope Street. In the absence of a cathedral, the Chapel had so far played a major role in the religious worship of Liverpool people, with its popularity among the higher ranks of society being well known. It is not surprising therefore to find the Committee most reluctant to lose such an asset and consequently keen to do whatever was in their means to preserve such a valuable and impressive edifice.

This was a fine example of engineering, although due to obstruction from the Council, the aesthetic appearance of the steps leading up to the portico was lost, as that body refused to allow sufficient space on Hardman Street. Sir James Picton, city architect and an historian, was not impressed, (although he was not a great admirer of the "Doric Mania" as he called it). He declared,

"It is undoubtedly the same building – with a difference. The narrow area of the new site would not allow of its full development. Cribbed, cabined and confined, its receding stylobate cut off close to the columns, it presents rather a forlorn appearance, the mere shadow of a transient taste, which never took any permanent hold among us."[4]

Others disagreed. The Reverend Mr Thom, writing in the year the Chapel was reopened, commented,

> "...not the slightest difference can be detected between what it was and what it is...The Church of the Asylum of the Blind now forms one of a cluster of public buildings, which by the variety, grandeur, and beauty of their respective designs, are eminently calculated to strike the eye of the beholder."[5]

The new school, situated alongside the Chapel and facing Hardman Street, was designed by Arthur Hill Holme. His brothers' construction company (Samuel & James Holme) were contracted to erect the building.[6] The work began in March 1850 and was completed in July the following year at a cost of £11,650. Prior to the opening, a grand ball was held in the new School Building just a few days after the consecration of the Chapel (which had been performed by the Bishop of Chester on 25 May).

By 11 July 1851 85 pupils had begun their new school-life in Hardman Street. Meanwhile, on the old Chapel site, the extension of Lime Street was opened in 1852, and the old main School building was demolished, although the land was not directly incorporated into the new extension. Shops were erected on the site which faced London Road. Only a few weeks before the opening of the School, the town received a visit from Queen Victoria, together with Prince Albert and their four children. It was a high point in a miserable year which had seen a cholera epidemic wipe out over 5,000 Liverpool people. (It was also the year that saw the deaths of Edward Rushton jnr., Stipendary Magistrate for Liverpool and Committee member for the School, and the 13th Earl of Derby who had twice served as President of the School.)

For days preceding the Queen's visit there was intense activity in the preparation and construction of scaffolding, stages and various decorations lining the streets through which the cortège was to pass. At the School, which lay on the route, pew-renters were to be allowed to stand on the front of the Chapel steps and it was estimated that the front of the School, including the windows, would accommodate 400 spectators. Each Committee member would receive six tickets for his own use and several more to distribute among benefactors and subscribers.

On the day of the visit, Thursday 10 October, there was the heaviest downpour the town had seen for a long time. Nevertheless, little was to

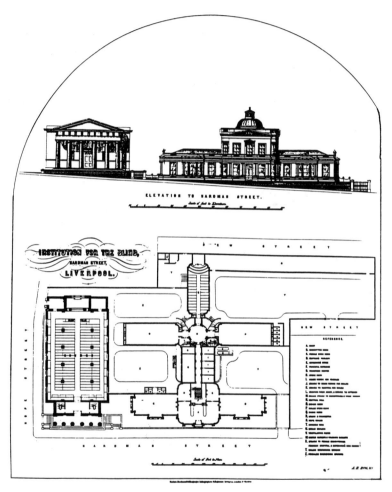

Plans of the new Hardman Street School and relocation of the Chapel (opened 1851). (Architect A.H. Holme.)

deter the crowds, many of whom had travelled from North Wales and the Isle of Man, and the route was heavily lined throughout. A cruise along the River was also on the itinerary, followed by a reception at the Town Hall. After a visit to the soon to be completed St. George's Hall, the Royal Party took the train from Lime Street for a similar visit to Manchester.

There were no significant changes in the running of the New School. Rules and Regulations were retained, with necessary adaptation, and trades taught were also unchanged. The upheaval may have been too much though for Alice Frodsham, who died in 1853 aged 77. She was an original pupil of Henry Dannett's School of January 1791 and had been at the School for 62 years. She was the 17 year old "decent, regular woman" of his 1793 Final Report.

There is no doubt that Henry Dannett would have been overjoyed at the development of the School during the first half of the century, especially the role played by the Chapel. The position of Chaplain would probably have been one he would have relished. Yet it would have been difficult for the School to have done better than the appointment of Edward Hull, who was still at the Chapel, now on its new site.

Shortly after his appointment, Edward Hull had been described as a preacher in whom, "...the candid critic can discover so little either to condemn or to admire." He was not thought of as the most eloquent of speakers in his early days, yet it was also believed by his congregation to be "...bad taste or hyper-criticism in placing him elsewhere than in the first class of orators". The literary, moral and scientific journal, *The Hermes*, in which these comments were made, regularly featured a biography of eminent Lancashire clergymen, and their third edition included a profile of Mr Hull. They were not as impressed as his congregation evidently were:

"He appears to be rather free from glaring faults than characterised by any striking beauties; careful to a letter in the rules of rhetoric, but regardless of every adventitious auxiliary. His reading is strong and deliberate; but marked with something of monotony, from a too-general emphasis; and is painful to many of his hearers, because laborious to himself. This is evident from the almost constant motion of his head, and the difficulty he evinces in finishing his longer periods."

A rather unforgiving description; nevertheless, *The Hermes* felt it only fair to offer advice on how to improve in those areas where they believed he was obviously deficient.

Hardman Street School and Chapel from St. Philip's Churchyard 1852.

> "We would respectfully suggest to the reverend gentleman, a longer rest between his sentences; as calculated both to relieve himself and give greater effect to his delivery...This gentleman's sermons would doubtless be heard with greater interest were they accompanied with a little action...We are quite of opinion with the Spectator on this subject, that proper gestures and vehement exertions of the voice cannot be too much studied by a public orator; that the best discourses are improved by a natural accompaniment of the arms and by a judicious modulation of the voice."

Despite trying to lay the foundations for American television evangelicalism, *The Hermes* did have complements for the chaplain.

> "The style of this gentleman is elegant; but rather that of the accomplished scholar than the ingenious orator. He is evidently well read in the Classics, Ecclesiastical History, and general Philosophy...Upon the whole he must be called a good preacher; and it is due to Mr Hull to observe, that few men are more attentive and sedulous in the discharge of their duties. Since his appointment to the present charge he has distinguished himself by a zealous endeavour to enforce a due observance of the Lord's day..."[7]

After almost 50 years in the pulpit of the Chapel, Edward Hull died on 6 January 1867, aged eighty. His pulpit fame was by then well established, and although he did not have the bigotry which might have developed in late age, he had undoubtedly, according to his contemporaries, been left behind by the bulk of those amongst whom he spent his latest years. On his death, the local press reported,

> "The Chapel of the Asylum became, under his care, the most fashionable place of worship in the town, and a visit to the Blind Church was equivalent to seeing one of the lions in the town. That a position so peculiar should affect the style of Mr Hull's preaching was all but inevitable; that it did not affect it for evil was greatly to his honour."[8]

His style of preaching had become famous and greatly admired. In later years his eloquence, theological intellect and faultless elocution all contributed to his celebrity. As a man he was highly cultivated and widely sympathetic. Keenly interested in the development of intellectual progress, he rarely publicly interfered in local or national politics, although he was the author of several literary contributions to contemporary causes. He was frequently warned by the Committee for preaching sermons for charitable causes other than the one which employed him, although mounting debts at the School during the 1850s necessitated an Appeal by Hull at his solicitous best. On Sunday 9 October 1859, the 40th anniversary of the opening of the Chapel, he preached a sermon which by his most eloquent and sympathetic character he appealed to the benevolent nature of his congregation. The discourse was later published to enable his appeal reach those outside.

The change of locality and the improved construction of the School were looked upon as most beneficial to the health and comfort of the pupils, but the change of circumstances in the course of the last century was not as favourable to the finances of the Charity. It was inevitable once Schools began to open in many of the larger towns in England (especially now that Henshaws had opened in Manchester and a second school in Liverpool – the Roman Catholic St. Vincents), that the School would assume a more local rather than national role. The obvious result of this was the reduction of public support. As Hull's Appeal informed his congregation,

"Liverpool was then [in 1819, on the Chapel opening] a resting place for all travellers passing to Ireland and the West of Scotland, and this Institution thus became known to the wealthy classes of the whole of the United Kingdom, who freely contributed to its support. The amount of subscriptions in the year 1819 was no less than £1,373"[9]

Of that amount, £524 came from outside of Liverpool. Forty years on that total had dropped to only £78. From the locality, £815 was received in 1819 compared with £660 in 1859, despite a fourfold increase in the population of the town. Most of the wealthier merchants had ceased to reside in the town, and, according to Hull, "...a change has also taken place in the habits of the upper classes." Pew rents were satisfactory, but the benefits previously received from the collections on the door had diminished considerably. "The casual frequenters of the Chapel...", Hull informed his listeners,'...appear to have lost sight of its private character, and the purpose for which it was erected...large numbers of persons, whose appearance indicates them to be well able to contribute towards the support of their afflicted brethren, pass the plates without contributing anything whatever."[10] The collection after his sermon realised £167.

Edward Hull's obituary stated:

"He deserves especial record as a clergyman in whom there were no professional weaknesses, and the tribute of secular administration is paid the more readily because it is seldom indeed that a minister deserves such honours while maintaining in a high degree, the dignity and efficiency of his sacred office. The "Blind Church" may gain a popular successor to its late incumbent, but it is doubtful whether the Church of England in these days of silly millinery on the one side, and bitter bigotry on the other, has not ceased, for a time at least, to produce such men as Edward Hull."[11]

His successor was the Reverend Mr Alexander Whishaw, who took only a few months to incur the collective wrath of the Committee. His crime was to appeal to his congregation for two annual collections "for the benefit of three or four Great Societies of the poor and for foreign and home missions". He proposed this only on a trial basis so as to prevent any injury to the Charity, but the Committee, still mindful of the dire straits of the previous decade, from which the School had since recovered, were determined not to return to such a position and consequently censured the Chaplain.

It was not a happy period for this particular Board of Governors. Shortly afterwards their administration came under the open scrutiny of the press and the people of Liverpool in a damaging case of alleged fraud within the School.

The unpleasant sequence of events which took place during 1869 were in consequence of the persistent questioning of the financial affairs of the School by one man, Samuel Goodacre, a member of the Committee. For four or five years Goodacre had noticed what he felt was high expenditure within the stock and grocery accounts and suggested to senior members the need for investigation. Despite promises to that effect, no inquiry was instituted to look into the possibility of excesses. This Goodacre found rather galling and quite frustrating. There is no doubt that an element of misplaced snobbery was evident. Goodacre, although a successful businessman, was in the eyes of several Committee men, a mere "Grocer", with respect to his trade. As one newspaper of the day put it, "[Goodacre] by some unforseen accident obtained a seat at their board. Between the position of the manager of a bank, an attorney, a cotton-broker, and other such equally exalted personages of the Committee, and that of Mr Goodacre, Grocer, the line of demarcation is broad and well defined. This he ought to have known too, that the honour of a seat at a board comprised of such distinguished individuals, was honour sufficient in itself, without seeking to elevate himself by attacking abuses..."[12]

By April 1869 Goodacre decided it was high time for positive action. Unable to solicit support though private channels, he decided to "go public". At a special meeting of the Committee held on 13 April 1869 to elect a successor to their late President John Drinkwater, Goodacre reported that numerous goods at the School were not purchased on the best terms and could be procured for less cost elsewhere. He was requested to liaise with the Treasurer, Courtenay Cruttenden, and make an initial report at the next meeting before any decision should be taken regarding the possibility of an official investigation.

Enough errors and questionable figures were discovered by the two men to warrant a report to the Committee. Meanwhile, it had got abroad that such a report was to be expected at the meeting of 4 May, which stirred interest among the press. They promptly turned up requesting admittance to the meeting. The Committee, appalled at the thought that such business would be reported to the public before they had had a chance to even assess the situation, promptly barred their admittance. Goodacre, who no doubt, had a hand in their being there in the first place, objected to this decision and declared that he would report the intended proceedings to the press before the meeting anyway, irrespective of the outcome.

This action was to be decisive and certainly contributed to his downfall. Even if he was entirely correct in his claims, it would be so far removed from what appeared to be held dear by the majority of this Committee as to be completely irrelevant. This after all, was ungentlemanly conduct.

Goodacre, however, was a realist. When he spotted blatant bad business practice he wanted it put right as quickly as possible to protect those who would obviously suffer for its neglect. He had given up long ago waiting on the word of "gentlemen" and certainly did not trust the outcome of this meeting to go the way of a mere grocer. Sadly, this point of "ungentlemanly conduct" was to overshadow the investigations and act as a diversion from the real issues at stake. A four man sub-committee was set up to report on the claims, but a meeting was also called on 8 May, three days after the reports appeared in the press, to move to censure Samuel Goodacre. The meeting was extensively reported in several local newspapers and makes unpleasant reading. The Committee's open hostility to Goodacre was quite evident but was unquestionably without support in the town. When he was permitted to speak, he was barracked, and when going into the specifics of how much more the School were paying for certain provisions, he was reminded that, "this was not a grocer's counter". He was never forgiven for "betraying" his station. The motion of censure was carried. "I must say," remarked the Chairman, "Mr Goodacre is in a most unenviable position." The matter, however, was far from over.

The press, inevitably, had a field day. Overall support was given to Goodacre. Initially, this was due not to the question of the possible irregularities in the accounts, but to the treatment meted out to Goodacre at the hands of his associates. In the opinion of the press, the Committee had failed on several counts. They had obviously taken too long to look into Goodacre's claims. They had let personal differences interfere with the interests of the Institution and their reliance on the support of the people was miscalculated. Once the debate in the press was unavoidable, any credibility left was undoubtedly erased once the public witnessed the unjust treatment and reprimand of the man, who in their eyes, had the sole interests of the Charity at heart with no reason for personal gain. Furthermore, the continued unwillingness of the Committee to admit the press or even issue statements, merely created suspicion, however erroneous, that discrepancies did exist and a cover-up was being attempted. What else were people to think when Goodacre's request to have a shorthand writer present "for his own protection" during his interview before the Sub-Committee was turned down? Letters began to flow into the newspapers in support of Goodacre as the debate continued, which had now escalated into one of the main issues in the town and was to remain so for several weeks to come.

Finally, on 8 June, the Sub-Committee published their report.[13] It completely vindicated Goodacre, who, in the meantime, had furnished the Committee with quotations from several suppliers, all of whose goods were less than the School was paying for them. To the further chagrin and embarrassment of the Committee, the figures promptly appeared in the papers. The Report found numerous examples of the purchase of overpriced goods and in the accounts of the Shop, discrepancies were found in the supply of raw materials and stock both sold and in hand. In addition, the grocery accounts also showed a weekly purchase of 270lbs of meat, of which 46lbs could not be accounted for.

The person held responsible for this serious state of affairs was the Superintendent of 20 years, Henry Addenbrook, who vehemently denied malicious intent and refused all calls to resign. Addenbrook was allowed time to explain his actions or at least to suggest how the accounts came to be in such a state and four days later submitted a careful and intelligently worded tract. His extensive statement, despite receiving careful consideration from his superiors, was deemed inadequate, and at a special meeting on 15 June he was given notice to quit the School by 1 October 1869.

The press, who had been admitted to the final meeting to hear the inquiry into the published Report and decision of the Committee, slated the

Management of the School within their pages. Several members of the Committee were heavily criticised regarding their behaviour over the past weeks and their conducting of the School's affairs, especially the Auditor, Treasurer, and the Vice-President, Messrs. Lister, Cruttenden and Mills respectively. The call by certain sections of the press for a public inquiry and positive action against the Committee would have to wait for the Annual Meeting, which was still some five months off.

The embarrassment to the Committee and bad publicity for the School continued. In one paper (known for its frequent radical and satirical views) an attack came in a lengthy, waggish poem entitled *'Ode to Samuel Goodacre'*,[14] which pilloried each member of the Committee in turn, except, of course, their hero. Then, in September, it was found that Addenbrook had been receiving £22 4s a year intended for the extra accommodation of a female pupil, money which never reached the Charity, a practice which had continued for several years. Finally, just four weeks after his departure, it was also found that Addenbrook had been receiving 6s per week for many years from the Cook for the fat and dripping off the meat, which she in turn had sold for her own profit.

At the following Annual Meeting held on 14 January 1870, few subscribers were in attendance and the Committee, who had already appeared with a cut and dried list of their nominations for election for the coming year, had little trouble in seeing its approval by such a small number present.

Samuel Goodacre had been excluded from the list.

8
EDUCATION OR INSTRUCTION?

"A man is isolated by everything that renders the acquisition of knowledge difficult and tedious, and his isolation is diminished by everything that facilitates his power of self-education."

Dr Thomas Armitage
The Education and Employment of the Blind (1871)

"Education of the blind absolutely fails in its object in so far as it fails to develop the remaining faculties to compensate for the want of sight."

Dr Eichholz (1909)
H.M. Inspector of Special Schools

During the first seventy years or so of the School's existence, formal education had never been a serious consideration. The 'educational role' of the School was quite simple; to provide technical training in a trade to a level which would enable the pupil to become independent and self supporting (or at least, 'less burdensome'). This, of course, included music, which was taught primarily to qualify pupils to secure work as church organists, piano tuners, or music teachers.

This ideal was a manifestation of fundamental utilitarianism, developing in late eighteenth and early nineteenth century England. Based on the "greatest happiness of the greatest number" principle, the Schools' founders and subsequent guardians aimed to train successfully as many pupils as possible – but only up to a degree where a level of "happiness" could be attained (in this case, independence and self sufficiency), when they would then be encouraged to become part of this new society and put their skills to the test. The School was not about producing "high fliers" at whatever cost.

Put into contemporary context, such a scheme was undoubtedly admirable, and initially one without equal in the kingdom, but little heed was being paid to the appeals of Diderot, 'Demodocus', Haüy, and Blacklock, all writing in the later eighteenth century, with regard to the intellectual consideration of the blind person.

'Demodocus', for example, in his *Edinburgh Magazine and Review* article of 1774 (alluded to in chapter one) stated,

"...The most important view therefore, which we can entertain in the education of a person deprived of sight is to redress as effectually as possible, the natural disadvantages with which he is encumbered, or, in other words, to enlarge as far as possible his sphere of knowledge and activity. This can only be done by the improvement of his intellectual imagination and mechanical powers, and which of these ought to be most assiduously cultivated, the genius of every individual alone can determine."

Haüy's radical methods have already been discussed in the first chapter. The sole objection to his Institution – of which he himself tells us in the second section of his *Essay on the Blind* – relates to this point; "Had you the idea," he was asked, "when teaching your pupils all the branches of education you propose, of peopling the republic of letters and arts with savants, professors, and artists, each of whom, though blind, shall be capable of making a distinguished figure in these conspicuous departments, or can they even be certain of deriving the means of subsistence each from the labours of his own vocation?" "People have done us the justice," replied Haüy, "to admit that we have accomplished the first object of our Institution by offering an amusement to well-to-do blind pupils; but, however, we do not claim that the most skilful of our pupils can ever be put in competition, in any way, with the most ordinary artist who can see. But we recommend them to public benevolence."

A rather disheartening and paradoxical response regarding the potential of human achievement to come out of revolutionary France of the 1780s. Despite this acceptance of the unlikelihood of their methods producing a profusion of artisans, an emphasis on intellectual education continued in France well into the nineteenth century.

In England, and here Liverpool was not alone, methods were entirely in favour of instruction in forms of manual labour – to produce artisans, and to remove the burden placed on charity and annuity. This principle was, at first, applied quite vigorously, to the exclusion of all intellectual teaching. By the 1830s, however, a new trend was becoming common, that is, where a part of the day was given over to learning, but not at the expense of the working day. Schools by this time were of two types; those which taught pupils a trade or skill, then after a fixed period sent them away, usually after furnishing them with a few pounds or tools to start them off; and those which were closer in nature to "homes", where they trained their pupils in a craft, then continued to provide shelter for those who required it, or deserved it from their good conduct, frequently in exchange for producing saleable goods. The Liverpool School was, as we have seen, mainly of the first type, although it was not uncommon for pupils to be allowed to stay longer than the statutory period if it was felt their circumstances required it.

Again, by the 1830s, the former type, although popular in England and Ireland, was beginning to be generally abandoned to be replaced by "homes", which were already exclusive in Scotland. It was also found that due to a reduction in the continuous turnover of pupils under the Homes Scheme, economies were made in running expenses (for example, less stock "lost" as a result of training) and larger profits gained from a consistent trade in saleable goods.

The home system was now increasingly promoted due to growing concern over the welfare of pupils once they had left establishments. Studies of former pupils of various schools showed that it was not uncommon for those who had acquired great skills and had left their School with a good character, to be unsuccessful in maintaining themselves. Sadly, it was also found that there were frequent occurrences of them being readmitted in a destitute state. At a meeting held in Manchester during March 1834, relative to the erection of an institution, (which would later become Henshaw's), the committee appointed to make the necessary enquiries also assured the meeting that in Liverpool the need had long been felt for a home for the blind, who could not provide for their needs with the wages earned outside the establishment. Feelings were aired but little was done.

The success of education hinged on the pupils' ability to read. Today, we immediately think of Braille as the means by which the blind may spurn their disadvantage. Yet, that system has only been universally recommended in this country since 1868.

When Louis Braille "invented" his system in 1828, the method of reading by the use of raised characters was already several centuries old. The first recorded instance was c.1517 when Francisco Lucas of Saragossa, Spain, contrived a set of letters carved on thin tablets of wood, which was followed by a similar invention to that of Braille in 1550, by Girolimo Cardano (1501-1576), a physician of Parvia in Italy, who mentions his system in his *Natural History*. There were at least a further seven inven-

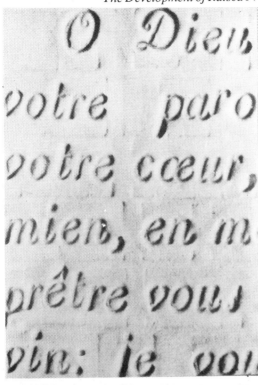

Left: a. Valentin Haüy type for beginners 1784.

Below: b. James Hartley Frere's Type 1838 (the first raised type used by the Liverpool School).

THE BRAILLE ALPHABET, WITH CONTRACTIONS.

The large dots represent the raised points of the Braille letter; the small simply serve to indicate their position in the group of six.

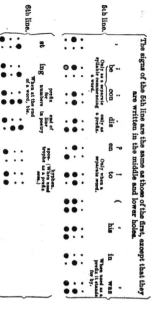

1st line.
A | B | C | D | E | F | G | H | I | J
 | but | Christ | | every | from | God | have | | Jesus

2nd line.
K | L | M | N | O | P | Q | R | S | T
 | Lord | | not | people | quite | right | some | | that

3rd line.
U | V | X | Y | Z | and | for | of | the | with
unto | very | | you | | | | | |

The signs of the 2nd, 3rd, and 4th line are formed from those of the 1st by the addition of lower dots.

4th line.
ch | gh | sh | th | wh | ed | er | ou | ow | w
child | | shall | this | which | | | | | will

The signs of the 5th line are the same as those of the first, except that they are written in the middle and lower holes.

5th line.
be | con | dis | en | ? | to | (| ' | his | in | was
Only as a syllable commencing a word. | | | | Only when a separate word. | | | | | | When used as a prefix it stands for by.

6th line.
st | ing | press for numbers in poetry | end of line hyphen. | apos-trophe. (When used as a prefix sem.) | hyphen. (When at the end of a word, &c.)

The signs of the 1st line when preceded by the prefix for numbers stand for the nine numbers and the cipher.

c. Braille 1829.

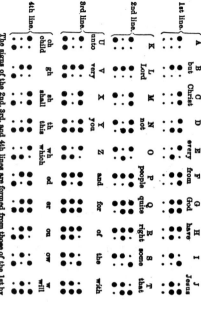

GALL.

ALSTON.
PQRSTUVW XYZ.
ABCDEFGHIJKLMNO
1234567890.,;:.—!?()

LUCAS.

MOON.

SPECIMENS OF ALPHABETS.

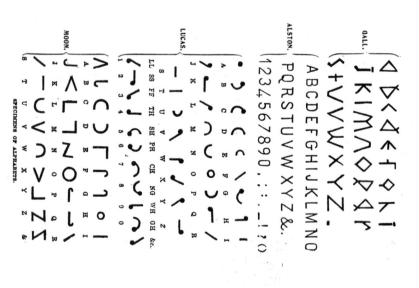

d. Gall 1827, Alston 1838, Lucas 1838, Moon 1847.

140

tions over the next two centuries before Valentin Haüy printed the first embossed books for the blind.

Louis Braille, who was later a pupil at the Paris School founded by Haüy, invented his Domino Six system in 1828. He had been inspired both by Haüy's books, which were still in use at the school, and a coded system of reading by raised dots which had been invented by a military man, Captain Charles Barbier, initially to enable men under his command read battle instructions during the night. During the early 1820s, Louis Braille was selected, along with a companion, to help test Barbier's system.[1] Louis felt this system was too limited (as it was necessary to understand Barbier's Code before beginning to read) and began to develop his own, which by 1824 he had tested on his fellow pupils. Louis was then aged just 15. He adapted his system to include musical notation and with further refinement, he finally published in 1829 his short 32 page guide book (with a long title), *Method of writing language, plain chant, and music, by means of raised points for the use of Blind Persons:* "Author, Louis Braille, tutor, Royal Institute for Blind Juveniles, Paris".

His invention appeared stillborn, making no immediate impact on the authorities and receiving much opposition, even from other teachers in the school. Still without support, it was 1837 before the first book in Braille was published; a popular text book already in use, entitled *A Summary of French History, Century by Century*. He was not to see his method adopted in his country in his lifetime. Opposition and conservatism continued well after his death in 1852, and it was not until the 1870s that French institutions began to make positive moves towards its official adoption.

In Britain, Scotland led the search for a similar method. In 1832, the Edinburgh Society of Arts offered a prize for the best type to enable the blind to read. Out of the six entrants the award was given to Mr Alexander Hay, a blind man of Edinburgh. Still unconvinced that they had found the definitive system, and believing that further investigation was warranted, the Society decided not to adopt Hay's system and instead offered a gold medal the following year in a competition which was given greater publicity. This time, 15 competitors entered, 12 of whom used their own system of characters rather than the Roman type which had been preferred so far. Despite these moves towards arbitrary methods, the medal was awarded to Dr Edmund Fry of London, in favour of his plain Roman type.

Although there was widespread acknowledgement of the need to introduce an accepted system of raised characters, (and to begin treating the intellect of the blind person the same as any other), many learned men continued to believe in the use of the Roman type pioneered by Haüy. This, to be fair, was understandable, as teachers were afraid of further demarcation and segregation of blind pupils from sighted pupils, which may have resulted from the blind having their "own language". Furthermore, it was felt common sense to continue to use letters (now in their raised form) that were already known to many before their sight was lost.

Abbé Carton, who had come to England from Bruges in 1838 to survey blind establishments in England reported,

"The largest number of blind is found among the poor, and the greatest misfortune of the blind consists in their isolation. All our efforts should tend towards bringing them near to ourselves, and to make their education as like our own as possible, and not to think that a special institution is needed for teaching them to read. If the characters in their books are those which we teach to other children, ordinary schools will be able to admit from their infancy these unfortunate beings, who have been hitherto kept afar off under a false pretext; and their misfortune will lie less heavily upon them, their intellect will be developed, and the advantage they will derive from their stay in special establishments will be in harmony with what they will have learnt before entering them."[2]

With the benefit of hindsight it is easy to criticise the apparent lack of awareness regarding difficulties faced by the practicalities of using a Roman system but such beliefs were understandable. Yet Carton put forward a good case for integration;

"If the young blind went to school with other children, they would take part in their games and would be strengthened by the exercise. They would be obliged to rely more on themselves; for from natural indifference the children who had their sight would often leave them to themselves, or would be satisfied to direct them by words, which would be still better. Choosing the ordinary character would render all this possible, and the teaching of the blind would thus become as simple as that of others."[3]

Richie, writing almost a hundred years later, realising Carton's deductions had been drawn from insufficient data declared,

"The best way to prevent the undue isolation of the blind has been shown by experience to be to give them the machinery best adapted to their use and so enable them the more quickly and efficiently to keep abreast of the intellectual life around them."[4]

Abbé Carton was certainly not alone in his belief in the Roman method. James Gall of the Edinburgh School and John Alston of Glasgow had already pioneered such systems (with modifications) and had also published discourses on its use, together with suitable books for their pupils.[5] Their methods continued in use in their own school and several others for many years to come.

Other systems were adopted elsewhere with varying degrees of success. Thomas Lucas, a Bristol man who had opened a school for a few blind children in his town, invented an embossed type, a stenographic shorthand, which he brought to London in 1838, hoping to see it put into general use. The result was the founding of the London Society for the Teaching and Training of the Blind which published numerous works using his type.

James Hartley Frere, a blind man from London, had invented a phonetic system based upon a contemporary shorthand known as Gurney's. In August 1838 he was allowed into the Liverpool School to try out his system on some of the pupils. Each word was embossed according to its pronunciation, and the names of the characters – combined or sounded together – gave the word. He assisted the pupils with twelve rules in verse, the last of which was

> "Whene'er the proper rule don't yield you satisfaction
> On trial, you will find the word is a contraction."

Frere's type was the first system to be used at the Liverpool School, although with little success, despite £38 being immediately allocated to the purchase of reading books, and the appointment of a teacher in 1841. Its complexity led to its failure, for the simple linear signs of which it was composed represented vocal sounds instead of the alphabet. Yet the last of the English systems, that of Moon, was based on Frere and met with outstanding success; out of all the English types of this period it is the only one still in use today. He had devised his type by 1847, after becoming completely blind in 1839 at the age of twenty-one. He began printing books using his characters, in a small workshop adjoining his Brighton home. By the late 1880's, there were more books using his type than any other in Britain. The Moon Society, which had been founded to publicise the system, was flourishing and he had received an honorary doctorate of laws from the University of Philadelphia. The Society was taken over by the National Institute for the Blind in 1914, where books and periodicals in Moon Type are still published, mainly for those who cannot adapt to Braille or have less sensitivity in their fingers.

a. Louis Braille.

b. James Gall, nineteenth century educationalist of the blind.

c. John Alston of Glasgow, nineteenth century educationalist of the blind.

d. Thomas Rhodes Armitage, founder of the British and Foreign Association for the Blind (1868).

Shortly after Frere's 1838 visit to Liverpool, the School was subject to open criticism regarding educational policy – or the lack of it.

"Liverpool, the oldest asylum for the blind in the country, remains stationary in this march of improvement; at the eleventh hour, we understand that Frere's stenographic books have been introduced there; but there is no onward progress at all comparable with the instruction which is imparted at other asylums – no geography, no arithmetic, no geometry – all subjects in which the blind, as their annals inform us, are capable of attaining to excellence. We must yet hope that this institution, in the midst of an intelligent population, will overcome the obstacles which keep it in the background while others are advancing. Whether the evil be in its constitution, or in its management, we cannot say; possibly it was intended only for a manual labour and a singing establishment"[6]

By 1842, when this was written, only Liverpool out of the established schools had not adopted the "Roman letter" together with a programme of education. Placed in perspective, however, it was only five years since English schools had first addressed the question. Numerous papers had appeared during this enlightened period, all addressing the question of the Education of the Blind (some of which have already been referred to), which had a substantial effect on educational developments in the mid to late nineteenth century.

The roots of this movement came from a combination of two areas of change and transition. Firstly, the natural development and discovery made by compassionate men, working among the blind where they understood the need for a system to enable their pupils to read. This promoted a growing awareness that the mind of a blind person needed intellectual stimulation just like any other and should be treated as such – which ensured that change was inevitable. Most schools were still in their early days, as were their methods.

Secondly, there was a new stimulus in philosophical theory regarding general education. Throughout the 1820s, liberal thought was developing and encompassing wider areas. The factory conditions endured by thousands of young children brought increasing attention to their plight and many believed in the need for legislation to improve their lot and to provide schooling.

Henry Brougham introduced his Parish School's Bill in 1820, "for the better education of the Poor of England and Wales" which met with fierce opposition, not least from dissenters and Roman Catholics, and was withdrawn. Undaunted, he published a pamphlet entitled 'Observations on the

Education of the People', the outcome of which was the formation in 1825 of the Society for the Diffusion of Useful Knowledge.[7] This was followed by James Mills' article on 'Education' which appeared in the *Encyclopedia Britannica* of 1825 which stated, "An institution for education, which is hostile to progression, is the most preposterous, and vicious thing, which the mind of man can conceive."

By 1832, with the passing of the Reform Act, the balance of power in the Commons passed to the newly enfranchised middle classes, and popular education therefore was regarded more than ever as a matter of urgency. The following year, John Roebuck, who had taken Brougham's place as the champion of popular education, declared to the Commons, "Education means not merely these necessary means or instruments for the acquiring of knowledge, but it means also the training or fashioning of the intellectual and moral qualities of the individual, that he may be able and willing to acquire knowledge, and to turn it to its right use."[8]

Roebuck's ambitious plan of state education for all children in a variety of subjects, plus a trade, was given keen attention and debate by the Commons before its rejection. Nevertheless, in 1833, as a result of Roebuck's proposals, the Government made its first grant to education, allocating £20,000 towards the erection of school houses.

It is not surprising, therefore, given the developments in educational theory and a growing awareness of the needs of the blind, mainly by those who had close ties with blind institutions, that change would be seen to be needed in those establishments. Changes over the next three decades, where they were introduced, were the result of independent experimentation by schools acting on their own initiatives by introducing methods developed either by their own teachers and administrators, or by other institutions which had come to their notice through published discourses for just that purpose. A universal body to help control such developments was still a long way off.

At the Liverpool School, which had now become rather unique for the wrong reasons, an official reading programme was not introduced until 1862. This is not surprising, despite Baker's vociferous comments. In its capacity as the oldest institution in the land, which had pursued the technical training of its pupils since its inception, the ideas and beliefs of successive Committees were now firmly entrenched, in what they thought,

REGULATION OF TIME.

	ON WORKING DAYS.		ON SUNDAYS.
	From 1st April to 30th September.	From 1st October to 31st March.	The whole of the Year.
To rise in the morning at	¼ past 5 o'clock.	¼ past 6 o'clock.	½ before 7 o'clock.
To go to work at	½ past 6 ,,	7 ,,	...
To attend prayers at	¾ past 7 ,,	¾ past 7 ,,	½ before 8 ,,
To breakfast at	8 ,,	8 ,,	8
To return to work at	¾ past 8 ,,	...	...
To dine at	½ past 12 30	½ past 12 — 30	½ past 1 ,,
To return to work at	2 ,,	2 ,,	...
To sup at	½ past 6 ,,	½ past 6 6·30 ,,	5 30
To go to prayers at	6 30	6·30	8
To go to bed at	¼ past 9 ,,	9 ,,	9
To attend church at	...	...	10·30 a.m. and 6 p.m.

DIETARY,

. TO BE VARIED AS OCCASION MAY REQUIRE.

DAY.	BREAKFAST.	DINNER.	SUPPER.
Sunday	Coffee and Bread and Butter.	Beef and Potatoes.	Tea and Bread and Butter.
Monday	Tea and Bread and Butter.	Rice Pudding and Broth.	Tea and Bread and Butter, or Bread and Milk.
Tuesday	Ditto.	Suet Pudding and Hashed Meat.	Ditto.
Wednesday	Ditto.	Bread Pudding and Stew.	Ditto.
Thursday	Ditto.	Beef and Potatoe Pie.	Ditto.
Friday	Ditto.	Yorkshire Pudding and Stew.	Ditto.
Saturday	Ditto.	Bread Pudding and Pea Soup.	Ditto.

Extracted from the School Rule Book 1869.

by experience, was best for their charges. Furthermore, the town of Liverpool was founded on a port built by industry, trade and manual labour – intellectual development was for those who ran it – many of whom had sat on this very Committee since 1793.

After the agenda of the School's Annual General Meeting of 1862 had been discussed, the Treasurer then "spoke more especially as to the amount of time expended in having various books and Newspapers read to the Pupils".[9] This was at the expense of the time which should have been spent in the workshops. It was a reaction to this, therefore, that it was proposed at that meeting to teach the pupils to read for themselves, using the "raised Roman Character". The published Annual Reports for the next 20 years or so would carry an up to date standard assessment on the progress of pupils' reading, of which the following was the first.

> "All the Pupils capable of learning are taught to read by means of a raised type. Out of the 74 Pupils now in the School, 50 can read. The Pupils generally, who can read, have a portion of Scripture, in raised type, presented to them on leaving the School."[10]

Although the School had received criticism following the numerous papers published on the Education of the Blind during the 1830s and 40s,[11] the School had considered moves to teach reading as early as 1798, when the Committee purchased a "reading apparatus" from a Mr Carson. No details are known as to what form it took, nor the Arithmetic Apparatus purchased for five guineas off Thomas Spence of Whitehaven two months later, nor the writing machine donated by John Casson a month after that in January 1799. The minutes of the Annual General Meeting of 8 January 1799 recorded,

> "Mr John Casson, having by means of Mr Roscoe and Mr Dawson represented to the Committee that he has invented an instrument by which a person entirely blind may write and read with tangible characters, and that the same includes also a compendious method of writing music which may be read by the blind, and an easy mode of solving arithmetical questions; which invention he has after many years labour brought to great perfection. And the meeting being informed that when he has obtained a certain number of subscribers he intends to make the same publick, and to sell the instruments at five guineas each. Resolved:- by the meeting that the Committee do subscribe for five such instruments for the use of the Charity."[12]

On 6 September 1816 the Committee were obliged to give their thanks to Mr Molineux for "instructing musical pupils in the Madras System invented by Doctor Bell".[13] Again we know no detail of the method.

By 1822, the Committee were of the opinion that the pupils could be successfully taught to spell and read, also to learn arithmetic and even to print books, but despite their good intentions no official plan was introduced.[14]

Just a few months before reading was made compulsory, the School received a printing machine in August 1861 from a Mr Waldeman of Schiott in Copenhagen, but again, detail is frustratingly scanty and researches have proved fruitless. A month later there was another donation; nine volumes of music in raised type given by Captain James J. Rees of Hick Street South, Brooklyn, New York. It is feasible that he may have attended services at the Church and been sufficiently moved to return to the School with his gift after his visits to the port.[15]

By the 1860s it was clear that Educational legislation was long overdue. In 1868, that most famous citizen of Liverpool, William Ewart Gladstone, became Prime Minister, placing the Education Department in the charge of W.E. Forster, who introduced his Education Bill in 1870. It did not create a new national system of education, nor a completely compulsory system, nor a free system, but despite being a compromise, the Act was a brave attempt and laid important foundations for the institution of State education.

Although the blind were not mentioned (despite strong representation made to the Government) they were not excluded from compulsory schooling. In several centres arrangements were made for their attendance at the newly established schools. The decade that followed, partly as a result of this Act and the end of *laissez-faire* Liberalism (marked by Disraeli's administration and its increased social reform), was an important one for the education of the blind.

The Worcester College, the only school to prepare boys who were blind for the Universities and the liberal professions, was established, as was the forerunner to the Royal National Institute for the Blind, the British and Foreign Blind Association, founded by one of the greatest figures in the education of the blind, Dr Thomas Rhodes Armitage. This centralised organisation adopted Braille (now almost 40 years since its invention) and strongly recommended its use above all other printing types (together with Moon for those with less sensitive fingers). A survey taken in 1871 revealed that Moon Type was in use in 38 institutions, Lucas by seven, Roman by four, Frere by three and Braille by only four.[16] It was to be a slow and arduous task to persuade institutions to discard their own well tried systems, many with libraries now well stocked. The Association promoted their recommendation by printing and publishing Braille books, maps, and music and supplied writing frames and other educational apparatus.

The first training college for blind teachers, The Royal Normal College and Academy of Music for the Blind, was founded at Norwood, Surrey in 1872, and in 1879 the Gardner's Trust was established when Henry Gardner left £300,000 for the relief of the Blind. The Charity Organization Society, formed in 1874, appointed several committees pursuing various lines of inquiry relating to the improvement of educational and industrial training for the blind. Their findings showed inadequacies in all departments and the Organisation pressed for a Royal Commission to secure the necessary reforms.

During this period, there were also a number of conferences on the Continent, beginning with Vienna in 1873, where common problems between institutions were discussed and attempts at standardisation were made. The first British Conference was held at York in July 1883. Most of the leading figures in the blind world attended including Dr Armitage and Mr Campbell from London, Mr Harris from Leicester, and Mr Humphries from Henshaws. Liverpool was represented by Mr Brunton and Mr Bryson (Superintendent and Secretary).

Increasingly, recognition was being given to the necessity of a general inquiry into the overall condition of the Blind in England Wales and Scotland, and in July 1884 the Duke of Westminster called a Conference in Grosvenor House with just that plan in mind. Exactly a year later a Royal Commission was set up with a brief to

"investigate and report upon the condition of the Blind in the United Kingdom, the various systems of the education of the blind, elementary, technical and professional at home and abroad, and the existing Institutions for that purpose, the employment open to and suitable for the blind and the means by which education may be extended so as to increase the number of blind persons qualified for such employment."[17]

After four years' labour their report was published in July 1889, a comprehensive survey of the world of the blind, which remains today a mine of information for the student. The report pressed for an improvement in

T. Addison of Coniston (pupil 1889-93).

technical training, a great increase in workshop accommodation, and a general adoption of the Saxon System.[18] It recommended that responsibility for education and training should be laid upon the State and that compulsory attendance at school should be enforced on blind children from 5 to 16 years. It was also recommended that

"From 16 to 21 the School Authority should have the power and the duty to assist all necessitous blind persons to maintain themselves while learning a trade. Those who become blind from 21 to 50 should equally receive help from the School Authority."[19]

"The Commission's Report...," declared Richie, "...was a historic landmark. It was a monument of the best opinion of the day on all aspects of the blind problem. Much of its advice has been ratified by events, and on the strength of its recommendations the 1890 and the 1893 Education Acts were added to the Statute Book."[20]

The English Act was known as the Elementary Education (Blind and Deaf Children) Act 1893 and aimed at extending to blind and deaf children the education made compulsory by the Act of 1870.

Institutions already in existence were to receive junior pupils whose fees were to be paid by the Education Authority that sent them, who in turn received a grant from the Treasury. Although the Act was welcomed, it meant that children of the age of five had to attend school even if it meant separation from their parents. This was felt by many to be too young.

Schools were now to be certified and inspected by the Board of Education, which raised standards in accommodation, education and equipment. Many schools could not meet the requirements and relinquished their elementary departments. The Liverpool School found itself in a similar position after a visit from Mr Sharpe, H.M. Inspector, who condemned the Hardman Street Building as being absolutely unsuitable to the new requirements as laid down in the Act. His words were to determine the far reaching decisions soon to be made by the Committee regarding the future of the School.

A PERIOD OF TRANSITION

"It is a clear historical fact that educational change rarely, if ever, takes place for educational reasons. It is almost invariably dependent on social, political, and economic factors."

Sylvia Harrop
The Merchant Taylors' School for Girls, Crosby,
– One Hundred Years of Achievement 1888-1988

"Yesterday afternoon the new building, which has been erected in Wavertree in connection with the Liverpool School for the Indigent Blind, was formally opened in the presence of a large number of subscribers and sympathisers with the work of the Institution. The building, which is commodious and well equipped, stands on an excellent site fronting the open country. The ceremony was gracefully performed by the Lady Mayoress in the absence of the Countess of Derby, who was unable to be present owing to indisposition...Mr H.J. Wilson (secretary of Gardener's Trust for the Blind) proposed a vote of thanks to the Lady Mayoress for her presence. That institution was the pioneer of all other schools of the kind in this country, and he could not help thinking that in future history this century would be described as that in which care for the blind first began. Schools had been established all over the country, and school boards had also started classes for the blind in several towns. The education of the blind was of the utmost importance and school authorities were now responsible for it, as they had to make provision for suitable elementary education for all blind children in their district under the age of sixteen. He congratulated the city and the committees of the School upon having such a large well planned institution."

Liverpool Daily Post, 13 January 1899.

Once it had become clear that certification of the Hardman Street School by the Board of Education would be unlikely to be maintained, following the terms laid down in the 1893 Act, the Committee realised that swift action was needed to enable the Charity to care for children, who by law, were now entitled to an education.

It was decided to erect a separate building to cater specifically for junior school children. Public subscription would fund the project, which received a massive boost of £10,000, approximately a third of the total cost of the scheme, from a donor who wished to remain publicly anonymous, but was known to the School as Miss Mary Loiusa Hornby.

Miss Hornby, born in 1837, was the second of three daughters of the

Reverend Mr Thomas Hornby, one time vicar of Walton Parish Church. She was the cousin of Hugh Frederick Hornby, a wealthy merchant of Wavertree Hall, a great collector of books and prints (the whole of which was bequeathed to the City Library on his death together with £10,000 to provide a suitable building for the collection).

Inspired in her youth by Florence Nightingale, Mary Hornby became a nurse in the Franco-Prussian War, and was later a ward sister at Magdalen Hospital, London. After she returned to her native Liverpool, she became involved in district nursing in her own parish of Walton, entirely at her own expense, and made regular visits to the Walton Workhouse. Her experiences there led to her founding a home for destitute and neglected children in Walton. She had cause one day to take in a small blind boy, whose needs drew her towards a growing interest in the care of the blind. She started a blind family, and secured the help of two sisters; the Misses Allen, one of whom, thanks to Miss Hornby, became the first Matron at the Wavertree School.

When the Wavertree School was opened in 1898, for which she had also donated £30 under her own name (a similar amount came from the Patron, Queen Victoria), the blind children from Miss Hornby's Home were transferred to the Wavertree School, although her Home still continued to work for the blind. It became a hive of industry, especially in preparing Braille books, and Miss Hornby later founded the Braille Writer's Society. The Library at Wavertree School was soon filled with costly Braille books, and the City Library received similar gifts to become the centre for blind literature before the Blind Library was opened in Manchester to cater for the Northern Counties. The books were largely typed by blind people whom she paid for the work, and many copies were made by her own hands. For 14 years this special work went on and thousands of volumes were sent out far and wide from Aberdeen to Cairo in the interest of the blind of all nationalities and languages.

One of her later schemes was to invest a considerable amount of capital to provide a number of annuities for blind people. In recognition of her lifetime's work Miss Mary Hornby was presented with a silver casket by the Lord Mayor of Liverpool in 1911. She was described by the Revd. Thomas Lund, who had become the School Chaplain in 1884 after the death of the Reverend Clement Appleyard, as

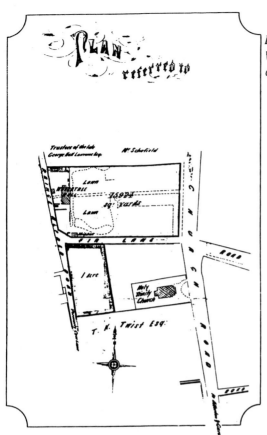

Left: Plan of Wavertree Hall c.1890

Below: Sketch from the 'Liverpool Daily Post' 11 January 1899.

NEW SCHOOL FOR THE BLIND AT WAVERTREE.

"the bent little figure, growing more bent with time, rendering it almost impossible in her later years to look into her face. It was a pity, because there was kindness there, written so plainly in the tout ensemble of expression, which was not only beautiful to see, but was the negation of the little nervous brusquerie of manner which some people could not understand, and of which she was only too conscious and deplored as part of her natural handicap. But those who knew her best loved her most, and that is the finest verdict you can pass on any life."[1]

Mary Hornby retired to Worthing in Sussex and there that remarkable woman passed away aged 76 on 3 April 1913.

The urban development of Wavertree today is a stark contrast to the rural community of the late nineteenth century which lay on the outskirts of Liverpool. The village was best known in those days for its large windmill, the village green lake, and the lock-up, the latter which still stands today. Although the village is one of the oldest in the area, evidence of a much earlier community was discovered in the mid-nineteenth century, when Bronze Age funerary urns were discovered near the Green by workmen in 1867, together with arrowheads and other grave goods.

The village also had its Hall, which stood in enclosed grounds bordered by Church Road, from which the road to Woolton ran, and Cow Lane (now Prince Alfred Road). The Hall was positioned on the Cow Lane side of the grounds, and in its final days overlooked the newly laid out recreational fields known as the "Mystery". (So called as when the land was donated to the people of Liverpool in 1895, its benefactor wished to remain anonymous. Today he is widely believed to have been Philip Holt of the famous Liverpool ship-owning family.)

Yet a further mystery surrounds the origins of Wavertree Hall itself. The precise date of its erection is unknown, but it is possible that it was not the first Hall to stand on the site. When the 1896 demolition of the Hall was taking place to make way for the new School, portions of an earlier building were found, which consisted of rough hewn timbers fastened with wooden pegs and remains of what was probably a thatched roof. It is conceivable that a medieval hall once stood on the site.[2] A sandstone horse trough was also uncovered which now stands proudly at the front of the School.

One of the earliest known residents of the Hall was Richard Percival, who belonged to a family with an ancient heraldic pedigree. His grandfather was Mayor of Liverpool in 1651, who purchased the Allerton estates from the Lathom family in 1670. By 1736, the family were in heavy debt and Richard Percival found it necessary to dispose of the Allerton land, selling it to the Hardman family, although he retained Wavertree Hall where he remained in poverty for almost 30 years.

A legend surrounding scandalous events of the mid-nineteenth century is still spoken about today, especially to visitors at the School who are struck by the site of the fine wrought gates standing at the front of the School, with no apparent driveway. In 1856, a daughter of the owner of the Hall brought shame upon her family when she eloped with her lover, a lowly coachman. Leaving at high speed in their carriage, they passed through the gates which then stood at the end of the drive. Her father was so outraged, that he ordered the gates to be sealed and never opened again. A clause to that effect was inserted in the deeds of the Hall, and to this day the gates remain securely locked.

The gates observed by the visitor today, however, are not the originals. In October 1955, it was found necessary to remove the gates, which were designed during the Queen Anne period, for restoration due to their deteriorating condition. Sadly, they were found to be beyond repair, but before being scrapped, perfect replicas were made which stand today in place of the originals. As for the eloping daughter, it is said that her carriage, still travelling at great speed, slipped on the cobbled cattle path as it passed the Green and careered into the Wavertree Lake, where she was drowned.[3]

In 1895 the Hall, which was now owned by Herbert Edward Smith and his sister Edith Grace Smith, was sold to Eleanor Stolterfoht and Matilda Madden, who in turn conveyed the Hall and grounds to the School the following year. Coincidentally, the first Vice President of the new school (the Committee of which entirely comprised ladies, with the Countess of Derby as President) was Mrs. Ireland-Blackburne of Hale Hall. Her husband's grandfather was John Ireland-Blackburne who was Mayor of Liverpool in 1788 and Chairman of the School for the Indigent Blind in 1802. His residence in those days was none other than Wavertree Hall.

The School opened in November 1898, taking in children from the ages five to sixteen, when they would then be transferred to Hardman Street for technical training. The new building was placed on the upper portion of the site, away from the Old Hall which had stood on the lower

The original gates of Wavertree Hall (date unknown c.1899-1920) (J. Waite).

site. The Hall was found to be unsuitable for use as a school and was of little architectural interest, hence its demolition. The principal entrance to the new School was situated in the centre of the main bloçk, standing about 50 yards from the road and approached by a driveway from Church Road. On either side of the principal entrance was a waiting room, the Committee Room, Matron's sitting room, the Master's office and officers' dining room, and behind them a range of five classrooms, each entered from a central corridor, which ran from end to end of the building. The classrooms were separated from each other and from the corridor by glazed screens, which, "...imparted a light and cheerful appearance, admitting perfect supervision of the whole range by the teacher".[4] There was a fully equipped gymnasium, a sick ward, nurses' rooms and a dining hall. On the first floor were the dormitories, plus wardrobe rooms and officers' bedrooms. Large day rooms and workrooms were in the basement. There was also a double lift between the three levels and "telephonic communication" between various rooms for the staff.

The Building, faced with grey brick, Rainhill stone and red Ruabon brick, was designed by Messrs. H. and A.P. Fry of Liverpool, and officially opened before a large gathering of dignitaries on Thursday 12 January 1899 at 3pm.

After the opening ceremony, Henry Wilson, aforementioned Secretary of the Gardener's Trust, took the opportunity to make a forceful speech criticising the inadequacies of the 1893 Act.

"The system of education for the blind was not yet complete", he declared, "for it was utterly impossible for children turned adrift at the age of 16 to earn their own living in the world when they had not been instructed in a trade. The Act of 1893 did not go far enough. The age ought to be extended for technical or secondary education; or, as recommended by the Royal Commission on the Blind, provision ought to be made by the school authorities to give liberal allowances to those between the ages of 16 and 21 while learning a trade...Besides the question of the care of the blind while they learned a trade, there was the question of institutions in which they might work afterwards. If men worked at home and had to spend time in soliciting orders and selling their goods, and had to purchase material at retail prices, they were hopelessly handicapped in competition with others."

Wilson continued to criticise the lack of prevention of blindness.

"Little had been done in the past to prevent blindness. It was appalling to read in the report of the Royal Commission that it was estimated that there were 7,000 blind people in the United Kingdom who ought never to have been blind. In nearly all those cases blind-

159

ness had resulted from inflammation of the eyes soon after birth. This was a disease which could nearly always be cured if taken in time, and knowledge of this could not be too widely spread among the poorer classes."[5]

Wilson's informed appeal regarding the care of the adolescent blind had not impressed the Mayor, William Oulton, who rose to his feet to object to the use of state aid for those between the age of 16 and 21.

"One of the greatest advantages to be derived," he declared, "was increased independence and self reliance on the part of the students, and the less they interfered with them and the less there was suggestive of their incapacity, probably the better it would be for the formation of that strength of character which was likely to be one of the results of the improved methods of tuition."

Wilson was only too familiar with such unsoundly based political rhetoric. One can almost feel his utter despair and frustration on hearing such words. As secretary of an organisation which was spending a great deal of money trying to alleviate the plight of many in this age group, he was well aware of the reality of the situation and the acute hardships faced by many ex-pupils who were frequently consigned to an early taste of abject poverty. Surely there was no lack of independence to have an option of state aid if all else failed.

In Liverpool many ex-pupils found themselves in the Liverpool Workshops for the Blind in Cornwallis Street. It had begun in 1859 as the Home Teaching Society, founded by Miss Wainwright in Birkenhead, who saw a need for suitable provision for those who had were no longer in the care of institutions, and to provide a facility and outlet for their technical work. Initially, it functioned as a home visiting arrangement, with teachers helping with reading, but it quickly included industrial training and opened its first workshops in 1861 in a large room under Hope Hall, just across the road from the Hardman Street School, moving to 37 Bold Street shortly afterwards. The Society received a huge boost from the Town Council in 1867 with the donation of 1,000 square yards of land in Cornwallis Street, where a new Workshop was completed by 1870. In 1906, to encourage closer cooperation and harmony between the School and the Workshop it was decided to introduce an interchange of representatives on their respective Committees.

The Liverpool Workshop for the Blind resided in the Cornwallis Street building until 1990, providing employment and an outlet for traditional goods such as baskets, hampers and mats, together with high quality domestic ware – paint brushes, table linen, towels and bathrobes.

160

On leaving the School numerous pupils took up a new option recently established in London. The Blind Tea Agency of 37 Pratt Street was begun in 1891 by Mr C.E. Dustow, a blind man, in order to find employment for blind persons selling tea and other consumer goods on commission (which in 1909 was approximately 20%). This was not a charitable institution but a commercial undertaking which soon had several hundred agents on its books. The work was not easy and many found problems in securing regular custom.

Several letters still exist in the School Archive, received from Old Pupils facing acute difficulties and appealing for help. So many make for pathetic reading. The Committee were not unmoved by the sad circumstances faced by many of the School's former pupils and decided to set up an Old Pupils Fund specifically to alleviate such distresses. Aiding over 100 pupils each year, it was based on the "Saxon" System, a continental approach to aftercare vigorously promoted by Dr Armitage, and was recognised as an essential requirement by the Royal Commission, no doubt on his instigation.[6] This question of provision for those above 16, both from an educational and employment point of view, featured prominently on the agenda of the International Conferences for the Blind in Westminster in 1902 and Edinburgh in 1905, and continued to be debated for the next two decades.

The Conferences were continuing the trend set in the later years of the preceding century as a necessary open forum to discuss matters regarding all areas of care for the blind, including educational and technical developments, medical care and the prevention of blindness. The international exchange of ideas was actively encouraged, and by the 1914 Conference, papers were read by representatives from Canada, Australia, Uruguay, Syria, Brazil, India, U.S.A., Russia, China, and Denmark. There was even a lecture by the Managing Director of Selfridges on "Salesmanship", a reflection of how seriously the development of successful commercial operations was now being taken.

Again, officers from the Liverpool School attended the Conferences. During the Manchester Conference of 1908, delegates were invited to come to Liverpool for a day, where large numbers visited the School and attended a reception held by the Lord Mayor at the Town Hall. The meet-

a. Pianoforte tuning lesson.

b. Dining room.

c. Basketmakers.

d. Shoemakers.

163

ing was presided over by the President of the School, Henry Wade Deacon, and a lecture was given by Walter Littlewood, Headmaster of Wavertree, on "Recreations for the Blind". Three and a half acres of grounds at Wavertree had given the teachers ample opportunity to develop ideas. Soon after the opening of the School the children were taking part in numerous outdoor activities, such as football, cricket, running on a specially adapted track and gardening in the spacious grounds. The children had also been granted free use of the newly opened Wavertree Swimming Baths which they visited twice a week. Other children joined the Scouts and Guides recently founded at the School.

During the first decade of the new century, music continued to be a strong subject, especially at Hardman Street. In 1905, under the instruction of Arthur Pollitt, who had just been awarded a music doctorate, three pupils were examined under the Incorporated Society of Musicians, all of whom passed and one with honours. Several more were successful in gaining Gardner's Scholarships which entitled them to admission to the Royal Normal College and Academy of Music for the Blind. Dr Pollitt was consistently achieving good results with his students during his time at the School, and his efforts were justly rewarded in 1909 when one of his pupils, Zachariah Hughes, obtained the Teacher's Diploma of Trinity College, London, becoming an Associate of that Institution. This was the first teacher's diploma gained by a pupil of the School.

Dr Pollitt was undoubtedly helped by a work produced by his predecessor Edward Watson. Mr Watson, who was using Braille music notation in his teaching, saw the need for a standard Braille text which could be used in the teaching of music. While at the Hardman Street School he embarked on his project, which he completed by 1900. The Committee expressed great interest in his work and were looking into publication costs when he decided to leave the School. His *Tutor*, a manual of carefully graded lessons, was published the following year. Novello & Co. published an ink-print copy in 1902, which according to Watson, "was more particularly intended for the use of seeing teachers of blind music students or for those who might wish to assist in the musical education of the blind in any way."[7] His textbook was still the official manual of British schools thirty years later.

Despite the high standards annually attained by many of the pupils, it was found after "long and very careful inquiry into the earnings and conditions of the pupils who had been taught Music and Tuning as a source of livelihood" that the teaching of those subjects was not producing the desired results once the pupils had left the Institution. Sadly, the Committee felt obliged to close down the Music Department at the end of 1912, although singing and "glee" classes were formed to "sustain the interest and pleasure of the pupils". Economic viability was still of paramount importance even as late as 1912. One hundred and twenty two years after John Christie had struck upon the idea of teaching music to alleviate the suffering of the blind, his Plan was to be laid to rest.[8]

Nevertheless, it was only three years before music lessons were reintroduced, to be taught, the Committee resolved, as a "recreation to a limited number of pupils, which will enable them to accompany on the piano those pupils to whom special facilities are granted for voice training".[9]

There were moves during this period to institute a nationally recognised certificate for those wishing to train as teachers of the blind, and to achieve the professional status which it deserved. The Liverpool School supported the developments and received numerous groups of students from Edge Hill College for practical training. By 1908, after meetings at the British and Foreign Blind Association, it was decided to establish an examining body; the College of Teachers of the Blind, which would grant diplomas to successful candidates. Both the College and its awards were recognised by the Board of Education. Three teachers from the Liverpool School graduated with honours in the first year, one of whom, A.A. Cowan, became Headmaster of Wavertree the following year. By 1912, an Association of Teachers had also been founded, which soon became a professional body of considerable strength and influence. It amalgamated with the College of Teachers in 1924.

Medical care continued to be of paramount importance at the School, although the sad loss of George Walker was suffered in 1909. Surgeon of St. Pauls Eye and Ear Hospital, Mr Walker had been Honorary Surgeon to the School for 35 years. He had supported the School since 1864, and had served on the Committee since 1877, including the office of Vice-President. Many pupils had benefited from his skills, several having left the Institution with sufficiently recovered sight to enable them to earn a living as sighted persons. He was succeeded both at the School and St. Pauls by his son, Arthur Nimmo Walker.

There were further losses to the Charity in 1913, and together with the resulting reorganisation in the form of the new appointments, there was quite a new atmosphere in the School. Henry Wade Deacon had resigned the Presidency in 1912 after 13 years in the Chair; and less than two weeks after Miss Hornby's death in 1913, the School also saw the passing of the Revd. Thomas William May Lund, Chaplain of the School for the past 29 years. A memorial service was held in the Chapel attended by the Lord Mayor, the Bishop of Liverpool, and numerous dignitaries, friends and relatives. The address was given by Reverend Lund's lifelong friend, Reverend Charles Foster Gunton, who was appointed as his successor shortly afterwards.

Thomas Lund was born in Sneinton, Nottinghamshire in 1843, the son of a vicar. Educated at Sidney Sussex College, Cambridge, he became curate of St. Phillip's (opposite the Hardman Street School) in 1866. From there he took up a ministerial post in Manchester, before returning to Liverpool in 1884 to become Chaplain of St. Mary's, the School Chapel. There he exhibited a magnetic power as a preacher, regularly filling the Chapel, which had no parish of its own to draw from. His sermons revealed a remarkable breadth of mind, force of character and an exceptionally high standard of intellect.

He was one of the most enthusiastic art connoisseurs in the city and he collected many examples of pictorial, photographic and sculptural work which he exhibited at his home and in the Chapel. He annually toured Italy and on his return would give illustrated lectures showing his fine collections of photographs. Invitations to lecture to societies on art subjects were frequent and he had numerous books to his credit. "His death was a serious loss..." reported the Committee, "...not only to the School, but to the intellectual life of the City, and he will long be missed as an eloquent and earnest preacher."[10]

Within the School, the pupils were faced with three Superintendents within four years. Thomas Taylor, who had died in 1909 after 20 years in office, was replaced by Walter Littlewood, the Headmaster of Wavertree. When Mr Littlewood resigned in 1913 he had served the School for 17 years as Schoolmaster, Headmaster and Superintendent. As the cloud of war hung over the country, Mr Cowan, Headmaster of Wavertree for only three years, left the School to take up a similar position at the Bristol School. He was replaced by Mr E. Gledhill of Preston School for the

Revd. T.W.M. Lund (Chaplain 1884-1913).

Sir Henry Wade Deacon, elected to the Committee 1896 President 1900-19, 1927-30.

Edwin Green, President 1938-1944.

Harold Smyth (President 1945-51).

Blind, who was returning to the School where he was formerly Assistant Master.

The coming of war inevitably had an effect on staffing levels. Within weeks the Defective Sight Class was suspended, as a replacement for the Teacher, Mr S.S. Jones, could not be found. Mr Jones had volunteered at the outbreak of hostilities, and received a Commission in the 15th Middlesex Regiment. Only days earlier he had heard that he had passed his Teacher's Diploma at the College of Teachers of the Blind.

The Hardman Street pupils played their part too in the war effort, supplying the troops with large numbers of mittens, socks and gloves. Chairs and frames were re-seated in cane, for use on hospital and transport ships. Four pupils, having completed their training as basket makers found a position at Southport where they worked on a Government supply contract, and five Old Boys had recovered their sight sufficiently to enable them to join His Majesty's Forces.

Sad news was received from the Front of the death of Lieutenant-Colonel Arthur Nimmo Walker, Honorary Surgeon to the School, who was killed in France on 24 September 1916, while serving in the Royal Army Medical Corps. This was a great loss, not only to the School, but also to the medical world. For many years he had carried out pioneering work in the treatment and prevention of Opthalmia Neonatorum (infantile blindness) and was universally regarded as an authority. It was indeed his life's study, and through his skill and knowledge in this direction many thousands of young people were saved from becoming blind. He practically revolutionised the treatment of this grave disease, and one of his brightest and most successful ideas in coping with infantile blindness was the innovation of having the mother in hospital while her child was under medical and surgical care. The School were unable to replace Mr Walker until the end of the War when they turned to the Royal Infirmary to secure the services of Dr T.H. Bickerton. Dr Bickerton, who later wrote *A Medical History of Liverpool*, sat on the Committee until 1932, and like George Walker before him, he was succeeded by his son Dr H.R. Bickerton who in turn served the School until 1943.

Mr Gledhill, who due to illness, had been exempted from the Headmastership, by an arrangement with the Board of Education, until the end of November 1916, resigned his post on that deadline and died shortly afterwards. Due the scarcity of trained teachers of the Blind, the School were obliged to appoint Mr T. Gillespie, a retired schoolmaster of Bristol, as temporary Headmaster of Wavertree.

After helping the School out of a difficult situation, Mr Gillespie stepped down the following year when LLoyd M. Davies, recently released from the Army, resumed his duties as Assistant Master. His stay was a short one too, however, as he left after only a few months to take up a similar post at the School for the Blind, York. This state of affairs prompted the Committee to suspend the position of Headmaster, and to make the Superintendent directly responsible for Wavertree (the Superintendent already held jurisdiction over both Schools, including Headmasters). Samuel Stevens, formerly of Henshaws, who had taken over this post on the resignation of Walter Littlewood in 1913, was thought capable of such a role.

These were also the heady days of women's suffrage and just as the war had had a catalytic effect, due to the shortage of manpower at home, on the growing acceptance of women carrying out tasks formerly of the male domain, so too did the School play a rather reluctant part in promoting the Women's Cause. The search for suitable schoolmasters had become an acute problem by 1917, when the Committee, no doubt heavily influenced by the Ladies Committee of the Wavertree School, decided to tread new ground and follow a precedent set in other parts of the country, which was by now, becoming quite commonplace.

"The retirement of the remaining sighted Assistant Master, Mr Norbury, to take up work in India, has further reduced the staff of male teachers, and the Committee have, owing to the dearth of suitable male teachers, been compelled to fill their places with female teachers, and they are gratified to report that their work has proved eminently satisfactory and great credit is due to them for carrying on the educational work in so adequate a manner."[11]

The coming of peace also brought numerous social reforms, not least of which was Fisher's Education Act. The powers of Local Education Authorities in regard to every type of education, including that of the blind, were re-stated and enlarged under the Act. It reinforced the provisions for medical inspection and the treatment of school children, thereby laying the foundation of much preventive work in blindness. Furthermore, the Government grant to blind schools materially increased. Under this Act, the vocational training of the blind became an obligation on the Local Education Authority.

Two years later, the Blind Persons Act of 1920 was placed on the Statute Book, which made it the duty of County Boroughs and Councils to provide for the welfare of the blind. Old Age Pensions were extended to blind persons of 50 years of age instead of 70, and it was also made illegal for any appeals to be made on behalf of the blind by non-registered charities. Blindness itself was given a narrower definition than that which was given in the Education Acts. Additionally, it also placed a duty on Local Education Authorities to provide for, or secure, the technical education of a Blind person. It was a memorable Act.

A third Act during this period was passed in 1921 which effectively consolidated all previous Education Acts into one Statute. Reforms had also taken place in the raising of funds for the Blind. This was entirely due to the efforts of the British and Foreign Blind Association, recently revamped with new headquarters, a new name and new leadership.

The new premises were opened in Great Portland Street by King George V in 1914, and under the Presidency of Mr Arthur Pearson (later Sir Arthur) the Association was known as the National Institute for the Blind. Arthur Pearson, who had recently become blind, was a driving force with a great knowledge of the advertising world and much influence in Fleet Street. In the words of Richie, "He was soon able to show to an astonished and rather slow going blind world, what could be accomplished by hustle, flair, daring, and a wide acquaintance with the advertising media."[12]

His energies soon turned to the care of soldiers and sailors who had lost their sight in battle, together with the raising of funds for that purpose, and a large publicity organisation was rapidly built up, soon catering for the whole of the country. The response of the public to these philanthropic efforts was so generous that a rare situation developed in that funds began to outstrip needs. In consequence, the N.I.B. began to make substantial grants to local institutions. However, it was decided that to continue to receive N.I.B. funds, institutions must refrain from carrying on with independent collections, and apply instead for a percentage of funds collected by their local branch (although this did not apply to the solicitation of subscribers). In 1918, such a system commenced in Liverpool, initially with a grant rated at five per cent of the N.I.B. (Liverpool Branch) annual income, which amounted to £462. Two years later, the percentage system was abolished and a fixed grant was awarded, the first being £500.

The School, however, was desperate for additional funds and the President swiftly replied to the N.I.B.

"...The amounts we have received from your Institute have been of the most timely assistance in carrying on at Hardman Street, but I find the ever increasing cost of maintenance a sore burden. Our debit balance at the Bankers is growing in a manner that haunts me all the time. Do you think that your Institution could make us a special grant this year, of say, £1000 in view of our present position and the fact that our present arrangements with your Institute precluded any special appeal locally? We have something to show at Hardman Street for the money we have had to spend. We are most excellently equipped in all our Workrooms, and must, at all cost, retain our present staff of technical teachers. It is not without great searching of heart that I make this appeal, but I feel certain that in any event, I shall have your sympathy..."[13]

Sympathy, sadly, was all the School did receive – the appeal was turned down. This state of affairs highlighted at a very early stage the drawbacks of the new system.

Abortive attempts to find a solution to the problem were witnessed as early as April 1920. Money was now being raised in areas where local institutions had previously known little competition, which gave rise to widespread feelings of dissatisfaction and resentment. By the mid-1920s positive legislation was sorely needed and it came by way of a scheme drafted by the Ministry of Health and adopted by the N.I.B.

The scheme enlarged the Council of the National Institute by electing additional representatives of local agencies throughout the country. Provided that agreements, where possible, were entered into in each area, (deciding in each case whether the local society or the N.I.B. should be the collecting agent); the money thus collected was to be distributed in agreed proportions.

At the end of the War, financial problems were also being faced by the Committee in the running of the Chapel. Matters had become so serious that it was decided to place the whole business before the Lord Bishop of the Diocese. At that meeting it was decided not to replace the recently retired Chaplain with a full-time incumbent, but instead attach a clergyman to the position without actually being appointed Chaplain or to take on the full duties previously required from such a post. This would immediately save the the School £100 per annum. Such moves, however were clearly inadequate and the running of the Chapel continued to be a financial nightmare, until by 1926 there was an accumulated deficit since 1910 of

£3,225, which was being met annually out of the general fund of the Charity to the detriment of its usual beneficiaries.

In addition, several other factors were now acting against the very existence of the Chapel. Firstly, there had been a general change in the church going habits of local people; secondly, there was a diminution in the residential population in the Hardman Street area and the extra-parochial nature of the Chapel was now a handicap (i.e. no parish of its own). The funds received from pew-rents and offerings had in the past largely off-set the running costs of the Chapel but now scarcely anyone outside of the School attended services. Thirdly, 1924 saw the consecration of Liverpool Cathedral which stood only a few hundred yards away from the Chapel. There was also less need for a Chapel attached to the School, now that the children had been removed to Wavertree. For those actually in Hardman Street it would not be too inconvenient for them to attend St. Luke's nearby, should the Chapel close.

In August 1926, it was decided by the Committee to inform the School's solicitors of the problem of the Chapel, and to place in their hands the necessary legal documentation on which the Chapel was founded. The Committee felt that closure was the only option, but as the documents revealed that the function of the Chapel was determined by Statute (the Act of 1829), which also involved legal ties with the Lord Bishop and the Liverpool Corporation, negotiations became protracted and complicated. It was certain that nothing could be done without an Act of Parliament. Furthermore, the original grant of the Chapel land was made by the Corporation in trust that the land would always be used for a Chapel, otherwise a reversion would become effective. The Corporation, therefore, had to be consulted throughout. The Lord Bishop, meanwhile, informed all that as the matter involved consecrated ground within his jurisdiction the final decision regarding the use of the Chapel and the land was his alone, and he would not become a party to decisions made by the Corporation. He also declared that de-consecrated buildings must be demolished and not used for secular purposes, although he had power to waive this, adding that that the Chapel building was a good one and he might do so in this case.

Henry Wade Deacon, who was handling the Chapel "problem" on the Committee's behalf, felt that after closure, if effected, the Charity should be allowed five years to find a suitable use for the Chapel, otherwise the land would revert to the Corporation. On this basis the Town Hall began to draw up a de-consecration Bill to present before Parliament.

Meanwhile, as is usual in the case of the imminent closure of notable buildings, suggestions were soon made by the public to the Town Hall as to the reuse of the Chapel. Before the year was out Mr Rushworth of the City organ manufacturers and music stores, wrote to the Lord Mayor suggesting it should be used as a centre for cultural and educational life, especially as the City was scarce in venues for concerts, recitals, lectures and so on. Not surprisingly, Mr Rushworth also highlighted in his argument the fine acoustic properties of the Chapel and its modern organ, being understandably fearful of their destruction. Mr Rushworth did not give up easily, and a year later wrote to Henry Wade Deacon to repeat his ideas, going so far as to suggest that the building should be renamed Lunn Hall in lasting memory of a notable Liverpool citizen who had done so much good work for the city.

The Corporation were about to lodge an Omnibus Bill in Parliament, and within this Bill a clause was included, which would, if passed, authorise the discontinuance of services and the closure of the Chapel. Section 220 of the Liverpool Corporation Act of 1927 sealed the fate of the Chapel when it received Royal Assent in May 1927. The last service was held on 17 July 1927, when the Lord Mayor, Sir Frederick Bowring, attended the morning service. The Committee now had five years to determine the future of building.

By the following year it was reported by the Committee that extra accommodation was required to give full effect to the work now being carried on in the School. Workrooms were needed by the girls to complete their training and space was also required to cater for physical education and dancing. The Committee had been aware for a long time of the urgent need of employment of girls of the School following their training, and wished to make special provision for them within the new project.

Following expert advice and examination of costs involved, the Committee took the decision to demolish the Chapel and erect new premises, which as well as providing the accommodation for the above, would also present the School with a spacious and attractive new shop on the Hardman Street and Hope Street corner.

Chapel prior to demolition (18 September 1929).

Sanction from the Corporation was slow in coming and took just over a year to obtain, finally being received in March 1930. Demolition commenced immediately and took only a few months. The last part of the building to be taken down was the front colonnade, which was romantically described by a contemporary as, "standing with an almost heightened dignity amid ruins".[14] This example of classical architecture was to be taken down and preserved for the second time in its life, initially being placed into storage while its uncertain future was debated. Sixty years later it was to become the centre of an unusual mystery (see Epilogue).

Tenders were invited to erect the new building which would contain a Sale Shop, Offices, Workrooms for Girls, Rooms for Domestic Training And Recreation Rooms under the design of Architects, Messrs. Minoprio & Spencely of Liverpool and London. The tender of William Thornton & Son Ltd for £21,768 was accepted by the Committee and work on the new building commenced in late 1930.

Anthony Minoprio and Hugh G.C. Spencely, were two young architects trained in the Liverpool University School of Architecture, who had already made their mark by winning important competitions in other parts of England. Their scheme, however, was not without difficulties; there were, for instance, several different levels on each floor of the old building; both street frontages had to be set back; the façades had to relate with that of the old building, which was small in scale, and yet complement the appearance of the adjacent Philharmonic Hall; and finally, alterations to the Old Building could only be made during the School holidays.

The construction was of solid brick walls faced with Portland stone, and on the street fronts was a fine series of sculptured panels by John Skeaping. Each subject related to the life and work of the School, representing the reading of Braille, and trades such as brush-making, knitting and basketwork. The most remarkable feature of the exterior was the bronze doors, designed and modelled by James Woodford, who had won the Rome Scholarship in 1922 and had carried out a number of significant works including a large group on the Town Hall at Nottingham. It was decided at an early stage in the design of the building to emphasise the importance of the entrance to the ground floor shop by a pair of doors, and the comparative simplicity of the façade served as a foil to the rich bronze reliefs.

SCHOOL FOR THE BLIND

HARDMAN STREET, LIVERPOOL.

②

Opening of the New Extension
BY
The Right Hon. The Earl of Derby, K.G.,
On Monday, 31st October, 1932, at 3 p.m.

L ORD and LADY DERBY, the MAYORAL PARTY and MEMBERS of the COMMITTEE will assemble in the Board Room of the School at 2-45 p.m., entering by the old main entrance in Hardman Street. Other guests will enter by the door in Hope Street, and will proceed to the Upper Work Room, in which the opening ceremony will take place.

The Right Hon. THE LORD MAYOR (Alderman J. C. Cross, J.P.) will take the chair and invite Lord Derby to open formally the new extension.

A vote of thanks will be proposed by Mr. WM. J. SMITH, and seconded by the Rev. ALLEN BROCKINGTON, M.A., PH.D.

After the ceremony all departments of the School will be open for inspection.

Tea will be served in the Dining Hall.

Programme for the opening of the new extension 1932.

176

a. Drawing of planned new extension to Hardman Street.

b. Hardman Street 1932.

The doors were ten feet high by five feet wide and were adorned with six reliefs, again symbolising the life and work of the School. The two upper motives were "Christ healing the Blind" and "The Cured giving thanks". The four lower groups represented crafts and trades; one making a wicker basket, another a leather bag, and two women engaged in chair seating and knitting. Below were groups of brushes, socks, tools, basket work, knitting, and a calf and a lamb symbolising the leather and wool used in various crafts. The design of the handles was inspired by a clump of reeds growing in a stream. A small bronze door was also positioned at the side entrance in Hope Street. Here the sculptor composed three motives tied together by a border of reeds and a base of water. The upper relief showed a man gathering reeds; the middle one girls working round a table, and the lower showed two of the machines used by the girls in the School. Both doors were superb examples of bronze craftsmanship and were cast by the Morris-Singer Company of London. Full size plaster casts of the doors were exhibited at the Royal Academy in the summer of 1932, where they attracted considerable attention.[15]

The New Extension was completed and fully equipped in September 1932. A few weeks later on 31 October, Lord and Lady Derby, the Mayoral Party and Members of the Committee entered the Hardman Street School by the old main entrance and assembled in the Board Room at 2.45pm. Other guests entered by the side entrance in Hope Street and proceeded to the new Upper Work Room where the Parties met at 3pm for the opening ceremony.

The Lord Mayor, Alderman J.C. Cross took the chair and invited Lord Derby to formally open the New Extension. Afterwards, a vote of thanks was proposed by Mr William J. Smith, the new President of the School, which was seconded by the Revd. Dr Allen Brockington, a member of the Committee. (He also penned the words which can still be seen today engraved above the new Hope Street Door – see illustration.) The ceremony finished, the guests began to tour the School where displays of work were exhibited by the pupils, before returning to the dining Hall for tea.

The proceedings were overshadowed, however, by the absence of the man who had devoted considerable time and effort to the running and continued success of the School since the previous century. Only weeks before the Extension was officially opened, Sir Henry Wade Deacon, in his eightieth year, had passed away on 29 July at his residence, 8 Ullet

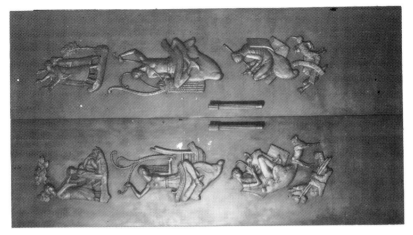

The bronze doors, Hardman Street (front).

Bronze door (Hope Street entrance).

179

Road, Sefton Park. He had been one of the most prominent figures in the political, social and civic life, not only of Merseyside but of Lancashire; his activities ranged from long service on Lancashire County Council and the Widnes Education Committee to valuable work for voluntary hospitals, especially as Chairman of the Liverpool Royal Infirmary, and later as Chairman of·the British Hospitals Association. In 1930 he laid the foundation stone for a grammar school in Widnes which was to bear his name (where, coincidentally, this writer was educated). In 1931, he received a Knighthood for his public service and later that year the University of Liverpool (where he had been a member of Council) conferred upon him the Honorary Degree of LL.D.

In his younger days he had worked for the Widnes alkali manufacturers Gaskell, Deacon & Co., founded by his father, but on its absorption into the United Alkali Company (forerunner of the chemical giant I.C.I.), he retired from active business and turned his attention to public and philanthropic affairs. This was to the good fortune of the School, who soon secured his services by electing him to the Committee in 1896. After overseeing the construction and opening of the Wavertree School, he was elected President in 1900, serving until 1911, with a second term from 1927 until his death. His funeral was held on 2 August at the Cathedral where the School was represented by several of its officers. The organ was played by Henry Goss-Custard, who had been music-master and Chapel organist at the School as well as Cathedral organist for many years.

Successes in educational achievement continued throughout the 1930s. In 1934 two pupils, James Rigby and Walter Bate, were awarded honours in the Home Teachers' Examination, James also being awarded the "Arthur Pearson Prize" for attaining the highest marks in the country. In that same year, twelve Wavertree children were entered for the Trinity College of Music examinations; all passed, seven with honours.

While the educational standard was maintained, the physical well-being of the children was not neglected. Many of the children participated in the Scouts and Guides, the former receiving a national shield for winning a competition for Schools for the Blind. The School had also enjoyed success at a Sports Competition organised by Henshaws at the White City Stadium in Manchester in June 1934. The Schools from Leeds, Preston and Sheffield also took part, where inevitably, the Liverpool team took to

Wavertree in the 1930's. Arithmetic with Mr Crocker.

Wavertree in the 1930's. The running track (pupils are using guide straps invented by the headmaster C.V. Egerton-Jones).

the field in their red strip. There were 36 events in all, which ranged from the under eights' "Tot's Race", to the senior relays, and included, of course, the essential tug of war. The day was a great success with displays of skill and determination reflected not least in the prowess shown by the "Reds" who returned home triumphant with the Junior Championship Trophy and two Senior cups.

The event was repeated over the next few years; the Hardman Street team winning the Championship Trophy in 1936 and 1938 (although in 1937 the Liverpool children were prevented from attending due to an outbreak of chicken-pox at Wavertree). The Hardman Street Pupils took the event seriously and were aided by the Liverpool University Guild of Undergraduates in the use of their ground for training. Competition in any event with Manchester was not to be taken light-heartedly.

Matters in Europe, however, were also becoming serious and were soon to have a profound effect on the School.

10
WAR AND EVACUATION

"I had a sense of freedom...so I was in favour of moving from the School. I wanted a change after being in that School for five years. I can't remember anybody shedding any tears or anything like that...and they were all very jubilant on the coach going to Rhyl. It was the first time that a lot of them had ever been through the Mersey Tunnel."

The outbreak of the Second World War had disastrous effects on the national system of education. Even before the declaration of hostilities, thousands of children had already been moved to rural areas, away from those zones deemed to be under threat.

The story of the evacuation has been widely told in a plethora of accounts, and many more appeared while this work was in preparation, primarily to mark the 50th anniversary of the beginning of the War. Many recall the difficulties faced by children on their reception into an alien environment; frequent stories of harsh treatment; and numerous reports of inability to adjust.

Others had never left their home town before, and to many it was akin to a long holiday. Regarding schooling, certain areas operated a shift system where both the home school and the evacuated school would use the same building on a rota basis for a reduced number of hours. Another scheme was to use a village hall or some other adapted building for both billeting and schooling (which were rarely adequate), and a third method entailed integration into the existing school, causing overcrowding and inevitable difficulties.

Despite the obvious drawbacks, there were positive benefits gained from the evacuation. There were new experiences for teachers and children alike, new interests, fresh approaches to work, and freedom from old routines. Rural and urban England had been brought together as never before.

The evacuation movement was not always compulsory, which resulted in large numbers of children remaining in danger areas. Figures varied enormously; 97 per cent, for example, remained in Rotherham, and 67 per cent in Liverpool. The average number that remained in high risk zones was 80 per cent.[1]

Those that stayed behind suffered from a total disruption in their education. Once the evacuation had been effected, the Government ordered the State Schools in those areas to be closed, and to be taken over by civil defence organisations or the military authorities.

In some areas, home education was organised, but this was far too inadequate. Crisis point was reached by 7 February 1940, when the Board of Education ordered L.E.A.s to make preparations for the resumption of compulsory school attendance.

The billeting of special schools was an even greater problem. Almost exclusively, they were re-established as residential schools in the reception areas. At Leatherhead, the Royal School for the Blind handed over its buildings to the Government on the outbreak of war, and after a short period of evacuation, the residents were housed in hostels in the neighbourhood, so that training and employment could be resumed. The Birmingham Royal Institution for the Blind took early precautions by building eight concrete shelters, each capable of accommodating 50 people. When the war came, however, all pupils under 16 were evacuated to various rural establishments, which included the transfer of senior boys to Worcester College. In 1940, the Northern Counties Association for the Blind opened the Cinderella Home at Honley, near Huddersfield, for the accommodation of blind persons from danger areas, and the following year the Royal Normal College was evacuated from Norwood to Rowton Castle, near Shrewsbury, where it remained until after the war ended.

At the Liverpool School, matters were well in hand before the pupils left for their holidays in the summer of 1939. Families of the pupils were warned that if the situation in Europe worsened they should be prepared to receive notification from the School regarding an early recall to enable a total evacuation. By the time that Britain and France had declared war on Germany, the pupils were already relocated in Rhyl, far away from Liverpool, which was widely believed to be a certain target for enemy air raids.

Danny Peacock was a 13 year old pupil at Wavertree in 1939 and had been at the School since 1934. He recalled his feelings during the weeks running up to the outbreak of war.

"We were well aware of the crisis in Europe, as we used to have gas mask practice in the class room. We knew about Czechoslovakia in 1938, but we never had the news sources that we have got today, so it didn't mean a great deal to us. We knew there was a war on, I think the general attitude was 'Britain will win, they won the last one'. We did know about evacuation, although we never had any contact with other schools, but many of us had brothers and sisters and we learned the news off them. Then we were warned before the holiday, and sure enough we were called back early to be evacuated. The children were coming from all over, the Isle of Man for example, so it was a lot to organise."

Before the War, the Wavertree children were all boarders who were only allowed home during the end of term holidays. To them, there was an overall feeling of excitement when the news of the evacuation was learned. There was no question of spending extra time away from their family, as was the case with other school-children, as that burden of separation had been imposed when they entered the School. The School was to be transferred to Rhyl where daily life would be resumed with as little change as possible. There, several buildings would be taken over for the exclusive use of the Liverpool School. Many of the additional hardships which were to face other school children billeted among alien communities would not be experienced by the children from the School for the Blind. There would be settling in problems, of course, but essentially there was much for the pupils to be excited about in the knowledge that the School was to move lock, stock and barrel to a North Wales sea-side resort for an unlimited period.

By 1939, the School had become a prison to Danny Peacock. He did not believe he was isolated in his feelings.

"I don't think we were that concerned about the move because we were already confined to the School in most cases. We were already boarders and you couldn't go home at weekends in those days. You had one two-hour visit, every third Saturday in the month, from two 'till four, so you were a prisoner anyway. I think it was more excitement than anything else, just getting out of Wavertree – nobody seemed to be bothered by the thing, it was just excitement. We could go home at holiday periods, that was the only time. This was right up to 1939. Our families came in on the third Saturday, and after the two hours were up they used to ring the bell, the visitors said 'goodbye' and...they could write to you, and you could write to them – one letter a week I think it was – or a a post card – but there was no physical contact. I remember my Father having to get me home when my grandfather died in 1936, and I thought, what a wonderful thing to be getting out. I think he was buried on a Thursday."

There was a strict regime imposed on the pupils which had been the norm until the outbreak of the Second World War. To many pupils, in retrospect, it was a throwback to an earlier period. One pupil certainly had little affection for the Superintendent.

"The Superintendent, he should have been in...well... he would have been dismissed from Walton [Gaol] to be honest. Actually terrible. He would never stand a chance today. But, of course, they tell me most places were like that. But it was a prison before the war. You used to get caned for whistling on the corridor or jumping down the stairs. It's a different institution today, of course, but then it was very brutal. That all ended in 1939; when the War started everything changed, and nothing was the same after. After the War was over and following the Education Act, local pupils used to go home at weekends; of course, the parents...in fact everybody, had a different outlook after the War. An outlook that they would never allow pupils to return to Wavertree under the pre-war conditions. Before the War you couldn't go home from one term to the other, and if you did have to go home for a special reason, everything had to be written down...how many hours before you were back; 'When will you be back?... Will you have them back for the next day?' People were over-exercising their authority in those days."

This harsh code was firmly entrenched throughout the School. Several members of the Staff had been at the School for many years and their basic methods were undoubtedly firmly rooted in the nineteenth century when they received their own education. The Assistant Matron, Miss Borthwick and Joe Crocker, the Schoolmaster for example, had been at the School since the turn of the century. Both were still there in the 1930s and Joe Crocker remained until 1944. Mr Jones, the Headmaster of Wavertree, was, according to Danny Peacock, of similar ilk to the Superintendent.

"Mr Jones really didn't have any time for the pupils. If we were in the dining room with old Miss Borthwick, sometimes a boy might go (whistles). She would shout 'Who's whistling? Go out to Mr Jones.' Jones didn't ask why you were sent, he would just say, 'Who sent you? Miss Borthwick? Put your hand out' ...(swish of the cane). Wicked!
Of course you couldn't compare those days with today. You couldn't complain to anybody. Education has come a long way since that brutality took place in Schools.
Years ago, we used to call Joe Crocker the 'Ear Warmer'. He was totally blind and he would put his arm on your shoulder, and if you didn't get your sum right – Bang! right over the ear! My pal George Holmes liked Joe Crocker, but he was a timid lad and rarely got a wallop. He thinks Joe Crocker was a brilliant teacher, but Joe Crocker in my opinion was brilliant to those he could teach but those who were backward he used to belt. He never admitted to himself he couldn't teach a slow pupil, he used to belt them on the ear, and Ernie Jones called him the 'Ear Warmer'. Terrible!"

The evacuation was planned for early September. Samuel Stevens, the Superintendent, recalled the organisation of the move.

"The evacuation took place on the 1st and 2nd of September. The pupils were on holiday, so responsible authorities and parents were notified by telegram, telephone and messenger – children coming from places as far removed from Liverpool as Nottingham, Northampton, Cumberland, and the Isle of Man. With a few exceptions the parents cooperated willingly. On the first day the Matrons of both Schools and members of the house staffs preceded the children to Rhyl, in order to make plans for their reception the following day. Vans were sent containing food, cooking utensils and bedding. The children and trainees slept in their respective schools on the night of the 1st September, and after breakfast the next morning they travelled by motor coach provided by the local authorities."[2]

Four coaches left Liverpool by 11 a.m. After picking up the pupils from Wavertree and Hardman Street they then made their way to Rhyl via the new Mersey Tunnel. Danny remembers clearly his feelings about the move and the events of that September morning in 1939.

"Speaking for myself and on the attitude of the others, we were quite looking forward to it to be honest. I didn't see any remorse in any of them, and I remember all the lads walking around and talking to the girls more freely, which they weren't allowed to do. They didn't seem to bother much what they did, breaking the rules and so on, because I think that they could sense that there was a change taking place. Personally I was glad, I remember doing something – a few of the lads did it, John Warley did it and I did it – on the morning that we were leaving, we were walking around the grounds and we lit a cigarette up, which we would NEVER have dared to do, and we smoked openly, John Warley and one or two others. I remember we smoked this Woodbine and d'y' know, we said, 'Right! you damn well cannot touch us now, we're free!' I'll always remember that – it was the first cigarette I'd ever had in my life – how I got it I can't remember!

We didn't care if anyone saw us, because we knew very well that the buses were going to come that morning and they dare not cane us anyway, so...I don't know, I had a sense of freedom...so I was in favour of moving from the School. I wanted a change after being in that School for five years.

I can't remember anybody shedding any tears or anything like that...and they were all very jubilant on the coach going to Rhyl. It was the first time that a lot of them had ever been through the Mersey Tunnel. Really, they just couldn't believe that looking through the coach windows these lights were going by all the time, and all those that could see [i.e. partial sight] were straining to get close to the windows to look at the Tunnel lights. And that for some was probably the first experience of the Tunnel in their lives and for some the last...the Tunnel was a great experience and the distance in the coach was exciting as well. We'd never been that distance in a coach before."

"When we arrived," continued Danny, "we had tea in the garden to begin with...we were exploring a lot, wondering when we were going to go out on the promenade. We realised there was going to be more freedom going to the beach and playing football on the shoreline." That night, after arduous preparation by the house staff, all pupils quickly settled down in their own beds. There would be no "roughing it", not even on the first night. A diary kept by the Senior girls tells us of that first night.

"While a number sat out in the garden of our new temporary home, quite a number sang in the library while Jean played (Jean Freman – a senior girl) the piano, and some right good shouting there was.

While this was going on, officers were very busy bed making and everyone seemed to be smothered in bed clothes for a while, carrying them here and there. Senior girls' dormitory was a lovely room, with a window forming the whole of one side, with an another smaller one. Hence lots of sunshine. But to the beds; there were six on the left side, four on the right, with a path of beds in the middle of the room.

Naturally, care was necessary moving about our new quarters. Eventually, quietness reigned, at least to some extent, for all the pupils were a-bed. Decided to call to see the girls. There was great excitement as they were trying to locate a 'knocking sound' – strictly speaking, it was a banging on the floor. Eventually we found it to be the Wavertree boys in the room above playing Germans!"[3]

There were four buildings taken over by the School, although initially they began with two, the former North Wales School for Blind Children (founded in 1903) in Russell Road, and College Clwyd next door. "In a short time", according to Samuel Stevens, "it became evident that more "living room" was necessary if the regular school routine was to be followed. I was directed by the Committee to look for further accommodation and mainly due to the good offices of members of the Rhyl Rotary Club, two houses of the large Villa type were rented – Northgate House for girl trainees, and Penrhyn Lodge for Senior boys. Both were run on hostel lines."

The Wavertree children remained at the Russell Road School, the girls having dormitories in the adjacent College Clwyd, and their lessons would soon carry on as normal in the School. The Senior boys meanwhile, daily walked the five minute journey from Penrhyn House in Queens Walk to Northgate, where they would continue their technical training with the senior girls.

There was certainly a change in the atmosphere among the staff and pupils. Even the stern Mr Stevens was beginning to relax, away from the stresses and confines he had been experiencing in Liverpool. He reflected on the early days of the evacuation.

"The children were excited at the thought of the seaside and the sands of Sunny Rhyl. The glorious weather experienced during September and October was a very valuable asset and enabled the children to be out paddling and sand digging most of the day and the first three weeks were regarded as an extension of their holidays."

Mr Stevens and his wife, who was Matron, were on the verge of retirement when war broke out and had been thrust into the complicated and taxing organisation of the move to Rhyl. Their continued services would be desperately required, at least until the the move was seen through.

Meanwhile, they secured a retirement home in Newmarket, a small village near Rhyl, where they would return each night, instead of sleeping on the premises as they had done in Liverpool. By September 1940, once it was clear that everything was running smoothly, Mrs Stevens left the School for her long awaited retirement.

The change in atmosphere was certainly felt by Danny Peacock, who was now a Senior boy and trainee at Penrhyn. He described the apparent change in the Superintendent.

"He relaxed his manner when we were at Rhyl, although we didn't really see that much of him, due to his duties being spread across four buildings and the fact that he went home each night. There was none of that stamping through dormitories and snarling, 'Come on... what's going on in here?!' He always spoke with a snarl and I don't know where he came from but he certainly had a bad upbringing in my opinion.

But attitudes seemed to change all round. We mixed more; the boys and the girls could talk to each other when they went to Rhyl, which you couldn't do at Wavertree. There were much more changes.

There used to be a law at Wavertree that you mustn't go down to the bottom of the grass to talk to the girls. There used to be a hedge by the path going along at the bottom and the boys and the girls used to stand together talking, and you'd get old Morgan shouting, 'Come on! Come on there!' and all the girls used to scatter.

All that had gone once we went to Rhyl. It was social freedom going to Rhyl after being in Wavertree. The pupils in my opinion were more happier than what they were in Wavertree. It was much more relaxed, and you never got the cane like you did at Wavertree. That had all gone. I can't remember Jones using the cane in Rhyl. He retired about 1953 and I don't remember him using it ever again. He was a changed man."

For the first two years at Rhyl, the senior girls kept a diary of their daily experiences. Today, the small black exercise book lies in the School Archive. Below are extracts from the Diary which give the reader a greater insight into the daily life of the girls and staff and of their joys and hardships.

Extracts from Diary of the Evacuation 1939-41
(kept by the Staff and Senior girls formerly of Hardman Street)
(Drawings by Arthur C. Black.)

November 1939

There was the chance of things becoming monotonous but we refuse to let them. Our shopping days were very exciting. Woolworths played an important part. More than once we walked in fours and fives towards Splash Point[4] where we found ourselves with the Prom to ourselves. When it so happened we sang and marched along.

A day was fixed for gas mask drill and the only suitable place was the dormitory. So there we assembled – all complete with hats on and respirators. An imaginary walk was fixed and suddenly Mr Dyson would give the alarm – "Off hats!..On gas masks!". That sounds easy, but we were not quite so quick. Not too bad really. Susie decided she would vary it by giving us weird and wonderful sounds...when wearing hers. We laughed a great deal...it was really funny! Quickly they came off and were placed in their cases, yet there was Lizzie, still with hers on, not having heard the 'all clear'!

Towards the end of our stay there, Elizabeth managed to walk into the glass case in the hall breaking her glasses and giving herself a shock, but soon got over it. A constant cry from the younger boys is 'Any cigarette cards?'

During our month's stay, which we enjoyed very much, Mr Stevens greeted us all very cheerfully, morning, noon and night. Although he was extremely busy, he found time to amuse and be entertained by the children. As soon as he approached, the children promptly said, 'Here's Mr Stevens', then sniff (of course), as they said they could smell him. One day, Mr Stevens told us he had a house for us, just a few minutes away from the school – 'Northgate'. We were all very eager to know all about it and so passed by on one of our walks and peeped into the garden. Then came the day for Miss Roberts and I to go up and prepare our workroom; so the girls amused themselves. Fortunately it was a lovely day, therefore they were able to sit out. So off to Northgate.

NORTHGATE

The house was fixed, for Matron had been busy for days seeing to this. Everywhere looked bright and cheerful. We immediately set to and arranged the workroom. Knitting machines – five of them at one end.

Again we move, this time walking, each one carrying her case and coat. In twos we set off, after bidding farewell and thanking Matron for her kindness. All excited, we walk for the first time altogether into our new home straight into the lounge. The sighted girls become busy and carry the cases upstairs. Then we all have a walk up to see our respective dormitories. Lovely! We're going to like it very much. Two of the bedrooms have hot and cold water. This is fine – five beds in the back room, six in the front and six in the 'loft' (as we christened the top room). The girls from this room come to wash in the others. It's quite free and easy, yet we do have discipline; we decide when and who go up first, although we change about of course. The wireless is in our lounge and we have a piano, and Richard, who never wearies of singing to us. This room of ours is really marvellous. During the day it is a workroom; immediately we finish, we sweep and tidy everywhere, then the finishing touch...down goes the rug...and its a lounge! Quick change isn't it?

The evenings pass quickly in a number of ways; reading, writing (it's amazing the number of letters we find to write), listening to the wireless, singsongs and reading aloud by the Teachers.

One Friday morning at 11a.m., we heard the air raid warning – a second elapsed before we realised what it meant. Immediately we shut the window, got our gas masks beside us and just waited for developments. Miss Roberts and I carried Hilda down and fixed her on the couch in the workroom. I went to the garden gate and asked one or two people if it really was a warning. No one seemed to be sure, then I saw the Air Raid Warden hurrying along on his bike and he called out, "Yes, it is". And that was our first experience. (The following day we read that a plane was seen in the Mersey and they too had the warning.)

Naturally, the postman was a great favourite. All of us expected letters, every post and every day. Not that our desires were fulfilled, but I must remark that Hilda seemed to be continually getting letters – sometimes two or three a post. Sad to relate that we had to leave her indoors when we went out walking. She was not too well; walking being out of the question, for her feet were swollen. Not once did she complain – no grumbling that she was lonely, but always cheerfully found a book to befriend herself or wrote her beloved letters.

CHRISTMAS IS COMING

More excitement! This was considerably prolonged for we started our Christmas shopping very early. Oh yes, there were reasons – it gave us something definite to shop for,

'We were very gay in the lounge, for we were all "Christmassy".'

191

and doing so early we were able to pick and choose. Then again, we posted them on because we were handicapped for room here. We had endless enjoyment – for if one didn't buy, the other did, and so on. One would get a better bargain than the other – such discussions!! Then, nearer Christmas, our parcels began to arrive. Well, needless to add this was more than ordinary excitement. If one parcel arrived we all were thrilled, apart from the girl to whom it actually belonged.

One day it was suggested that those living in 'safe areas' could return there for a fortnight's Christmas holiday. Several went home, leaving six girls; Nancy, Millicent, Jean, Elizabeth, Agnes and Hilda. They had a grand time. Mrs Williams was with them for the first part then Nurse and Miss Roberts. Of course, Mr and Mrs Stevens were here for the Christmas time and made things as they usually do – perfectly beautiful.

From the 20th to the 25th, time passed rapidly and parcels and letters poured in. One parcel addressed to Mrs Williams was brought into the lounge and opened amidst great excitement because of its size. A lovely box of toffees – but what a disappointment; inside, a card – "to the girls". Not even a share for Mrs Williams, although she secured the tin when it was empty.[5] Then another similar occurrence – two parcels – both were addressed to Hilda, but were for the six girls here for Christmas, so she had a little disappointment too, but we laughed about it all and thought it very kind of the girls who sent such sweet Christmas greetings. By this time, we were very gay in the lounge, for we were all 'Christmassy'. It was decorated with cards and looked quite festive.

But, to retrace our steps a little. The 18th December was a very jolly day; t'was Jean's birthday. Strangely enough, Matron threw a party. Not a word had been whispered, but when we went into tea, there it was; gaily decorated, the tables beautifully arranged – jellies, tarts, scones, crackers, fruit and sweets and last, but most exciting, a gift each. Mrs Williams gave us a number each and Matron gave us the gift that had the corresponding number on. We were brim full of excitement. In the lounge afterwards, we had a sing song, which we all enjoyed, possibly because we shouted some parts.

Another surprise was on Tuesday the 19th. About 9.45pm, when all were dozing or about to settle for the night, Mrs Williams appears with something and pops it into our hands. What is it? Why, 2/6d each, with Mr Stevens' greetings! Joy untold, for we are always hard up. Here we are now leaving for the Christmas holidays. Edna Riley went off on the Sunday by car. Vera too; her brother came for her on the 19th. On Wednesday. Mary Monks, Susie, Gertrude Edyvean, Florence Hankey, Dorothy Woodcock, M.J.Newby and Betty Jones went off with Miss Owen in her car. It was dark this particular morning and very damp, but we bravely trotted to the station for the 8.12am and the 8.26am. So we all went together and, after getting rid of the 8.12am lot, the others stayed in the waiting room, for there was a lovely fire there. It's as well it was dark that morning if this is how we looked.

We managed to go for walks on the Prom; once we got there it was really fine for we could walk in a string of seven with plenty of room to spread ourselves out.

Every time we came in, there were parcels and cards and letters – so that there was plenty of excitement.

Christmas Eve – while Mr and Mrs Stevens and staff (Miss Jones, Mrs Williams) were at supper, just the four – we, the pupils, sang carols outside the door. Suddenly, just after we had started singing, the door opened, and being so unexpected it put us off somewhat with the result that was disastrous – for we wanted to giggle! Mr Stevens called us in and gave us 5/-!

At last, Christmas Day is upon us. During the morning we had a walk – then into din-

'Coming home we had adventures, bumping into many people or people bumping into us.'

ner – roast pork. What a lovely meal and Christmas pudding. Tea time we had a meal – Christmassy tea and crackers and sweets sent by Miss English. The boys came for their meals and needless to say they enjoyed them.

Tuesday we all went to a Panto at the Queens. It was great fun, for we sang gustily and the Wavertree children were with us. Miss Roberts takes over duty for the next week. Mr and Mrs Stevens go off for the week and Nurse takes charge.

JANUARY 1940 – THE SPRING TERM

January 3rd brings us all together again. Dorothy Woodcock and Vera Davies were the only two not to return.

The weather from then on has been very cold – stormy and plenty of snow.

One or two birthdays this month and Mr Stevens very kindly gave us special teas – all as surprises too, for we had no idea until we walked into the Dining Room – we so appreciate these things! (say Jean and Edna Riley). In the lounge we had toffee and fruit and a jolly sing song. So you see, we make much of these things, therefore we all have jolly times together.

We have had, up to now, Wednesday afternoon and Saturday free when we go out in twos, with someone sighted as a guide. Sometimes we decide on the Pictures, but usually if it's fit we make the most of fresh air. The Promenade is such a fine one, and easy for us. When out for set walks with the Teachers we have gone inland, walking along a narrow path alongside the railway, then over a stile – for some of us the first experience of such. Laughs and laughs trying to get over gracefully. Another time, we missed the turning and walked too far, for some of us were very tired, and seemed to have completed a circle. Then there's the Botanical Gardens.

Sunday 28th January 1940

One of the worst days we have experienced; snow, rain and wind. So much wind that the snow will not stay on the housetops. It freezes as it comes down with icicles everywhere. The trees in the garden are a perfect picture – the ice forming lacy pictures everywhere. The little birds are looking for food, so we have given them some – they look so wet – poor little things.

Miss Jones stayed at Penrhyn Lodge today so Nurse supervised the cooking. Tea was a picnic in the Lounge because the Dining Room was cold and the means of heating cut off. The electricity has gone off completely, so candles are in great demand. Whether it is just us or general, we don't know yet until Mr Stevens returns from Penrhyn Lodge. Miss Roberts is in the lounge with the girls listening in to the wireless – no candles there, just a lovely fire. So, in spite of our little difficulties we are enjoying ourselves.

Hilda is feeling the cold for her little electric stove is not in use either. Nancy, Susie and Gertrude have been up for short periods with her. Nancy tells me she wore one of the red blankets off one of the beds. These look so warm and cosy and act as eiderdowns, one for each girl.

Phone call from Liverpool at 8pm. I went home and remained there for a week.

Monday 5th February to Friday 9th February

To my great surprise the girls want reading aloud by the Teachers, so we joined the library and luckily managed to get *Prester John* by John Buchan.

Weird noises during the night and the occupants of the loft decided t'was an owl, but this morning Nurse said "No". She decided t'was boys amusing themselves – That's that.

This week, no potatoes for dinner. Evidently transport's still affected. Susie in bed yesterday.

Called in to see Hilda and Susie – both lying comfortable. Hilda tells me she has diagnosed their sickness – Foot and Mouth Disease – great joke – for Hilda's great trouble is her feet swelling and funnily enough Susie's mouth is her cause for being there, hence the combined 'foot and mouth disease'. Hilda is always bright and cheerful and deserves a medal. The rest of us often have grumbles, with no real foundation. When we think like

194

this we feel ashamed of ourselves.

Wednesday afternoon, we managed to get out for our half day and then had to return because of the rain. Three of us, Riley, Betty and Joyce, sat in a shelter in spite of the weather rather than go indoors too soon.

Sunday 11th February
We went to church for the first time for about a month because of the bad weather. Very few there and something must have happened to the organ, for we had the piano, which is never as nice for hymns. Our walk materialised in spite of several attempts to snow. It was cold but we bravely faced it and walked quickly to Splash Point.

We listened to a wireless programme about the evacuation into North Wales, it was most interesting, for the children actually took part and spoke little bits of Welsh, one sang, one did her shopping in Welsh and so on.

'*We listened to the News and "The World Goes By" in the fire glow.*

Monday 12th February
Hilda is leaving us for a while, as she is going to the Alexandra Hospital.

Orders received from Mrs Macara [of the Hardman Street Shop] wanting more hoods, so a number of us are busy knitting mauve, yellow and green hoods.

Wednesday 14th February
St. Valentines Day! Mary and Florence received Valentines. Being half day, quite a number went to the Pictures to see *Nurse Edith Cavell* and thought it wonderful.

Tea time – Mrs Williams read *Prester John* and just as we were about to finish tea, and the reading of course, the lights fused, so out we came and into the Lounge. Seated around the fire we listened to the News and 'The World Goes By' in the fire glow. Later, Lord Tweedsmuir's funeral service was broadcast from Ottawa.

Friday 16th February

Walk first thing. Much sickness about. Met soldiers who were also doing their day's march. They called, 'Good morning' to us and sang and whistled as they cheerily passed us. T'was cold but bright. 2pm; Another walk, this time to Splash Point. No excitement of any kind. Had a reading of *Prester John* during tea and for a while after the 6 o'clock news. So ends another day!

Saturday 17th February

As we are not going out except in 'crocodile', Mrs Williams has a long list of shopping for us. Never was such a variety – stamps, curlers, soap, toothpaste, wool, envelopes, etc.

Hilda was pleased to have a visitor. She looks very well. In fact, much better. It is a very cheerful ward with a pretty green colour scheme. We listened to the wireless and felt thrilled to hear what our wonderful Navy had achieved – the removing of 300 prisoners from the *Altmark*.

Wednesday 21st February

Luckily, the girls went off on their own. Some walked to Abergele, others in the Dyserth direction and Prestatyn.

Thursday 22nd February

Walk at 9.30am on the Prom. The soldiers were having a keep fit class in shorts and vests. Further along there was a kit inspection. Later, a number passed here in full kit marching along and whistling. Their tin hats would be warm as it was such a beautiful sunny morning.

Friday 23rd February

Usual 9.30am walk to Splash Point. T'was lovely, the waves thundering against the Prom. Far out in the distance was a ship heading towards Liverpool – also a plane heading, apparently from it's direction, inland to Sealand. [R.A.F. base near Chester]

Letter and B.R.P. from Miss Rawlins. We always enjoy these. Mary Monks gone to bed this afternoon. Listened to London's welcome to the Ajax and Exeter crew. It thrilled us to hear it all!

Saturday 24th February

Girls out for the afternoon, then after tea we settled ourselves to listening in. We just managed to get the News and a despatch from the Front which was short talks by the various Chaplains and a Rabbi. As the wireless failed us we had a little sing song.

Sunday 25th February

Long walk instead of Church – still fresh air fiends. As we approached some jolly soldiers, they thought we might be Guides. We must have been marching well!

Monday 26th February

Great news – the first squadron of Canadian airmen arrived. Something to be proud of; firstly, their desire to come and help us, and secondly, the actual getting them over. Marvellous! Days like this make us talk about our anticipated joy ride through Wales. Yes, we are talking about a trip – to Criccieth, covering a great deal of ground and a number of beauty spots. We're saving up for this great event.

Friday 1st March – Gwyl Dewi Sant – Welsh Day!
We set off with a 'Bore Da!', and all day tried to express ourselves in Welsh. It afforded lots of fun. Daffodils in the Workroom of course!

Saturday 2nd to Thursday 7th March
March 6th – I went to see Hilda at the Hospital. In fact, Susie came with me to help carry all the food things. Matron sends nice things always; a dozen Jaffas and biscuits and we in the Workroom sent oranges too and a few stamps, while Nancy sent some biscuits – she evidently wanted to be one up on us. She was (Hilda I mean), much better, although whilst up for a few hours one day she had caught a cold.

Saturday 9th March
A letter from Mrs Wooding telling us of all the creepy things in Africa. During the morning, Joyce's sister arrives from Liverpool to take her back on the next train. Her Father is on the H.M. Hospital Ship and going away for an indefinite period. There was great excitement getting her off in five minutes.

More excitement – but not the right kind. Several girls very late for tea, having gone to the pictures.

We had a concert – each girl giving a "turn". It was jolly good fun.

Wednesday 13th March
The dates for Easter holidays have been fixed; March 20th to April 3rd. Train times are all arranged – naturally, much excitement. Some of the girls bought Easter eggs to take home.

Finns' Peace with Russia given on the 6 o'clock News.

We heard a most interesting talk given by Mr A.P. Herbert, M.P. on the River Emergency Service – making us realise there were people and clubs we knew nothing at all about, giving their services to This England of ours. Private motor boats, previously of yachting clubs, with their crews even now only wearing yachting caps and grey flannel trousers, help anything and everything on the river. A sort of humble maid of all work to shipping, who feel proud when they can help a barge along, perhaps one with 120 tons of cement. There are still ships up and down the River although Admiral Hitler says we have no trade and we are starving. These possibly bring us a few sandwiches, or a bag of nuts, or coal or maybe just sail up and down just for fun while we eat seaweed.

EASTER Friday 15th and Saturday 16th March
Great fun getting an Easter egg from Mr Stevens and 2/6d each. The first time this has ever happened – so we were very excited. We seem to be in and out of the Workroom – hair washing and generally getting ready for 'off'.

Our last sing song on the Tuesday was most enjoyable. This is to make up for the loss of our Wireless. Nice change – it always proves to be.

Easter holidays are individual secrets. All seem to have enjoyed the change, but all seemed pleased to meet again. So life here cannot be too bad. Probably when home, it was described as wonderful.

Thursday 4th April

Rather a rush at 7.35am, for the majority seem to be in bed instead of out and almost ready for coming down. This is probably the result of the bad habit formed during the holidays...getting up late!! Mr Smyth came to see us and was pleased to see us so happy and comfortable.

Friday 5th April – Grand National!

Great excitement! We've all chosen a horse – so that when we listen to the race this afternoon we will each have an interest. We are all looking forward to this, for it's the first time we have listened to the National away from home!

　...Nobody had any luck!

OUR GARDEN DEVELOPS – May

Today is Air Raid Practice again. A few of us have done a little gardening – for a garden needs a lot of looking after. The leaves constantly keep us occupied. What a back aching job weeding is – and endless! We have a whole evening of tidying up and we think it looks well...then, next morning, why, it's ready for us to be busy again.

　Hilda has returned from hospital, but unfortunately is in bed again.

Tuesday 7th May

Managed to plant a few Pansies and Forget-me-nots and hope to plant Delphinium (Larkspur) and Antirrhinum (Snapdragon) this evening. The gardeners are Florence, Edna, Joyce, Susie and Mary and latterly Elizabeth has joined us. Great enthusiasm for the photography! Snaps here and there! In fact all over the place. Its all fun – but might prove too expensive....we'll see!

Friday 10th May

Snaps not so bad! A glorious morning, but what news! Belgium, Holland and Luxembourg all invaded by air and land. Whit Holiday cancelled.

　Gas masks to be carried again. No travelling – only if necessary. Planes over the Thames – not successful – driven off by anti aircraft and our fighters.

　News at intervals; 8am, 10.30am, 12 noon, 1pm, 4.15pm and 6 o'clock.

　Hilda left us today for Walton Hospital.

Tuesday 21st May

Glorious day! Tonight we'll be very busy gardening – watering...for our new watering can has arrived. Our plants, the ones we actually planted are flourishing – the pansies are beautiful. We have A.R. practice from the workroom, fortunately our "spot" is near and we get there very quickly. No 1 O'clock News today, for our wireless has let us down.

　Whit Monday passed happily, for the day was ideal and we were all out. We visited the fair at the Marine Lake and had a gay time. Florence's Mother came for the day on the 18th, so more fun for Florence, out with Mother and showing her Rhyl.

　Heard this morning that May Bowen isn't well again. We are all very sorry about this and intend to write to her.

　Ankle socks have come into fashion...and lying on the grass at lunchtime, sunbathing.

'Tonight we'll be busy gardening...our new watering can has arrived.'

A CHRISTMAS OF BANSHEE WAILING

December 16th

Today we celebrated the coming festive season by holding a Christmas party – a dinner. Matron Cormack surprised us all when we saw it. She had smuggled the crackers, boxes of chocolates for the girls, cigarettes and tobacco for the boys and sweets for all, into the building without our knowledge.

The dinner was marvellous. If Lord Haw-Haw could have seen it, it would have broken his heart and caused him to wonder whether his blockade was quite as effective as he hopes it to be. Even Lord Woo Hou might have had something to say with regard to the quantity of food consumed per person. We all sang with true feeling "For he's a jolly good fellow!" when the Superintendent came in.

December 17th

Going home day! Everyone was up betimes and away we went to the station. What a time, getting all into the train and settled. Back again to work for those of us who were left – beds to dismantle and everything generally to pack up before settling down to our holiday.

December 20th

While seated in the lounge we were suddenly disturbed by gunfire which continued for some time. At 8.15pm the warning was sounded and we had perforce to retire to our shelter – the cellar. We put down the carpet and settled ourselves for a long vigil. Our thoughts were on Liverpool which was definitely bearing the brunt of the attack of wave after wave of bombers. Tempers were bearing thin at 1.45am when, the gunfire lessening, we decided to go to bed. Matron and Miss Gallimore sat up until 3.30am but retired to bed to await the 'all clear' at 4.30am.

'What a time, getting all into the train and settled.'

December 21st

Tonight, gunfire started early, the barrage being very intense. However, since the alert did not sound, we went to bed. Matron and Miss Gallimore went to bed, or at least attempted to, but the gunfire and the sound of planes was so near that it hardly seemed policy to stay in bed. The girls, however, slept through it.

December 22nd

The holidays being in the air, we decided to celebrate by going out to tea at Robins'. For many of us it was rather an ordeal but we all managed very well and thoroughly enjoyed ourselves. Coming home we had adventures, bumping into many people, or people bumping into us. Arriving home we went to bed. An hour later we were brought very suddenly to the consciousness of the fact that the Air Raid warning was shattering our peace. Downstairs to the cellars we hurried. Having been up two nights, Matron decided to bring mattresses down to the kitchen. We did so accordingly. Just as everyone was settled in bed, the 'all-clear' sounded. Matron came into the kitchen and said, 'Now girls, the 'all-clear' has sounded and I think we will all get back to bed!' The maids, exhausted, simply gasped and said, 'Oh! Matron!' We decided to stay put and spend a fairly comfortable night in novel surroundings and positions.

December 23rd
Once again the sirens sounded, before bed-time. Mattresses were brought down and again the 'all-clear' sounded, but we spent the night where we were.

December 24th
Christmas Eve! We made a final tour of the shops and came home to rest and sing carols.

December 25th
Being Christmas Day went to church, coming home to a lovely Christmas dinner; goose and potatoes, boiled and roasted, sprouts and pudding, with nuts, fruit and dates. After dinner we rested until tea time. After tea Miss Poulton, Matrons' friend, came in and sang to us for hours. How we enjoyed ourselves.

December 28th
We went to Wavertree for tea and the kiddies played with us. The piano and wireless were in great demand, we sang and danced.

January 2nd
We had a visitor today, Matron Stevens! We were pleased to see her and to wish her a Happy New Year.

January 7th
Back again to Rhyl. Holidays over, we had a great deal to talk about, each discussing their holidays with the other.

January 9th
Once again our rest was disturbed. At 8.30pm the banshee wailing shattered our enjoyment of the peaceful night. Since there was so many of us we went to the kitchen, the safest room in the house. Beds were brought down to the second floor and we went to bed. The 'all-clear' sounded at 1.20am.

On February 7th Matron told us that Hilda Quigg died in Hospital. (Hilda, who was only 32, had been suffering from heart disease for some time).

February 10th
Mrs Stevens paid us a brief visit this morning and spoke to us all. Today was really mild and sunny, much too nice to be indoors...

During the Blitz, Liverpool suffered some of the heaviest and most intense bombing of the War. Measured by weight and number of attacks, and number of casualties, Merseyside was Hitler's prime target outside London during the 1940-41 Blitz. By the end of May 1941 almost one and a half thousand people had been killed in Liverpool alone with a similar number seriously injured. There can be no doubting the wisdom behind the evacuation given those figures, especially when it is learned that Hardman Street had suffered damage and loss of stocks as a result of the enemy action.

The 'May Blitz' during April and May 1941 saw the most devastating period of the campaign.

"You could see the glow of the May Blitz on the horizon from Rhyl in 1941," recalled Danny Peacock, "Funny thing was, I wasn't worried at all, I only thought about my parents, that's all, hoping they would be all right. We always had a confidence that we would win. Of course, when you were young, well... The news was always well dressed up by the time it reached us. We always retreated according to plan! We thought how clever we are! Isn't that brilliant!"

Danny went home for the Christmas holiday in 1940 and remembered visiting Wavertree to pass the time. As he approached the gate to the driveway he was confronted by a soldier armed with a rifle who was manning a sentry box.

"He said to me, 'Halt! Where are you going?' I said, 'I'm just going in to visit the School.' He said, 'You can't get in there! Who are you?' I told him I was a pupil. He said, 'It's full of Frenchmen and you won't be able to understand them anyway.' Well, I still went in and the boiler-man, Billy Stewart, was there and he told me, 'All these Frenchmen are just waiting to be repatriated.' They had come over from Dunkirk, but he told me that many were reluctant to return and had changed their minds about fighting, believing that Britain didn't have much of a chance anyway. Sometimes they would get a pass and go down to the Coffee House, although they had to be back at a certain time. This bloke Billy Stewart also worked there as a barman. He could speak a little French and he could understand them.

After they'd left the School I visited Wavertree again and there were crowds of kids and women all over the place and Billy Stewart said, 'This shower are all from Scotland Road – they've all been bombed out.' There were beds all over the classroom floors – all the furniture had been taken out, all the mattresses were all over the floors and in the basement. So it was still used, but as a shelter for the homeless for those who had lost their houses. The Ministry of Works had taken it over.."

Hardman Street, meanwhile, had been requisitioned on 16 June 1941 by the R.A.F., although they did not secure the entire building, as the Music Room and the Boy's Lounge had been rented to the Thames and Mersey Marine Insurance Company since February of the previous year. Both would remain for the duration of the War.

The School stayed at Rhyl until after the end of the War, the Juniors returning to Wavertree in May 1946 and the Seniors to Hardman Street in November of the same year. At Rhyl, life had continued as normally as possible, training continued as before and both Schools were well supplied with Braille Books by the National Library for the Blind. Regular visits were made to the performances of the local Repertory Company and the girls frequently performed at concert parties, sometimes for the soldiers stationed nearby.

The Shop at Hardman Street remained open throughout the War and continued to sell goods made at Rhyl. The School and ex-trainees were also supplying the Government and Shipping Companies with clothing, baskets and other wares, including hampers for parachutes.

As peace was declared in May 1945, so Samuel Stevens finally decided his work was complete. The Annual Report of 1945-6 carried the following announcement:

"During the year, Mr S.E. Stevens, the Superintendent of the School, retired after more than thirty-two years of honourable and faithful service. He had worked untiringly to place both Schools in the forefront of the Blind Schools in this country. The welfare of all the pupils was always his constant care, and he will be long remembered by them. During his long term of office both Schools were extended and brought into line with the latest requirements. In addition to his work for the Institution, Mr Stevens gave of his best to the various organisations in the larger Blind world, especially to the work of the College of Teachers of the Blind. At the outbreak of war in September 1939, instead of retiring Mr Stevens took on the arduous task of transferring both Schools to Rhyl, and settling them down to work with their accustomed smoothness and guided their fortunes until the end of the war. The Committee are very sorry to lose him and in thanking him for his long and devoted service to the Institution wish him a long and happy retirement."[6]

His replacement was Edward Keates, Superintendent and Secretary of the Ripon and District Hospital. The nation was moving into a new period of social and educational reorganisation, which would have a considerable effect on the School. The new man must have qualities which would be able to cope with the new measures and have an approach quite different from that of Samuel Stevens. Keates' appointment would be purely administrative. Danny Peacock saw an immediate change in the role of the Superintendent.

"Mr. Keates was more of an administrator; the only time he ever saw a pupil was if a pupil wanted to see him – he never knew any pupils names. He never knew them at Wavertree. He used to come in to Wavertree on a Tuesday and a Thursday between two and four to see the Matron. They used to go into the sitting room and have tea, then he would go out of the School and never meet the staff or anything. Very remote really, to pupils and staff. When Mr. Keates took over, it was clear that he was from a different era altogether. He was a mild man and a bit more religious than his predecessor, so you had no brutality with Keates."

Both Schools returned to Liverpool in 1946, but it was not only a changed City affected by war-time ravages they were returning to. The structure of education had been changed during their absence. The pre-war system had been swept aside by a new Act of Parliament and the School was to undergo a complete reorganisation.

The educational system had suffered its own war-time damage, but just as there were those prepared to reconstruct the ravaged cities, so there were those who would do the same for education and look for ways to improve on the existing framework.

At times of war and destruction it would seem that minds are turned towards education in a reaction to the waste that has gone before, in an attempt to prevent its recurrence and to look to the future with hope. It may be no coincidence that the major Education Acts of 1870, 1902, 1918 and 1944 were passed in times of conflict.

11
EDUCATIONAL RECONSTRUCTION

*"All the problems of special education were not solved by the 1944 Act.
In some respects problems were created by it...The provision of special
educational facilities in the ordinary school is still woefully inadequate. Where the special class exists, it is all too frequently regarded as a
poor relation. Schools tend to concentrate on the examination successes of the brighter children, and while many dedicated teachers do
excellent work in the special classes, others await the day of transfer to
the 'A' stream. Moreover, there is often a lack of realisation of the true
needs of the children in special classes. Teachers are unaware of the
particular learning difficulties of individual children, and the shortage
of educational psychologists makes the solution of the problem no easier."*

Dr D.G. Prichard
Education and the Handicapped 1760-1960 (1962)[1]

The foundation for the Education Act of 1944 was laid in a 1941 Green
Paper, later streamlined by the *Educational Reconstruction* White Paper
of 1943. The Green Paper found that much of the accommodation for
blind and deaf children was old with inconvenient distribution. Yet it was
still acknowledged to be adequate – an indication of the declining numbers of such handicaps, rather than evidence of excessive provision made
in earlier times.

The White Paper, however, was a reflection of the low priority given to
the needs of the handicapped child by administrators, politicians and the
public, and dismissed special education in a short paragraph. Despite
these shortcomings, the 1944 Act reacted positively to calls from earlier
reports and recommendations to bring special schools within the general
education framework. It was time that the handicapped ceased to be a
class apart and the stigma attached to special schools removed.

Whereas earlier legislation had dealt separately with the education of
the handicapped, the new Act laid down that the provision of special educational treatment was merely part of the general duty of the L.E.A.s to
ensure that children were educated in accordance with their ages, aptitudes and abilities. Even in the consolidating Act of 1921, blind, deaf,

"defective" and epileptic children were treated as a separate class. In the section of the 1944 Act which detailed legislation regarding the education authorities" provision of primary and secondary education, the L.E.A.s were also required to ensure that provision was made for pupils who suffered from any disability of mind or body by providing, either in special schools or otherwise, special educational treatment.

The Act instructed L.E.A.s to "provide for the education of pupils, in whose case the disability is serious, in special schools appropriate for that category, but where this is impracticable, or where the disability is not serious, the arrangements may provide for the giving of such education in any school maintained or assisted by the local education authority".[2] This was a serious attempt to address the needs of the individual child, recognising that handicaps existed in varying degrees and that it was undesirable to continue to categorise and segregate without any considered measure of flexibility towards integration.

The effectiveness of the Act was hampered by its own shortcomings – not so much in the lack of provision of special schools, but in the lack of provision of special educational facilities in the ordinary schools. Regulations were laid before Parliament the following year by the Minister of Education, increasing the recognised categories of handicapped children from five to eleven.[3]

Changes were to be made in the case of the existing category of the blind. Pupils were now to be educated in residential schools. Schools that had been founded for daily attendance would have to close. Secondly, the mandate given to L.E.A.s to give special education in the ordinary school would *not* apply to blind or deaf children.

Two new categories of handicapped children had been recognised following the recommendations of the Committees of Inquiry of 1934 and 1938; the partially sighted and partially deaf. They were to be treated as separate handicaps, and schools were requested to concentrate on one of those handicaps only.

Numbers of registered blind children had been dropping dramatically since 1925; at the end of the War the number had halved, and by the mid-1950s, blindness in children was mainly the result of hereditary, congenital, and developmental defects. In 1937, for example, there were 5,050 cases of Ophthalmia Neonatorum – that figure was reduced by 75 per cent by the end of the 1950s. Facilities in 1945 were consequently judged to be adequate and despite the disorganisation caused by the War there were thought to be enough places to cater for the declining demand.

During the War, however, a newly discovered disease was beginning to show a marked increase. First identified in 1942, Retrolental Fibroplasia, as it was known, was affecting a growing number of infants, which continued until 1955 when its cause was eventually realised. Numbers fell as dramatically as they had increased. (During 1951 and 1955, 38.4 per cent of children born blind suffered from this condition – this was to fall to 10 per cent over the next five years.)[4] The disease was caused by excessive use of oxygen on premature babies (sometimes referred to as "oxygen tent babies").

Although numbers swiftly declined after 1955, affected children needed care and education during the 1950s and 1960s. Their numbers substantially affected school totals and put pressure on a section of special care that until this outbreak, was beginning to have less demands placed upon it for accommodation.

Following the 1944 Act and Butler's general revision in education,[5] the newly formed Ministry of Education placed reorganisation of Blind Schools on the agenda in tandem with ordinary education. Concerned that consultation with the respective bodies should take place, the Ministry set up conferences throughout the country to address regional reorganisation. In the North West representatives from educational establishments and L.E.A.s were invited to meet with a Ministry delegation at Manchester Technology College on Wednesday 21 February 1945. (The North-West Region was to comprise of Cumberland, Westmorland, Lancashire, Cheshire, North Wales, and parts of the West Riding of Yorkshire.) Representatives were sent from Henshaw's in Manchester, Preston School for the Blind and the Liverpool School for the Blind. (Attending on behalf of the Liverpool School were Chairman Harold Smyth, Vice Chairman, Mr Mines and Superintendent Samuel Stevens.) The Liverpool Catholic School, St. Vincent's, was not involved as it was recognised that as a sole Catholic foundation the School's purpose was national and not local.

Three new regulations dominated the discussions.

1. universal residential education (although local day scholars would be allowed)
2. new requirements regarding size of classes and schools before classification would be awarded and
3. the separate education of the partially sighted.

The division of schools into primary and secondary was not to be compulsory for blind schools but it was clear that it was preferred by the Ministry.

During the Conference, the ages and number of children to be cared for was assessed and it was decided that provision would be made for (a) nursery education (b) junior (c) senior (although this would not conform to the standard definition of secondary schools) and (d) continued education and training after 16.

James Lumsden of the Ministry elaborated on a scheme, although not ideal, provided some immediate solution for the problem of reorganisation, remarking that there had been "a disinclination in the blind world to accept anything but a perfect scheme". Lumsden had begun to formulate this scheme as early as June 1944, following his H.M.I. visit to the Liverpool School at Rhyl. In his confidential report to the Ministry he declared, "I feel strongly that some scheme of amalgamation of the Lancashire blind schools is the only way to secure a good education for their children: all the units are too small."[6] Lumsden's scheme partly entailed eliminating the Bolton School, and closing the small schools at Oldham and Burnley (or adapting them for other purposes).

The worst fears of the Burnley representatives had been met. Perhaps being only prepared to accept a "perfect scheme", they promptly rose to their feet and walked out of the Conference. (In fact, it was later decided to close both the Oldham and Burnley Schools and reorganise the Bolton Thomasson Memorial Blind Council School as a primary school for both sexes.)

The Ministry pressed on. It proposed to turn the Preston School into a Partially sighted residential school, which appeared to be well received by the authorities. Children under seven would be taken out of their present schools and, if accommodation was available, be sent to the Sunshine

Home Nursery School at Southport.[7] Wavertree was to be adapted to take all children from 7 to 11 plus, and Henshaw's to take the Seniors. Those children about to enter senior education who showed exceptional promise would be sent to Worcester College for Boys, Chorleywood College for Girls, or the Royal Normal College where they would generally remain until they were 18. It was intended that the changes would become effective on 1 September 1945.

Henshaw's and Liverpool were willing to effect the changes, although both schools were still in a state of evacuation. Reforms would be delayed until hostilities were at an end and buildings made secure for a safe return of the children.

Harold Smyth pressed the Ministry on the question of general funding and the wisdom of nursery schools retaining children until the age of seven. He met with little success to both queries. Grants were available, he was informed, but would only be made for new premises. Bosworth-Smith (of the Ministry who was Chairing the meeting) expected Voluntary Societies to "do their best to raise funds for this purpose". He stated that it was the intention of the Ministry to ensure that the fees charged by the Voluntary Societies should cover full charge for maintenance as it had been felt for some time that they had been keeping down their fees "too close to the bone". Regarding nursery care, the age bracket had been set and the Ministry were quite immovable.

The structure of the education and training of 16-21 year olds was also discussed, although the absence of the Burnley representatives hampered the proceedings, and the conference ended without firm agreements. It was not until 25 November 1946 that an invitation was made by the Minister of Education to the Liverpool School to submit proposals for a Technical School for the North West Region based at Hardman Street. The continued existence of several training centres in the region was felt to be no longer justifiable. The offer to Liverpool was on condition that provision was also made for the continuance of the students' general education.

The offer was quickly accepted by the Management Committee of the Liverpool School. Vocational training was to consist of basket making, boot and shoe repairing, brush making, and hand, flat and round machine knitting. Other trades could be taught to those over 21, such as mat making, but their training would be a matter for the Ministry of Labour and

National Service. Training was to be given by full-time instructors and kept separate from the workshops.

The Ministry philosophy behind the scheme was that training in each trade should be made comprehensive enough to enable the students to become "satisfactory home workers or employees at any workshops at which they may become employed, and not merely to conform to the requirements of local workshops". Hardman Street had already introduced this programme several decades earlier. Residential status was not compulsory – "independence and tidiness" were to be encouraged.

The main change at Hardman Street was to be seen in the introduction of compulsory general education, which was to be given in working hours. General education had already been introduced on a narrower basis some years earlier, although this was given during the evening. Housecraft was to be introduced for both boys and girls, which would cover cookery, housewifery, laundry, personal hygiene, marketing and food values, and care of clothing. Evening discussion groups were to be encouraged to study "aspects of life which may not be familiar to those who have spent most of their lives in boarding schools".

Despite the reorganisation brought by the 1944 Act, the changes regarding the 16-21 age group were wholly inadequate. During the War large numbers of able-bodied blind, mainly in the workshops for the blind, turned from peace time production to meeting the needs of a nation at war as government orders flowed in. Many more blind men and women were absorbed into sighted industry. In 1942, all Employment Exchanges in the country were authorised by the Ministry of Labour to give favourable consideration to applications for work from suitable blind persons, and by the close of hostilities in 1945 about 2,000 blind persons, many of whom had hitherto been classed as unemployable, were engaged in open industry. Although numbers fell with the return of those on active service, there were still around 1,500 men and women working alongside sighted workers in factories and workshops by the early 1950s.

These positive steps forward were further enhanced by the introduction of the 1944 Disabled Persons Employment Act, which enabled the Ministry of Labour and National Service to arrange vocational training for disabled persons, and compelled employers who had a substantial number of employees to engage a quota of disabled (not necessarily blind) workers.

It was disappointing therefore, in view of the gains made in so many areas and the lessening of social stigma, that such an opportunity for radical change in adolescent education was forsaken. Those trades confirmed by the Ministry for the Hardman Street Technical School in 1946 would not have been out of place in the Liverpool Asylum of 1791.

Three other Acts introduced after the War would also affect the blind, just as they would affect every citizen in the country. They were the National Insurance Act 1946, the National Health Act 1946, and the National Assistance Act 1948. The latter was of special importance as it entirely superseded the 1920 Blind Persons Act and largely too the Blind Persons Act 1938. The duties of the Local Authorities laid down in the 1920 Act were reaffirmed, but it went further than earlier legislation by detailing specific forms of care; registration, advisory services, provision of work in workshops and at home, marketing of goods, hostels for work and trainees, recreational facilities and support grants for the needy. Legislation had now been confirmed therefore, to care for the Blind from infancy to old age.

After the interruption and upheavals resulting from the return from Rhyl and the introduction of a new educational structure, the Liverpool School tried to settle into its new role. For the technical students, although their trades were still rather limited and were designed for a future in the Workshops for the Blind or home based work, there was now an improved opportunity to enter open industry. There was also a fresh impetus at Wavertree where academic aims were set for senior places at the two colleges of grammar school status.

The successes of the two Liverpool establishments differed greatly over the next few years. Both schools were performing well academically, but were finding the the transition difficult.

At Wavertree, promising pupils were regularly securing grammar school places. Music students were achieving excellent grades under the tutorship of Miss Flora Cann and pupils were consistently awarded the highest prizes in the National Braille Reading Competition.

Meanwhile, Hardman Street was not performing as well as had been predicted. Students numbers were still short of the expected figure of 60, which had been estimated at the outset of North West reorganisation. Al-

Exhibition of Hardman Street products at a local theatre 1949.

Taxi drivers' outing 1950...

...and 1977 ready to go!

214

though work was generally of good standard, the Committee were understandably keen to attract more students. By 1950 there were vacancies for 18 girls alone. Matters were no better in the workshop, where employees had been placed on short time during the previous year due to poor shop sales and falling orders.

Improvements were being made to both Schools to enhance and consolidate their new roles. A new Boot Machine Plant was installed at Hardman Street, while Wavertree received a new gymnasium and an adventure playground. The latter was known as the "Wilfred Pickles Pleasure Garden" named after the BBC Radio personality who officially opened the new recreation area and helped fund the project. He appeared on B.B.C. Regional News later that day to publicise the event.

Due to the kindness of various organisations, the pupils were able to enjoy several outings. In 1949, an invitation was received from the owners of Gwrych Castle, near Abergele in North Wales, to spend a day in the grounds of the Castle. It was a resounding success, and the outing became an annual event.

The following year the Liverpool Hackney Drivers' Club, then known as "Mocatra", invited the pupils and staff on a trip to Southport. On 20 September, 23 taxis set off on one of the most memorable outings experienced by the School. The organisers immediately extended their invitation for the following year and with remarkable dedication the commitment of the Taxi drivers has continued unbroken to the present (the organising body are known today as the Liverpool Taxi Drivers Blind Children's Outing Committee). The event is now a joint benefit for both Wavertree and St. Vincents and has moved with the times – the venue now being the theme park of "Camelot" at Charnock Richard. The outing remains a high-point of the year and maintains a long and happy association with a group of men and women which has not been limited to this event alone.

Sadly, during the late 1940s and early 1950s the School lost the services of several long serving teachers and governors. Mr Albert McCartney, an instructor in boot-repairing at Hardman Street, died in September 1946. A former pupil of the School, he had been appointed Assistant Teacher in 1918.

James Shipsides died in 1951. At his retirement six months previously,

215

he had completed 45 years service as a technical instructor at Hardman Street.

On 27 March in that same year the School saw the passing of its President, Harold Smyth. He had been connected with the School for over 43 years, serving as Honorary Secretary and Correspondent, and for the last six and a half years of his life as Chairman, overseeing the difficult period of reorganisation following the Education Act. His father, T.N. Smyth, also had close connections with the School.

The Chairmanship was taken over by George R. Stubbs, but the vacancy on the Committee was filled by John C. Smyth, son of the former Chairman. John Smyth, a partner with a Liverpool firm of Solicitors, followed his father into service on the Committee to continue a remarkable family association with the School, which has endured from just after the turn of the century to the present day. Appointed as Chairman in 1954, John Smyth has held that office until the Bi-Centennial year when he is expected to retire after 40 years service.

Shortly after John Smyth joined the Committee, Cecil Egerton-Jones, Headmaster of Wavertree, announced his retirement, which had been expected for some time. He had been at the School for 32 years and Headmaster for 29.

During the Headmaster's final years, the Wavertree School was still rather traditional in its outlook. An H.M.I. Report of 1948 declared Mr Egerton-Jones' methods and curriculum to be on "very formal lines". Keen to see a closer parity with ordinary schools, the Inspector, Miss W. Deavin, who visited Wavertree on a regular basis over the next few years, was eager to see the School develop as a "modern" infant and junior school. Appreciating that Egerton-Jones was "making an honest endeavour to reorganise", despite "being within about three years of retirement", she felt it was essential that he and his staff visited good sighted schools in the district to see the sort of activity and apparatus which should be introduced.

But by 1951, Wavertree had adapted only a little to the new demands placed upon it. According to Miss Deavin, "much remains to be done, the organisation is not helpful and the Headmaster is more than a little at the end of his tether. A dull and uninteresting school."[8]

216

The School was also attacked by the Ministry over the inadequacies of ophthalmic care. Records were "of the scantiest nature" and "as good as useless". It was found that the visiting Ophthalmic Surgeon was inefficient and the School were urged have him replaced.

This was certainly a difficult period for Wavertree. Despite the academic successes mentioned earlier, the Headmaster was undoubtedly finding the changes burdensome, especially with his retirement looming. New teaching methods were being called for, but it was clear that traditions were fairly well entrenched.

Nevertheless, changes were on the way. The School acted quickly regarding ophthalmic care, drawing up a new formula, which was given a trial period. Within months a new surgeon had been appointed.

General progress, however, would take a little longer. H.M.I. Miss Deavin clearly believed a change of Head would solve the School's problems as she saw them. By early 1953, she was becoming a little impatient and her discrimination against Mr. Egerton-Jones was quite apparent.

"There is little progress here. Head tells me he intends to retire at Christmas. He already has a hotel in Wales to go to![9]... There seems no reason why there should be a Headmaster when all the staff are women – it appears to be a case for a Headmistress who might civilise the place a bit..."[10]

Mr. Egerton-Jones retired to his Prestatyn home at the end of the summer term 1953. His appointment dated from 1921, although he had connections with Wavertree as far back as 1914 and 1915 when he had occasion to take temporary charge during the War. His last years at the School were certainly some of his most difficult.

Christina Wilkinson was a pupil at Wavertree from 1950 to 1957. She recalled her first impressions of life at Wavertree.

"I always wanted to go home! You got used to it though. I wasn't perpetually miserable. I remember the awful feeling of coming back to school at the beginning of term or after a weekend. This building, even to enter now is quite imposing. The paint-work was much duller then with the tiled walls. It was a very forbidding place to come into, you'd come up the steps, ring the doorbell, wait for someone to let you in, you'd have to walk off down the corridor and my mum would be saying, "Now don't cry, because if you do they won't let you come home for another weekend". Actually, she told me much later that she only used to say that because she'd be nearly crying too, and if I started so would she. It wasn't so bad once you'd made the break. Once you'd got among the other children and you were playing about you did feel better, and you adapted. I've seen it with children while I've been teaching. Children do adapt quite quickly."

Christina remembered Mr. Egerton-Jones. (Before she spoke, she listened for a moment as if to make sure we were not being overheard, then leaned forward and whispered. For a brief moment I expected him to walk in and march me out by the collar.)

"Oh I was terrified of him!! I don't think I spoke two words to him but I was terrified of him. He used to cane the bigger boys, not the girls or little ones, but every once in a while someone would do something really naughty and they'd get the cane at the end of assembly in the gym. I remember standing there, all us little ones, really frightened nearly wetting ourselves, if you'll pardon the expression!

I sometimes had to go to his room in the morning with a message from my teacher, Miss Wares, to remind him to ring the playtime bell. He was always very pleasant to me and one morning he said, as a kind of treat, that I could ring it for him. But I didn't know where the bell was and I was too frightened too tell him so I went and hid, and the bell didn't get rung that morning. I got the slipper off Miss MacLennan for that!"

Christina, who came from Bolton, took her grammar school entrance exam in 1957 and passed with credit, gaining a place at Chorleywood College for Girls. From there she spent three years at Salisbury Training College, where she qualified as a teacher in 1966. Her first teaching appointment was at Bolton Sunninghill School and a year later, in 1968, she came to Wavertree, where she has taught ever since.

Following the retirement of Mr. Egerton-Jones, the Committee appointed Miss M.A. MacLennan as Headmistress of Wavertree. For the previous 13 years she had been the Headmaster's senior assistant. She was a popular choice among Committee and Staff, and, of course, Her Majesty's Inspectorate. Within little more than two months of her appointment H.M.I. made a full inspection of the School covering three days in November 1953. "Considerable improvements had been made since the Headmaster retired" it was reported, "and there seemed to be no doubt that a great deal had already been done to make life happier for the children. The amount achieved so far augurs well for the future."

Hardman Street too fared well in the report.

"This department is efficient technically and run with an understanding of the needs of the adolescent blind, both for competent instruction and for companionship in a civilised home background devoid of institutionalism."

Wavertree 1955.

Despite the achievements being made at Hardman Street, it was facing its greatest crisis since its inception. Running costs were becoming a considerable burden, losses were mounting, and by 1955 numbers had become so low that a normal curriculum could not be taught. The year also saw the lowest admissions since the war.

The Committee were faced with additional problems in 1955 over Ministry plans for further reorganisation, which, on a happier note, were deemed necessary due to the decreasing incidences of blindness. Two conferences were held to discuss the proposals, which were; either (a) to have a single mixed secondary school serving the whole of the North of England, together with two primary schools, one to the east and one to the west of the Pennines, or, (b) two all age schools, again, one either side of the Pennines.

After extensive consultations, the former plan was adopted and Wavertree, in the role of Primary School West of the Pennines, braced itself for the increase in pupils and staff.

During 1956, the position of Hardman Street had become very serious indeed. There had not been any admissions at all during the year. Thirteen trainees completed their training in 1956 which left only a further 13 to begin 1957. On investigating the difficulties, the Committee found that the problems were very complex and were affecting all training schools generally. The strongest possible representations were made to the Ministry of Education and by December 1956, a Conference of all managers of Technical Schools in England and Wales was held to discuss the decline. It was found that among the reasons for the decline in training in traditional blind crafts was the increasing attractiveness of open industry. Yet it is arguable that the very nature of the training programme was severely outdated and little foresight was being shown in 1956, just as it had been lacking a decade earlier when the time was ripe for a complete re-evaluation of the role of the Technical School.

In June 1948 the Government had set up a Working Party to investigate the facilities existing for the employment of blind persons in industry. The report pointed out that residential schools had, up to then, generally led their pupils through industrial training to employment in a sheltered workshop. It was recommended in their final report that young people should be given the opportunity of choice between the sheltered workshop and open industry, against a background of knowledge of what both involved.

Advances were made by the R.N.I.B. with the opening in June 1956 of its new Technical School at Hethersett, which provided a programme similar to that recommended by the 1948 Working Party. Although experimental, it was a positive move to stave off looming stagnation. The opening of Hethersett certainly affected the intake at other technical schools, particularly Hardman Street. Following the meeting of December 1956, it was agreed with the Ministry to run Hardman Street under financial assistance, to allow for new arrangements to be made, until 31 July 1957, when it would close.

School life at Wavertree carried on as normal while the problems of the reorganisation were being thrashed out. At the beginning of the Autumn term of 1956 there was great excitement when it was announced that Her Royal Highness the Duchess of Gloucester was to visit the School on 26 October. It was almost 150 years to the day since the first Royal Visit to the Liverpool School for the Blind, when the Prince of Wales (who later became Prince Regent in 1811 and George IV in 1820) came to the London Road School and bestowed his Patronage upon the Charity.

The Duchess was received by the Chairman, John Smyth, who presented the members of the Committee, staff and pupils. A bouquet was presented to the Duchess by Vivien Thompson, one of the pupils, which was followed by a tour of the School.

By early 1958 the sale of Hardman Street to Liverpool Corporation for £47,000 was complete. Soon afterwards, the building took on a new lease of life in the role of the City's Police Headquarters. In 1982 after the Police had moved to their new Headquarters in Canning Place, the Hardman Street Building became the "Merseyside Trade Union Community and Unemployed Resource Centre" whose facilities included conference and function rooms, a small theatre, a bar and lounge and a basement recording studio. (The magnificent bronze doors were not lost to the School, however. In 1971, under an agreement made in the original contract of sale to Merseyside Police – which made provision for the removal of the doors if a new set were substituted – the bronze doors were removed to Wavertree where they were set into the wall of the entrance hall.)

Visit of the Duchess of Gloucester to Wavertree 1956.

Duchess of Gloucester escorted by the President John C. Smyth and Miss Maclennan on a tour of the School.

After the closure of Hardman Street, office premises were purchased in Smithdown Road, a short distance from the Wavertree School. This was initially on a temporary basis until facilities could be provided at the School. The office was to cater for the Administration of the Charity and was run as before by Edward Keates in his capacity as Superintendent. "Temporary" has lasted 32 years, and although the faces have changed, the Superintendent (who is now known as the Secretary/Bursar) and his staff are still there today.

The closure of Hardman Street marked the end of an Institution founded on ideals dating back to the eighteenth century. The future of the Liverpool School would now lie solely within an academic framework for the first time since its inception. Efforts could now be concentrated on Wavertree to take the School into the 1960s and beyond as a modern and innovative school for young blind children.

12
IN AND OUT OF THE MAINSTREAM

"Every child, no matter how severely handicapped, should have the opportunity to develop to the fullest extent of which he is capable, and that it cannot be right to exclude any child from the scope of the educational services."

William van Straubenzee[1]

Now that the burden of Hardman Street had been removed, and the Charity had benefited from the proceeds of the sale, the way was open to mount a programme of improvements at Wavertree to enable it to enter the sixties as a modern, forward thinking primary school. The changes planned initially were extensive and were to continue over a decade.

A main extension to the School was completed by July 1959, which included additions to the north and south elevations. Three classrooms were provided, three dormitories, bathrooms and washrooms and further staff accommodation. This was followed by renovations and improvements to the older building, which also brought a re-equipping and updating of the classrooms.

At the end of the 1960 summer term, Miss MacLennan resigned as Headmistress after 21 years at the School, her first appointment being made during the Rhyl evacuation. On 21 June 1960 the Committee appointed Mr. Derek Marks as the new Headmaster, who commenced his duties on 1 October of that year. Miss Diana Wares, who had been a teacher at the School since 1949, was appointed as Deputy Headmistress.

Born in South Armagh in Northern Ireland, Derek Marks moved to Tyrone with his parents where he spent his childhood. On leaving school he spent three years in the police where his experiences in dealing with young offenders prompted him to return to education to study for a teaching diploma.

While at training college in Belfast, Mr Marks would periodically help out at the nearby Association for the Teaching and Training of Deaf and Blind Children in Lisburn Road. After a brief appointment at Jordanstown, he left for England with his wife, where he took up the position of

Assistant Master at Birmingham Royal Institution for the Blind. Promotion came quickly and it was not long before he had become Senior Master at the School's new Lickey Green premises in Bromsgrove, where he specialised in helping children with additional difficulties.

When the Liverpool post became vacant, Derek Marks was at first hesitant to move. He and his wife were happy in the Midlands where they had settled down to what he termed "an idyllic life". "We were happy and relaxed there," he said, explaining how difficult the decision was to begin with. "Our daughter had not long been born and life at the School was good. The children and staff were marvellous and we had settled down well in our home."

Yet the Headship at Liverpool was a challenge he could not afford to pass up. Here was a school which was clearly being injected with fresh impetus in an positive attempt to fulfill its new mandate with committed support. Derek Marks knew where his future lay. "Besides," he added mischievously, "It was handy for the boat back to Belfast."

"When I came here it was a period of unrest in education generally. MacMillan had a phrase at that time regarding 'a wind of change blowing through' (referring to the changes in the African Continent). I felt that 'wind of change' phrase could just as easily be applied to schools. There needed to be a change. Most of the schools had come back after the War to the same old routine. There was a tendency to stick to traditional, formal methods and there was almost a disapproval of new ideas and innovations. There was an unrest in people of my age coming into the work, we felt it was time for a change. I suppose really that this prompted me to take up this challenge of going to a primary school, one with a very good reputation, a very formal school, and to try and bring some of the ideas that I had been associated with at Birmingham and put them into practice here. Liverpool was a school ready for expansion, it was a school with very keen young staff, and a very good deputy in Diana Wares. There was also Brian Hechle; very scholarly and academic, very particular and conscious of even the smallest obligations in life. They all made some of the biggest decisions much easier."

At the time of Derek Marks' appointment, there had been a dramatic breakthrough regarding the reading and writing of Braille. A new machine, the Perkins Brailler, had been developed at the Howe Press, Perkins School for the Blind in Watertown, Massachusetts, U.S.A. It was a vast improvement on the Stainsby-Wayne writer, which punched downwards, as this machine punched upwards, enabling the pupil to read immediately what had been written. There were only two machines in Britain – both owned by the R.N.I.B., which were slowly being sent round various schools on trial. After using one of the machines at an exhibition

a. Perkins Brailler training 1962 (pupils Diane Hurst, Dennis Freedman and Julia Williams) (Stewart Bale).

b. Language laboratory 1964. A lesson with Mr Hechle (Stewart Bale).

in London, Mr Marks felt that their introduction was essential, and approached the Management Committee requesting that the School obtain the machines and set the pattern for the future. Backing was immediate and an order was despatched to Massachusetts for an incredible 60 machines. The order was queried by the flabbergasted Americans. When the figure was confirmed, the shipment was flown over to Manchester Airport and rushed by special delivery to the School. Every child at that time who could manage to write started using the Perkins Brailler. Many children leaving for secondary school were allowed to take a machine with them, which meant that other schools would soon have to follow suit and introduce the new Braillers.

Meanwhile, the building programme continued, and by November 1963 a house was added on to the Main School Building for the Headmaster and his family, which enabled easy access to the School for administrative and supervisory purposes. A swimming pool was added in 1964, followed by an extensive landscaping project in the School grounds, which brought additional recreation areas for the children.

Although disruption due to the School improvements was to continue over the next few years, a fair degree of stability had now been achieved at Wavertree. Numbers had remained steady during the early sixties, averaging 85 per year. That number was now expected to drop due to the peaking of the "Retrolental Fibroplasia Bulge", although, in fact, the decrease was not as sharp as had been originally predicted.

The School had now achieved a reputation for sending very high numbers of children to Worcester and Chorleywood Grammar Schools and new steps were continually being taken in introducing wider concepts of education into the curriculum. Craft-work and House-crafts were taught, now that new facilities had been built, and included woodwork, pottery, and domestic skills. The Headmaster was keen to see a much higher degree of care and education at Wavertree for children not excelling academically who would need an awareness of general living skills and independence. Teaching was structured to meet the attributes of the individual.

French had been successfully introduced in 1962, which prompted the School to set up a Language Laboratory, financed by the Nuffield Foundation, to assist with the teaching and further development of the subject.

Under the auspices of Brian Hechle, it caused enormous interest and the Wavertree School received a number of visitors from schools and local authorities to inspect the equipment.

The School was increasing its profile on an international basis during the sixties. Contacts and experiences were gained in International Conferences on the Education of the Blind and several teachers from Blind Schools in Sweden, Jordan, Ghana, Nigeria, Hong Kong, Malaya, and Germany, came to Wavertree, frequently staying for long periods to study methods and techniques used at the Liverpool School. In 1965 the School for the Blind in Paris was visited by Brian Hechle and later that year a reciprocal visit was arranged for some of the Paris children to stay at Wavertree. The French children took part in routine school life and also the annual taxi-drivers outing to Southport.

In 1969, Brian Hechle was appointed Registrar of the College of Teachers of the Blind. Prior to this appointment, Mr. Hechle had held various other College offices and had been the Editor of the College Journal *The Teacher of the Blind*. During the mid-1970s, Mr. Hechle combined his duties at Wavertree with an appointment at the University of Birmingham, where he lectured on education to student teachers.

In 1967, the Fourth meeting of the International Conference of Educators of Blind Youth (ICEBY) took place at the Perkins Institute in Watertown. This was followed by a tour of the North American Schools for the Blind by Derek Marks and Edward Keates in 1967. The Headmaster and Superintendent visited schools in New York, Boston, Louisville, Baltimore, Philadelphia, New Jersey, Montreal and Brantford. Numerous aspects of school life were studied and visits were also made to sighted schools and a number of establishments manufacturing equipment and appliances for use by the blind. After the American tour the Superintendent and Headmaster also visited the School for the Blind in Paris.

Many of the schools visited seemed very keen to appoint a Peripatologist on to the staff for the instruction of pupils in Mobility (long cane method). This was of great interest to the two Liverpool representatives as it expanded the established Wavertree programme of mobility and independence.

On returning to Liverpool, their findings were reported to the Committee and a joint venture with St. Vincent's was set into motion to bring a Peripatologist over from the United States for six to eight months.

The Schools secured the services of Mr R. La Duke from the University of West Michigan. A training programme was initiated and Mr La Duke trained two members of the Wavertree Staff; the Deputy Headmistress Diana Wares, and Barbara Williams, as qualified mobility instructors. Training was intense and skilful and placed great mental and physical demands upon the blindfolded trainees, who pressed on, regardless of weather conditions.

"I can remember Diana and Rob La Duke walking around the snow covered streets in West Derby," Derek Marks recalled. "Diana had an aversion to people taking her photograph. Yet here she was walking around blindfolded with a long cane with everybody busy snapping away and making a cine film of her. If only she had known – she would have been lashing out with that long cane and using it for purposes for which it wasn't intended!"

The specialised work caused much local interest and, during the course, Barbara Williams appeared in a short BBC Television Documentary, which was followed by several interviews about the work on radio. A couple of years later, to continue the momentum gained from Mr La Duke's visit, Diana Wares spent a short period studying the use of Sonic Aid in Mobility at Nottingham University where a research programme was being carried out on the mobility of the Blind.

Gillian Wake was a pupil at Wavertree between 1971 and 1975. She had lost her sight at the age of eight and found the mobility training particularly helpful.

"It was quite good, especially for me as I had just lost my sight. I was taught by Miss Reid and Phil Thompson.
It was weird at first. We were taken over to St. Vincent's where they had laid tactile objects so we could find our way around the building. We would then have to find certain parts of the school. Once we had learnt that part, we were allowed outside the school onto the roads around West Derby. It was an ideal area as some of the roads are on a grid pattern and were easy to start off with. We were then asked to find certain roads. I can remember walking along and all the old women would be stood outside the supermarket going "Aah" in sympathy as I went past!
I remember my teacher Phil Thompson taking me for Mobility outside the School, where I learned to cross the traffic lights by the school gates. I told him that I didn't understand why one set of cars had to wait while the others could go. I remember feeling mortified with embarrassment when he explained that they would all crash in the centre if they didn't!.

a. Rob Laduke teaching the long cane method to Barbara Williams (Stewart Bale).

b. Phil Thompson shows Edward Hill the position of Clifton House (Elsam, Mann and Cooper).

Mr Marks and the Staff had recognised that such skills were important for when you came to leave school. I also had to learn Braille straight away and basic skill work with Miss Reid, then with Mr Delacruz and Mr Barlow. It was all very academic then."

In the late 1960s, the Wavertree School, which was now known as The Royal School for the Blind, Liverpool, following Royal assent in 1966, was keen to make further expansions and to improve accommodation. It was broadly felt among Committee and Staff that there were untapped resources at Wavertree and that the Primary status was too restrictive. It was believed that less frequent changes of environment would be in the best interest of the children, thus encouraging a stability while allowing emotional and educational maturation. In addition it was felt that pupils who were slow learners would benefit from remaining longer at Wavertree before moving to secondary education. The future integration into the primary school of children with additional handicaps was also being looked at while national and international trends and developments in this field were closely monitored. Overall, it was proposed to extend the educational facilities to include all ages up to 16 years. This involved the introduction of a pre-school unit and secondary accommodation.

Two adjacent sites became available during this period which were purchased by the School with a view to putting the plans into practice. The purchase of Abbeyholme Private School situated alongside the Wavertree School in 1966 was followed by the acquisition in 1972 of Clifton House which lay on Prince Alfred Road at the rear of the School.

The Abbeyholme building was found to be too costly to repair due to its derelict and vandalised state. Several plans were drawn up for the future use of the site which included accommodation for pre-school facilities, a special care centre for children requiring long term extra care, and accommodation for slow learners. The Committee discussed their plans with the Department of Education and Science (formerly the Ministry of Education) and awaited their approval.

Meanwhile, the School lost two of its long term servants. Miss Phyllis Humphries, who had joined the Wavertree teaching staff at the end of the war, retired in 1968. Miss Humphries had been a much valued teacher and was keenly missed.

Edward Keates, the Superintendent, retired on 31 July the following year after seeing the School through several upheavals and developments during his twenty five years. His replacement was Thomas C. Milburn.

a. Wavertree 1968 (Stewart Bale).

b. 21st Picton Cub Scout Pack are led through Buckingham Palace gates by Len and Audrey Brooksbank and Marian Humphreys (1972).

Mr. Milburn came to Wavertree in April 1969 from Abbotsholme School, Rocester, in the West Midlands. Born in Bedlington Station in Northumberland, the son of the village policeman, he was orphaned at the age of eight after his parents died from T.B. in the 1930s. The next eight years were spent at an orphanage in Harrogate, although he gained a scholarship to Harrogate Grammar School when he was eleven. On leaving School, Tom Milburn went into banking, which was followed by 17 years in the Treasurer's office at Northumberland County Council. He then became re-acquainted with residential institutionalism when he took the post of Bursar at an approved school in Stannington, Northumberland. This was followed five years later by a similar appointment at Abbotsholme and after three years there he came to Wavertree. Mr Milburn still holds the office of Secretary/Bursar as the school moves into its bicentennial year.

By the end of the 1960s it was becoming clear that the nature of special education was again beginning to change. As early as 1967 it was reported by the Committee,

> "The pattern of children being presented for education is changing. Certain trends, national and international, indicate that children with a visual restriction plus other handicaps, may be the norm for the Visually Handicapped Schools for the future."[2]

While the D.E.S. were still dragging their heels over the proposed reorganisation at Wavertree, a government enquiry headed by Professor M.D. Vernon, was set up to look into the Education of Visually Handicapped Children.

The Vernon Committee found that in one respect little had changed since 1934.[3]

> "Comparatively little experience has been gained in this country of educating visually handicapped children in ordinary schools."[4]

It was recommended that Blind and partially-sighted children should be taught in the same schools. Yet by 1977, five years after the report appeared, there were only two schools, with a total of 221 pupils, that provided for both blind and partially sighted children; the remaining 1,017 blind and 1,559 partially sighted were still in separate schools.[5]

The Vernon Report did acknowledge that the numbers of blind children were declining and that the physical condition of the children was generally becoming very much poorer, noting that in almost 50% of admissions there was, in some degree, an additional handicap. Wavertree, even by 1967, was itself a certain example of such statistics.

The Report, however, was received with disappointment by Derek Marks.

"There had been a tremendous build up of expectancy regarding the Vernon Report, but when it came out I felt it was an anti-climax. There were no decisions, no foundations to build upon, no experimentation. It was a non-starter and had little impact."

The Wavertree School was already fully aware of the gradual change in the nature of blind education which was reflected in the plans for the Abbeyholme site and Clifton House, yet DES approval was still not forthcoming. By 1971 it was decided to landscape the Abbeyholme area as a recreational playground until plans could be approved for its future use. Here the School were fortunate to receive support for the project from the Liverpool Branch of the Variety Club and on completion of the work it was officially opened on their behalf by the then current Miss World, Miss Cindy Breakspeare, accompanied by Sir Fred Pontin.

Clifton House, a large detached house in almost an acre of land, was in much better condition and plans were set in motion to provide accommodation for a pre-school nursery unit.

During the early 1970s, admissions again reached the nineties as Wavertree slowly began to take children with additional handicaps.

The positive work and foresight during this period was overshadowed however, by the death of the Matron of the School, Miss Roberta McGregor on 10 December 1972. She had been Matron for 18 years and her loss was felt so keenly that no announcement was made to the children until they had returned from their Christmas holidays.

"I think she was the outstanding personality, as far as I was concerned, of my first ten years in Liverpool," recalled Mr Marks. "She was a very dedicated lady from Arran in Scotland, she had a very good background as Matron, she had her nursing qualifications, she had a qualification in ophthalmia, she had various other qualifications too, but it was her human personality, her gentleness, the pride in the School and her desire to work for people who were not as well off as the rest of society, that made her a very unique person. She really was, I would think, the outstanding person of my first years here. Subsequently, when we built the new teaching block it was automatic that we should call it after her – McGregor Hall."

234

The number who attended the memorial service held in her honour at Wavertree Parish Church, was testimony of the great impact she had made on all of those who surrounded her during her time at the School.

By the mid-1970s, the School was undergoing a slow but major transformation. Its future clearly lay in the care and education of blind and partially sighted children with additional handicaps, and building programmes were now well established to cater for their future care. It was further decided in 1976 (with D.E.S. approval) to offer places to children of secondary school age, again with additional problems, whom the Local Education Authorities were having difficulty in placing in suitable schools. These children were also to be cared for in Clifton House.

The debate on integration of children with special needs into mainstream education came to a head with the passage of the 1976 Education Act. Under Section 10, Local Authorities were required to provide education for pupils with special needs in ordinary State schools, except where it was "impracticable or incompatible with the provision of efficient instruction in the schools" or where it "would involve unreasonable public expenditure". This legislation was placed on the Statute Books by the Labour Government and effectively took the carpet from under a sitting Committee formed three years earlier under the Tories.

The Committee of Inquiry into the Education of Handicapped Children had been set up in November 1973 with Mary Warnock appointed to the chair by Margaret Thatcher, who was then Secretary of State for the Department of Education and Science. (Various organisations had urged the Government in 1966 to set up such an enquiry.) Its terms of reference were "to review educational provision in England, Scotland and Wales for children and young people handicapped by disabilities of body or mind, taking into account the medical aspects of their needs, together with arrangements to prepare them for entry into employment; to consider the most effective use of resources for these purposes; and to make recommendations".

The Report[6] was published in May 1978 and made some 250 recommendations, the basic thinking of which was summarised by the following passage.

"The wider concept of special education proposed in this report, embracing as it does all those children in ordinary schools, who, though not at present accounted handicapped, need additional support in a variety of forms, is directly in line with the principle that handicapped and non-handicapped children should be educated in a common setting as far as possible. The great majority of these children will continue to attend ordinary schools in the future. Moreover, we have made very clear our determined opposition to the notion of treating handicapped and non-handicapped children as forming two distinctive groups, for whom separate educational provision has to be made. It follows that we wholeheartedly support the principle of the development of common provision for all children."[7]

The National Federation of the Blind and the Association of Partially Sighted Students and Teachers welcomed the report, as by accepting Section 10 of the 1976 Act, it opened the way for the education of visually handicapped in ordinary schools. Others were less enthusiastic. The Secondary Heads Association gave it a rather more allegorical reception.

"The Warnock owl has told the grasshopper to change into a mouse but if asked how this can be done suggests that owls only deal with policy. The words are welcome but not the five year waiting period."

Many welcomed the recommendations in terms of basic human rights but were sceptical about provision of funding and the complex planning and training necessary to carry out the ideas on committed and positive lines. A concerned Wavertree teacher later remarked in retrospect,

"A child of special needs requires all the resources that can be given and the teacher needs them too in order to benefit that child. At one stage I was quite taken with the idea of integration, it sounds highly desirable but the more I considered it the more I thought the child could lose out quite considerably.

How acceptable is integration to the staff of the School in which the child is being integrated? From my own experience in the ordinary school and experiences of friends and colleagues, I know how difficult it is when they try to cater for a child with special needs, even with some support. I would also question the level of support. Resources being what they are today, I do wonder what kind of a deal the special needs child gets with support. I would sometimes prefer the child to still be in a place like Wavertree which caters for them fully, rather than doing just a back up job under the supposed name of integration."

It was not proposed to integrate children with severe physical, sensory or intellectual difficulties and those with less severe disabilities who, despite special help, had been unable to perform well in ordinary schools.

Legislation followed in the form of the Education Act 1981, which was brought into force on 1 April 1983. Like many other pieces of legislation in the U.K. it was greeted by diverse emotions ranging from enthusiasm for what could be seen as an embodiment of a broad concept of civil

236

rights in education, to Neil Kinnock's frequently quoted "like Brighton Pier, good as far as it goes, but a poor way of getting to France". Legislation in this country is usually enabling rather than prescriptive, and in this case the Act was introduced at a time of economic crisis and cuts in Government expenditure. Consequently, L.E.A.s were given little incentive to implement the spirit of the new Act.

Much of the philosophy contained in the Warnock Report was adopted and formalised by the 1981 Act, significantly, the widening of parental opportunities to participate in decisions affecting their children's education.

As the summer term of 1982 was drawing to a close, Gillian Wake returned to Wavertree to spend a week helping out at her former school while waiting to begin a degree at University. After passing her entrance examination in 1975, Gillian had moved to Chorleywood College for Girls, where she gained a place at Liverpool University to read for a degree in Sociology and Psychology. Wavertree was well into its transition by the time of Gillian's visit. She recalled,

"I was absolutely amazed at how much it had changed when I went back, as most of the children by then had additional handicaps. Also, I couldn't get used to the fact that I wasn't one of the school children any more – it was really weird! I helped out generally, and stayed in the School. I really enjoyed my visit but it so exhausted me that by Friday I was so shattered, I thought, I couldn't take another week of this, crawling around on the floor with the children and being hit by cricket bats!

The atmosphere though was exactly the same as when I had been there originally, even though there had been a few staff changes.

The school I went on to when I was 12 was totally different, it made me realise what a good school Wavertree had been.

Compared with Chorleywood, Wavertree was so much more practical. Besides mobility, we did typing, craft-work, domestic work and other things that were useful. I could type at the age of ten. It was very practical and all the staff were very approachable. It really hit me when I went to Chorleywood how distant all the staff were. There was a barrier between 'us' and 'them'. The staff at Wavertree also had evening duties and would frequently be rolling around and playing with the children. I didn't expect much of that in college education but roles were very differentiated, academic staff leaving at four and evening staff coming on.

Wavertree was a much more realistic education, whereas Chorleywood was old fashioned and traditional. I didn't enjoy my time at Chorleywood at all. Obviously it had to be academic for the pupils to have a chance at higher education and qualifications, but it was to the exclusion and detriment of everything else as far as I could see. Wavertree had a good academic standard, it certainly helped me get to Chorleywood, but more important for me were the other things that happened there; the whole atmosphere of the place, it was somewhere where I felt all of the children were happy in."

a. Gillian Wake gives an impromptu music lesson (Elsam, Mann and Cooper).

b. Miss World, Cindy Breakspeare, visits Wavertree 1976 (courtesy of 'Liverpool Daily Post').

After I left I would much rather have then gone into mainstream education. There was no provision in the mid seventies, although a lot has been done since then."

Although integration was now legislated, problems were clearly evident in relation to support and provision of resources for the pupil. In higher education support was scanty and even help from the College sending the pupils was derisory.

Experiences of Gillian and another former pupil contrasted sharply.

"The College was delighted when someone got a place at University, but they didn't prepare you at all, so you went from a really safe, closeted environment to be thrown into a chamber of horrors at University with 8,000 students. I was brought up for a preliminary visit to look around the University for a day by my teacher acting on her own initiative, but that was it, there was no structured plan.

My friend, who was in the year below me both at Wavertree and Chorleywood, only lasted three days at Lancaster University. There was no reason at all why she could not have coped if she had had the right sort of preparation."

Gillian was to find help by default rather than by a structured plan of integration and support.

"I was on 40 Minutes, the BBC2 documentary. In 1982 I was one of a first batch to go into the new Mulberry Court Halls of Residence on the Campus. The T.V. people were wanting to make a documentary on Freshers Week at Liverpool University. The University were happy to see these new houses being publicised and I ended up being trailed around by a camera crew for my first week, so I wasn't alone, I was with them all week! They filmed me doing everything. They came back a month later and filmed me at the match standing on the Kop. I was expecting to be only in it for about three minutes but when I sat down to watch it on T.V. I couldn't believe it, every other scene was about something I was doing, it was so embarrassing! Going to the match, going to lectures, the pub, everything!

So because the camera crew were following me around, it was quite good for me as everybody got to know me, which helped enormously as the University was so unprepared for me too. Fortunately, I had a lot of helpful and cooperative fellow students, otherwise life would have been practically impossible. I would certainly have gone the same way as my friend at Lancaster. Chorleywood should have played a part in liaising with the University prior to my entrance regarding additional requirements. Nevertheless, of all the departments, I naively thought that my own University department [Psychology/Sociology] would be able to cope with me."

In 1982 and 1983 consultations took place between the DES and representatives of L.E.A.s and the voluntary bodies concerned with the provision of special schools for children with visual handicaps, to discuss the

a. Pupils David Peel, Lesley Powell and Wendy Laverick receive a typing lesson from Val Burgess (Elsam, Mann and Cooper).

b. Christopher Duffy, optacon training 1986 (Elsam, Mann and Cooper).

a: Pupil Joanne Winstanley receives Visualtek training from Christina Wilkinson (Elsam, Mann and Cooper).

b: Swimming pool (John Mills).

future of those schools. Regional Conferences were organised and invited to formulate plans within their regions for the period up to 1987.

Over the past decade pupil numbers in special schools had been falling. This was attributable to the general decline in the birthrate, medical improvements which had reduced the incidence of handicapped children, and the new trends of integration as recommended by the 1981 Act. It was clear that a measure of rationalisation was required regarding maintaining too many schools with falling numbers and also to avoid haphazard closures. In 1982 it was found that in special schools nationally, there was already around 30 per cent over-provision for the blind and around 20 per cent for the partially sighted. As a result of the deliberations, several schools were closed, wound down or adapted to other requirements. Among the casualties were the schools at Newcastle, York, Preston, and Bristol, which all closed, and Birmingham, once the largest school for the blind in the country, which planned to close in July 1991. The two colleges of Worcester and Chorleywood were amalgamated as a co-educational college.

Concerning visually handicapped children with additional disabilities, three schools already established as the main provision were to continue in their role, which were Rushton Hall near Northampton, Condover Hall near Shrewsbury, and Wavertree.

After the 1983 discussions involving the North West Authorities, the role of Wavertree was now extended to the "education of visually handicapped children with severe learning difficulties and other handicaps between the ages of three and 18, who would not be catered for in their local schools'. Wavertree would also accept day pupils.

During this transitional period Miss Diana E. Wares, Deputy Headmistress, retired at the end of the 1985 spring term after a period of service which spanned almost 37 years. Miss Wares left Liverpool for another school, although not quite on the same lines as at Wavertree. She had renovated a Victorian schoolhouse in Portgower, Helmsdale in North Scotland where she intended to spend her retirement. She was succeeded by Mr. Brian Hechle who was formerly Senior Master.

Sadly, in 1988, after an unbroken period of 79 years, the School Scout Troop and Cub Pack was disbanded. For half those years, 40 in all, Audrey Brooksbank had been responsible for the group on a week to week basis and had given considerable amounts of her own time on camping, training weekends, and a multitude of scouting activities. In 1962, Audrey Humphreys, as she was then known, received recognition for her work when she was awarded the Badge of Merit. Throughout her time with the School Pack Audrey was frequently assisted by her sister Marian. In 1966 the post of Assistant Scout Leader was taken by Len Brooksbank who already had long experience in Scouting and was a former King's Scout. Two years later Len and Audrey were married and together they continued to run the troop until their retirement.[8]

The change at Wavertree from a School providing academic education for ordinary blind children and those with a secondary handicap, to a School catering for the care and education of visually handicapped children with severe learning difficulties inevitably took time and presented many problems, not least in obtaining specialist staff. The full transition into the new role was completed by August 1989. Many of the staff had been at Wavertree since the fifties and sixties and faced a personal transition to adapt their skills and commitment to the caring and education of a new type of child. "Academic" attainment would now be a much lessened expectation.

Ron Delacruz was one of those teachers who faced the change-over. Appointed in 1966, he had initial reservations regarding his ability to cope after the transition.

"If I'd stopped and thought about it, I'd have been apprehensive, but on the other hand I've always taken the line that to teach a child you need to know the child first. And I think that once you get to know that child, particularly in a small group, you establish some kind of rapport, if it is at all possible, with that child. They become people with personalities of their own and that's where the impact lies; one to one.

It has been fun teaching the more academic children and a great many of my early pupils now have degrees – some are much better qualified than I would ever be, but it's also enjoyable to make a breakthrough with a child who is very handicapped, its very satisfying to take a child with difficulties swimming and see them enjoy the water or to enjoy conversation with them. I think you can achieve something there which is equally satisfying if not more so than the stimulus and feedback from academic pupils".

As 1990 drew to a close with the Bi-centennial looming larger, media attention began to focus on Wavertree. Two hundred years to the day that Henry Dannett's first media statement announced in the local press that plans were afoot to open a Blind School in the town, Derek Marks appeared on a regional television news in an item covering the work of the School. He declared,

"This School is special because the children are special and because the staff are unique; and also because the results that we get from making the children ready for society, to take their place in the world, gives us such a feeling of greatness and makes the children so superb. The School is like Liverpool's football teams, it can't be held down!"

The School is ready to face the challenge of the next 200 years.

EPILOGUE

*"This School is now fulfilling a specific role, it has a number of special-
ist staff, occupational therapists, speech therapists, physios; there is an
expertise being provided. These children with profound needs were
sometimes being overlooked, shunted about or being missed somewhere along the line. The school has now found and provided a role
which I would confidently expect it to take into the next century."*

Ron Delacruz (November 1990)
Teacher at Wavertree 1966-1991

At the beginning of January 1991 it was revealed that a most distinguished visitor is to come to the Royal School for the Blind, Liverpool,
for the bicentennial celebrations. On 22 March 1991, the Patron of the
School, Her Majesty the Queen, is to visit the School. It will be the first
time that a reigning monarch has visited the School, and the first Patron to
do so since the visit of the Prince of Wales on 18 September 1806, when
patronage was originally bestowed. Her Majesty will meet the pupils and
staff while making a tour of the School, and carry out an unveiling ceremony.

To realise the significance of the unveiling ceremony we must return to
the end of the 1920s and look again at the doomed fate of the Chapel. Although it was demolished, it was not completely destroyed. Correspondence was discovered in the School Archive which revealed that the contract for demolition made provision for the six columns of the Doric front-
age to be recovered and remain the property of the School. But if they had
been saved, what had happened to them? There was no specific reference
in the Archive, not even in the Management Committee Minutes where
such dealings would be expected to be recorded. All that was known was
that the columns were intended to be given to the Liverpool Corporation
Parks and Gardens Committee for "future use".

After a few strolls around local parks and fruitless searches through
numerous records, contemporary press reports were consulted. A small,
yet crucial reference was found in a snippet in the *Liverpool Daily Post* in
January 1930.

"All that remains of the demolished Church of the Blind at Hardman Street is the front
colonnade, which stands with an almost heightened dignity amid the ruins. Lovers of

architecture will be pleased to know that this colonnade is definitely to be preserved. It has been accepted by Liverpool Parks Committee for re-erection in one of the parks.

Which park it will be is not certain, but it has been suggested to the committee that the colonnade might be embodied in the new shelter which will probably be erected on the sight of the recently demolished mansion house at Camp Hill, Woolton. Though the committee has not yet definitely decided the matter, it has at any rate ordered that the colonnade shall be sent to Camp Hill provisionally."

Yet Camp Hill had already been searched without success. A telephone call to the Conservation Section of Liverpool Council's City Planning Office solved the mystery. The Columns could be found alongside the wall of School Lane, which bordered the Park, near the entrance to the Corporation estate yard. How could they have been missed?

On returning to Camp Hill, the columns were found straight away. Now separated into their original sections of three per column (see the faint joins shown in the Harwood print of 1829), they lay side by side by the wall, covered in earth, ivy, leaves, and sheltered by trees. Little wonder they had been missed! The plinths too, lay part hidden by the undergrowth. There was a feeling of excitement at finding tangible remains of what had previously only been known in documentary form, but a sadness too, for they had peacefully lain there, untouched and unused for 60 years.

Six columns obviously meant 18 sections, yet only 16 were evident. Again the Conservation Section were helpful. One of the sections could now be found in the centre of St. James's Gardens below the Liverpool Anglican Cathedral, mounted on a plinth, bearing an inscription informing the visitor about the history of the Gardens. There was no reference in the inscription to the former use of the stone section. The whereabouts of the other missing section remains a mystery. It may lie in a Corporation yard awaiting re-use or it could have been damaged during the demolition and removal.

By an unusual coincidence, given the time-scale since their storage, there was another party interested in the present situation of the columns. The reason why the Conservation Section were so well briefed as to the location of the chapel remains, was due to the fact that after almost sixty years, plans had recently been drawn up with the intention of re-using one complete column. (Not wishing to cast aspersions on the Conservation Section, I had expected an answer to my enquiry to take a reasonable time

The author with the column sections Camp Hill, Woolton.

Column section with inscription (St. James' Gardens, below the Liverpool Anglican Cathedral.

SKETCH VIEW OF PROPOSED WATER FEATURE.

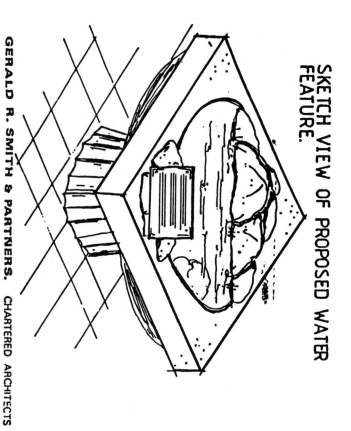

GERALD R. SMITH & PARTNERS. CHARTERED ARCHITECTS

a. Water feature with column section base, Wavertree (to be unveiled by H.M. The Queen, 22 March 1991).

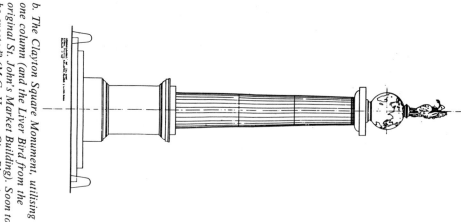

b. The Clayton Square Monument, utilising one column (and the Liver Bird from the original St. John's Market Building). Soon to be erected? (M.G. Hayes, City Planning Officer).

while researches could be made. Their reply, to my surprise, was immediate!) A copy of the plans was kindly forwarded for inspection.

In conjunction with the redevelopment of Clayton Square taking place at this time in the City centre, it was envisaged that a monument of traditional appearance could form a central feature and complement the nearby St. John's Market Precinct and the hi-tech design of the new shopping complex. The monument would have a historical significance. One of the Chapel columns would be placed on a new Doric plinth. On top, a globe would be positioned, and on the summit, a stone Liver Bird, the emblem of the City. This, however was not a modern sculpture. The Bird had once stood on top of the original St. John's Market Building of 1822 (designed by John Foster, architect of the original Blind School and Chapel, and situated adjacent to the same St. John's Church of which Henry Dannett was the former incumbent). The Bird, which is reputed to have stood on an earlier building of 1746, had turned up in an auction in Hereford(!) where it was purchased and restored by the developers of the new complex. It was suggested that the monument would also be a fitting reminder of the pioneering efforts of the philanthropists of late eighteenth century Liverpool and of those who ensured the continued existence of the School and Charity for two centuries.

Sadly, these plans remain unapproved, and in light of the financial burdens faced by the Council as we go to press, priorities clearly lie elsewhere.

Nevertheless, one of the column sections will return home, or at least, return to its former owner. Liverpool City Council have allowed of one of the four-ton sections to be removed to the Wavertree School where it will be incorporated into a water feature designed for the enjoyment of the children.

In 1990, in tribute to over 40 years of commitment and dedication in the caring of children with special needs, Derek Marks was awarded the O.B.E. The award was announced as he was celebrating 30 years as Headmaster of Wavertree.

Since Mr Marks and his wife, Lillian, arrived at the School, they have worked to make it a real home for the children. "The School is the centre of our lives", said the Headmaster, "Twenty-four hours a day, seven days

H.S.D. Marks O.B.E.

a. Thomas C. Milburn (Secretary/Bursar 1969-1991)

b. Ronald Wright B.E.M. (investiture made on behalf of H.M. The Queen by the Lord Lieutenant of Cheshire, Mr William Bromley-Davenport (right)).

a week – we can't see it as a 9–5 job. I think it is very significant that this city is charged with an atmosphere of challenge and enterprise – that atmosphere is a very infectious one."

When the notification of the award dropped through his letter box Derek Marks doubted its authenticity.

"When I received the letter I was very embarrassed and sheepish, I looked around the staff thinking someone was taking the mickey out of me. It took a while before the penny dropped!

You feel there are more people among your colleagues who are more deserving of the award and you feel too embarrassed to talk about it. I'm very pleased to be receiving this award, but the honour must really go to the staff and the School itself. Ever since its inauguration, it has pioneered care for the blind throughout the world. It was the first blind school to introduce language laboratories as a means of learning, and also the first to run independence training programmes. Independence is probably the most important and fundamental goal here at the School."

Understandably, the day at Buckingham Palace was a memorable one for the Marks family.

"It was a lot of fun. There were many people there involved in charity work and public life, such as Jimmy Saville, Mary Peters and Bruce Oldfield, and it was marvellous to be involved. It was rather nice to share a day with people who were as proud and embarrassed as I was. We were like a bunch of schoolchildren receiving a Christmas treat!"

Typical of his character, he caused laughter when the Queen spoke to him. Questioned about his time at Wavertree, his reply inferred that he didn't consider himself as the Head of the School, but that it was a position he felt he shared with a lot of other people. "Except," he added, "when the going was rough, then nobody wanted to be Head, least of all me!!"

By coincidence, in the same honours list was a former pupil of the School. Ronald Wright was awarded a B.E.M. for 40 years service to the Civil Service. A pupil from 1935 to 1944 and a former school pal of Danny Peacock, Mr Wright, who is completely blind, works as a switchboard operator at the Department of Social Security in Widnes. He has memorised the names and extension numbers of all personnel in the department – a total of 160 people.

The award of the O.B.E. to Derek Marks came as a fitting conclusion to a career due to end in the School's bicentennial year. Clearly rueful to-

Long time supporter of the School, broadcaster and children's author, Brian Jacques, presents a framed cover of his book 'Redwall' to the children. With them are Derek Marks and Ron Delacruz. (Courtesy of 'Liverpool Daily Post and Echo'.)

253

wards his looming retirement, he confided, "It will be very hard to shake my attachment to the School, it hasn't been a job at all, it's been something I've enjoyed doing all my life."

Still with a keen eye to the future he added,

"Rather than spend too much time looking back over the last 30 years, I prefer to look ahead – in 1991 the School celebrates its bi-centenary, and we have big plans to do even more as we enter our third century".

Those plans were given their first public airing in an official launch of the Bicentennial Appeal Fund on 13 November 1990.

Presided over by the Lady Pilkington D.L., the appeal will aim to fund the building of new classrooms, a hydrotherapy pool, remodelled residential accommodation for parents, the refurbishment of existing facilities, and to establish the School on a solid financial basis for the future.

A comprehensive fund-raising programme was set into motion with a target of £2.5 million. "Our target is a large one but the School architects have estimated all the plans at £4.4 million," said Lady Pilkington. "Several events have been planned," she continued, "which include concerts at the Philharmonic Hall, golf tournaments, a special fashion show at the Adelphi Hotel, auctions, and a summer garden party." Many other events are still to be announced.

The Liverpool Hackney Cab drivers, in continuing their long association with the School, would also bear stickers in their cabs and hand out appeal leaflets.

The School swiftly realised how many friends and supporters it has, as within six weeks of the launch of the appeal over a £$^1/_4$ million had been raised.

As we go to press, there have been numerous acts of generosity from individuals. Local plumber Sam Feeney, for example, is a long-time supporter of the Charity. After he heard the news of the appeal, he gave up his Christmas Day to dress up as Santa Claus and stride through the streets of Liverpool from 7am to 7pm with a collection box on behalf of the Fund. He first came into contact with the School 30 years earlier when he carried out repair work on the School's plumbing and has been raising money ever since.

The Lady Pilkington D.L., Bicentennial Appeal President, with children at Wavertree May 1990 (Elsam, Mann and Cooper).

255

Local broadcaster and children's author, Brian Jacques, is also closely involved. Mr Jacques, as a friend and patron, has actively supported the School for many years, and through the medium of his programme on BBC Radio Merseyside has done much to draw the attention of his listeners to the role played by the School. Through his co-ordination of fund-raising efforts, in conjunction with the Variety Club of Great Britain, Mr Jacques presented a specially adapted Sunshine Coach to the School shortly after the Appeal had been launched.

At the rear courtyard of the School, North West Water Authority have begun to construct a large water feature for the enjoyment and therapeutic use of the children. It is being entirely funded by the North West Water Authority, who are also carrying out the removal and re-design of the Chapel column section referred to earlier. It is this feature which will be unveiled by Her Majesty the Queen on her visit to the School. This author is proud to see his re-discovery used in such a way to contribute to the enjoyment of the children and act as a lasting tribute to the work carried out over the last 200 years.

Complacency at the School is rare. "There is much to be done," explained John Smyth. "We need to extend and further adapt the buildings, acquire new equipment and employ specialist staff. For as long as there is a need for such a service the School will aim to continue to be pre-eminent in the education of visually impaired children with additional handicaps and severe learning difficulties".

The Headmaster revealed the most basic problems facing some of the children.

"We want to teach our children a rhythm for living. Some of them need to be taught to wake up in the morning and to go to bed at night. Most children learn basic social skills by copying what they see, but you can't do that when you're blind. We want our children to go home able to dress themselves, eat properly, sleep properly."

For many of the children even these tasks are insurmountable and a favourable pupil-teacher ratio is essential. The success of the Appeal will ensure such measures are maintained. The bicentennial year is to be an intensely busy one with significant change and progress.

Progress there has been. Progress from the day when pupil Henry Arnold aged 17, secured the position of organist at Halsall Church in 1797,

256

Wavertree 1991: main entrance (Elsam, Mann and Cooper).

Wavertree 1991: Clifton House (Elsam, Mann and Cooper).

Wavertree 1991: McGregor Hall (Elsam, Mann and Cooper).

Wavertree 1991: the Replica Gates (Elsam, Mann and Cooper).

Wavertree 1991 (Elsam, Mann and Cooper).

to a day almost two hundred years later when ex-pupil Gillian Wake received a University Honours Degree and later became a Probation Officer.

As in the eighteenth century, so in the late twentieth century do voluntary efforts and voluntary organisations play their part and continue to show the way forward. We look to the future with optimism, but also look to the day when children no longer bear a handicap and this School can close, its role fulfilled.

Appendix 1
THE SCHOOL ARCHIVE

The archive at the School is extensive and holds books and documents dating from 1773 to the present. The majority of the items are in good condition, which is surprising given the number of moves of location they have suffered. In recent years they have been sorted, covered, and placed into boxes for future protection by the Secretary/Bursar, Mr Tom Milburn, to whom much credit must go for their present survival. (Although it must be said that many of his predecessors must have been keen to see their preservation too!)

During the summer of 1989, Mr Milburn's work was further enhanced by myself and Mark Nelson B.A.(Hons.) of the University of Liverpool, who compiled a thorough and detailed index with comprehensive referencing.

A very brief summary of the holdings are listed below:

1. Annual Reports 1793-present
2. Management Committee Minute Books 1793-present
3. Management Committee Waste Minute Books 1823-1958
4. Admissions Registers 1791-present
5. Visitors Report Books 1827-1899
6. Register of Legacies 1851-present
7. Medical Officer Report Books 1897-1927
8. Various Treasurers Books 1794-present
9. *An Address* Publicity Booklets 1808 & 1811
10. School Rules 1869 & 1893
11. *Essay on Blindness* – D. Diderot (English translation 1773)
12. *Education and Employment of the Blind* – Armitage (1871)
13. Various Chapel Books and Documents 1804-1927

Other holdings include various documents, journals, correspondence, statistical lists, newspaper cuttings, printed books and papers, sketches, plans, maps, antiquarian prints and dozens of photographs (several by Messrs. Stewart Bale). The Archive has recently benefited from the research required for the writing of this Book, as photocopies of documents relating to the School found elsewhere have been lodged.

The Archive is undoubtedly of great value to the social, educational, medical and family historian.

Appendix 2
RUSHTON'S LETTER

The following letter was written by Edward Rushton in 1790. Together with a second letter which contained his outline of an institution, it was intended for circulation around Liverpool Society and publication in the local press. His aim was to draw attention to the plight of the blind and gain support for his ideas (see chapter 2).

"Among the various calamities by which poor human nature is buffeted, perhaps there is not one which, upon close investigation, would be found more truly deplorable that that of the loss of sight. He who is in the full possession of this cheering sense, can have but a very inadequate idea of of the state of mind which is generally produced by its total privation. The rays of light may, indeed, for a time be voluntarily excluded, and thus the gloominess of the blind be, in some degree felt; but the mind, conscious that such an exclusion depends upon the will, cannot, on this account, be very materially interested. A human being, by the command of a Despot might be entombed in a dungeon dark as the eyeless socket, yet, even here, the consciousness of still possessing sight, and the hopes of being one day or other enabled to enjoy it, would lift him far above the dreary sensations of irrecoverable blindness;sensations which those who are blessed with vision cannot imagine, nor those who are bereft of it justly describe. The long night of the poor Greenlander is, undoubtedly, gloomy, but during that period, the Aurora Borealis, the Moon and the stars are so extremely luminous as to afford in some degree a compensation for his loss; besides, he is constantly cheered with a certainty of the return of the great lamp. Not so the sightless being! His loss has no compensation, his long, long night no brightness; nor can his mind be cheered with the expectations of returning light, for that he knows to be impossible, so that even Hope, the wretch's kindest friend, is to him, in this instance, utterly denied. How piteous then is blindness! The face of the country, with all its various beauties; the town, with its docks, piers, and stately edifices; the aspects of his friends, of his dearest relatives, of his partner and his prattling offspring, are all to him a blank – are all involved in a mass of thick black clouds, which no summer's heat can dissolve, nor wintry storms disperse. How deplorable then is such an existence! Even with a competence, how cheerless! But with indigence, how dreadful!"

Appendix 3
CHRISTIE'S LETTER

This letter was written by John Christie to Edward Alanson, the Surgeon, appealing for his help and support for the plans drawn by Rushton and himself (see chapter 2).

Liverpool,
September 22nd 1790

"Sir,

The loss of sight, particularly to those who well remember the enjoyment of it, is perhaps the most severe calamity that can befall a human being; but if to this calamity be added pecuniary distress, and to both, the consciousness of being burdensome to parents, to relations, or to friends, these united form such a load of woe as cannot be bourne by any feeling mind without those painful sensations of which words can convey but an inadequate idea. To alleviate those sensations, to lighten that burden, under which, I am persuaded, many of my fellow unfortunates at this moment labour, has lately employed my attention, and with all due deference to better judgements, I humbly think I have hit upon an expedient, which by enabling the indigent blind to procure, by their own exertions, a comfortable maintenance, would in a great measure, produce the above desirable effects. The profession of music is almost the only one in which the blind have any tolerable probability of succeeding; but as penury is too often the attendant upon blindness, it has happened not infrequently, that people in this unfortunate situation have been prevented from acquiring a knowledge of music by the inability of themselves of their connections to defray the necessary expenses of instruction. (This you well know, Sir, was exactly our case till the hand of benevolence enabled us to proceed.) To afford, therefore, a gratuitous instruction upon the harpsichord, violin etc. to the indigent blind of both sexes in and about Liverpool, is, in a few brief words, the outline of my plan. Let a few leading gentlemen give a sanction to the undertaking, for without this I fear nothing can be done. Let a room be appropriated to this use in some one of our public buildings; let a small subscription be obtained for the purpose of procuring a few necessary instruments, and the business in a great measure would be effected.

My brother and I have not a doubt but many more, who follow the profession of music, would, with pleasure, attend at certain stated periods in order to instruct those pupils only whom the voice of the subscribers should have regularly admitted; and thus, Sir, at a moderate expense, the helpless and broken-spirited would be enabled to struggle through a dark existence, with some degree of comfort to themselves, and with real satisfaction to the benevolent. Liverpool is already earmarked for the number of its humane institutions, and as it is the intention of such institutions to assist, protect, and cheer the wretched, surely something of this nature might be established for an unfortunate description of people, who, with a will to be industrious, are, by bodily misfortune, and the chilling hand of poverty, too often prevented from being so.

I am, your servant
John Christie

N.B. Those who contribute their time and attention, in order to instruct the pupils of the above institution, must necessarily be considered as subscribers."

Appendix 4
'A PLAN FOR AFFORDING RELIEF TO THE INDIGENT BLIND'

Henry Dannett drew up the following announcement in consequence of the decisions made at the second meeting at his house in October 1790. The entire document was placed in *Williamson's Liverpool Advertiser* on Monday 22 November 1790 (see chapter 2).

"They, who have always enjoyed the invaluable blessing of sight, can understand the greatness of its loss only by reflection: And ; et, it may easily be imagined, that the condition of blindness, even when accompanied with all the comforts and conveniences of affluence, is truly melancholy; how severe then must be its distresses, when associated with POVERTY!

But even this double misfortune, like all other calamities which befall our nature, admits of alleviation; it is the duty therefore, of all who can, to alleviate it; for it is the duty of all to do all possible good:– not to mention the sublime pleasure which will result to the mind from gratifying its benevolence towards this unfortunate and neglected class of our fellow-creatures.

Three objects are to be aimed at in affording relief to the blind poor:

First, To furnish them with some employment, which may prevent them from being burdens to *their family and the community*, or at least, render them less burdensome:

And, *Secondly*, That the employment be such, as gently to engage the mind without fatiguing it, and by diverting the attention of the blind from their unhappy lot, make them less a burden to *themselves*.

And, *Lastly*, that they be supplied with such a portion of religious knowledge, as may reconcile them to their situation, and teach them to be easy and contented;- and to this end, that they may be made acquainted with those parts of the Christian scheme in particular, which are best adapted to afford them consolation.

To answer these three views, a school will be opened, in which they will be instructed in music, that they may be enabled to become organists, and to teach music, if they are found capable of learning it; and all will be taught to make nets, to knot fringe etc.- And lastly they will be taught their prayers, and instructed in the doctrines and duties of Christianity every Saturday.

As many may be disqualified by age, infirmity, etc from learning any of these arts, or from receiving any benefit from the institution, – it is proposed, to afford them some pecuniary assistance; in the distribution of which, attention will be paid to the moral character of the objects.

When the pupils have learnt their respective arts, and begin to practice them, and earn money – it is intended that the blind shall enter into an association, for the relief of themselves and families, when disabled by sickness and age, in the nature of the MARINE SOCIETY, and the FRIENDLY SOCIETIES, which are found so useful in various parts of the kingdom, and from all which associations they are at present excluded.

Benefactions for the support of this CHARITY will be received at Mr. CRANE's, and Mr. GORE's."

APPENDIX 5
SOME PARTICULARS RELATIVE TO A PLAN, ETC.

A week after Dannett's published announcement (appendix 3), he then drew up 'Some Particulars Relative to a Plan, etc.' as an addendum to the published Plan. This was dated 1 December 1790 and appeared in the form of a printed circular combining both the Plan itself and the 'Particulars' shown below.

I.   That an advertisement be put into the Liverpool papers to call the indigent Blind together,to ask which of them will accept the offer, and to distribute them into classes of learners of music, learners of mechanical arts, and such as are disqualified for any art.

II.   That several rooms be engaged; one for the Blind instructed in music, the rest for those who are taught the other arts.

III.   That those be selected who are likely to learn music in such a degree, as may qualify them to become organists, and to teach music.

IV.   That spinets be hired during one quarter,proportional to the number taught, for them to practice upon at their own houses, and a harpsicord (sic) be bought for the room in which they are taught;- after the first quarter, that spinets be purchased for as many as are found capable of making a proficiency, to be lent them till they have learnt their art, and then to be given them.

V.   That when they are thoroughly instructed in music, and begin to gain a livelihood by it, they have a suit of clothes and decent linen given them.

VI.   That some person, who lives in the same family with the Blind, be taught to write and read music.

VII.   That the masters, who are so generous as to offer their labour gratis, be paid something for their trouble; and it is hoped that that pay will increase, when the good effects of the institution are seen.

VIII.   That the musical pupils be likewise taught some mechanical employment, as an agreeable variety, and that they may acquire something during the time they are learning music.

IX.   That a certain number of Blind learn church music, that they may be engaged and recompensed as singers at St.John's Church; and that at the end of the first two years, a sermon be preached, and continued annually, for the support of the charity:-

when the blind musicians and singers will display to their benefactors, the public, their musical proficiency.

X.   That after the first half year there be a public exhibition of all the Blind employed in their several mechanic operations, and afterwards, that this exhibition be annual; and at the same time a collection be made for the ASSOCIATION BOX mentioned in art.xiv – The first exhibition to be on Monday June 13th, and to continue the following fortnight.

XI.   That the Blind be supplied with work by the managers of the institution; who are to pay to each blind artificer the whole gains arising from his labour.

XII.   That the most diligent receive rewards, as encouragement, such as clothes, etc.

XIII.   That prayers be composed for the use of the blind, adapted to their peculiar situation; that they be taught these prayers and their duty every Saturday; and on Sunday, that those of the establishment go to St.John's, where seats will be provided for them; and those who dissent from it, go in a body to their respective places of public worship.

XIV.   That after learning their trades six months, the Blind be incorporated in to a society each of whom is to contribute two-pence weekly from his gains, as a provision for himself in old age or sickness; that he may,when 60 years old, or disabled by disease, receive three or four shillings weekly, in proportion as the Association Box will afford. To increase this fund for age and infirmity, Gentlemen will be solicited to become members of this BLIND FRIENDLY SOCIETY; which, it is hoped, will exhibit a model to shame into frugality, industry, and prudence, those lazy poor, who enjoy the sense of seeing, and the use of all their organs in full perfection, and yet choose meanly to live on common alms.

XV.   That an annual report be made of the expenditure of the money, and the good effected during the year; and that when the Institution is established and found beneficial, the plan when corrected, and amended by experience, be published, to produce imitation in other places.

XVI.   That the money collected be lodged in a bank, secured to the public by appointing Trustees.

From the whole it will be seen, that the Establishment is intended to afford relief to all;- to the youngest, as soon as they can learn music, which may perhaps be at about nine years of age;- to the middle-aged, by teaching them some art by which to entertain their minds, and to gain an honest living;- and to the old who are unable to learn anything, by affording them some assistance in clothes, money, etc. – and that one object of this Institution is, to attend to the morals of the blind of all ages, especially the young.

Liverpool
December 1st 1790.

H. DANNETT.

Appendix 6
THE SCHOOL OF INSTRUCTION FOR THE INDIGENT BLIND

On 29 December 1790, Reverend Dannett submitted the following announcement, regarding the opening of the new School, to *Williamsons' Advertiser*, which appeared on 3 January 1791 (see chapter 2).

THE SCHOOL OF INSTRUCTION FOR THE INDIGENT BLIND
Will be opened the second week in January,
in Commutation Row

At which place there will be an Exhibition of the BLIND, employed in the several Mechanic Arts, on Monday the 11th of July, and the following days of the same week, to show to the public the proficiency they have made. – Books will be left with Mr.Jones, Mr.Billinge, Mr.Crane, Mr.Preston and Mr.Gore, containing a list of the subscribers, with the sums subscribed. – Nearly £600 have already been given by liberal town to execute the plan. – The money received has been placed in the bank of Messrs. Caldwell and Smyth, who are generous enough to allow the Charity five percent. – Eighty-one blind Objects have given in their names. – The Mayor of the present year has obligingly consented to be the President of this new Charity. – The Arts, to which they are thought adequate, are the winding of Cotton, the spinning of Worsted, the knitting of worsted Stockings, the making of Whip-lashes, the winding of Worsted into balls and handles for the hosiers, the picking of Oakum, the making of Cabbage nets, Net caps, etc. the lining of Hats, Music, etc. – After the experiments have been made, the most lucrative and pleasant of these employments will be selected.

It may be proper to answer the weightiest objections, which have been made to the Plan:
1. It has been said "This institution will deprive the Blind of the benefit of Etherington's Charity"(*) – The managers of that Charity have been applied to and say it will not: – indeed their printed inquiries sent from Christs' Hospital plainly speak the same language to every unprejudiced reader's understanding. 2. "We shall have our streets filled with Blind Fiddlers". – Violins are excluded. 3. "The Blind are not equal to any of these Arts." – In Manchester, blind women wind cotton and line hats; in Paris, the blind make whips and whip-lashes, spin, weave nets, learn music so as to excel, etc. And what is done in Manchester and Paris, it is hoped, is practicable in Liverpool.

Dec. 29, 1790   HENRY DANNETT.

* 'Etherington's' Charity is actually the Charity founded by the Revd. William Hetherington, a governor of Christ's Hospital, London. In 1774, in the hope that his example would be followed, he gave £20,000 to enable the Governors to pay annuities of £10 each to 50 aged blind persons.

267

Appendix 7
QUALIFICATIONS, REQUISITE IN THE GOVERNOR OF THE BLIND ASYLUM

Extract from the Management Committee Minute Book, 27 August 1799.

Viz:
1. He must have an unexceptionable character for Integrity, Sobriety and Diligence; be exemplary in his conduct; - of gentle manners; - and good temper.
2. He must write a fair hand; - and have a competent knowledge of arithmetic.
3. It is desirable that he should be a married man and that his wife should be qualified to act as Matron; and that no young children should live with them.
4. He will be expected to give security for the due appropriation of all monies, goods, etc. committed to him.

Employments, viz:
1. He will be required to devote the *whole* of his time to the interests of the Institution and particularly to rise early in the morning, so as to see that the Blind attend and enter upon their respective employments at the stated hours.
2. He will have to keep a Day Book, Ledger, Book of Wages, and such other Books as may be found necessary; likewise an Absentee Book, and to make a deduction of 2d per hour for absence, unless for reasons to be approved of by the Committee.
3. He shall enter in the Books to be prepared for that purpose the different articles of stock, weekly, as they are manufactured.
4. We shall insist upon the men and boys coming clean and decently cloathed to the Asylum.
5. He shall take an account of all the stock, once a quarter, and lay it before the Committee at their Quarterly Meetings in January, April, July and October.
6. He shall collect all outstanding Bills once a quarter.
7. He shall attend in the Sale Room to sell the goods, taking all the pains he can to accommodate the Customers of the Asylum to their satisfaction; and behaving both to them and the strangers who may come in to see the Blind at work with the greatest civility and attention.
8. He shall buy in all necessary materials, if thereto required, first consulting some of the Committee skilled in the article wanted, till he shall have gained experience of his own.
9. He shall attend Church with the Blind Men every Sunday morning and evening, take down the names of the Absentees, and give in the same to the Committee at each monthly meeting.
10. He shall hear the men repeat their collects every Saturday when the visitors do not attend.
11. He shall record in a Book, to be called the Visitor's Book, every instance of misconduct which may merit the notice of the Visitors or Committee.
12. He shall deliver previous notices of each monthly or other meeting to the President, Committee etc.

13. He shall on no account receive from strangers or visitors of the Asylum any gratuity whatever, on pain of dismission. Nor suffer any gratuity to be received by the Blind or any other person.
14. He shall read the Rules of the Asylum both to the Men and Women, on the first Tuesday in every month; and shall request one or more of the Committee to attend whilst he reads them.
15. He will be expected to attend the Treasurer, President, or other officers of the Institution, with his accounts at their own Houses, whenever they require it.
16. He will be expected, as often as occasion may require it, to take out and deliver goods sold and to call for payment thereof.

The Matron's Duty

1. To overlook all the Women, instruct the Spinners etc., reel their yarn, prepare their flax, and spin herself when she is not otherwise necessarily employed.
2. To note any instance of irregular attendance, idleness, or misconduct amongst the Women in a Book to be called the Visitor's Book.
3. When the Governor is abroad on the business of the Asylum, she is to attend the Sale Room.
4. To take an account of the flax to be spun in the next week, and of the weight of yarn spun during the past week.
5. To hear the Women repeat their collects every Saturday, unless they have before repeated them to one of the Visitors.
6. She shall take no fee or reward from any visitant of the Asylum on pain of dismission, nor suffer any to be received by the Blind or by any other person.
7. To attend the Women to church every Sunday morning and evening, and to keep an account of all absentees (except those who are engaged as singers at some of the other churches) which account she is to give in to the Committee at every regular meeting.
8. To attend particularly to the cleanliness of the Women and of the House.

Appendix 8
EXTRACTS FROM THE RULES of the
SCHOOL FOR THE BLIND, 1805

The pupils when they are first sent to the School are to be clothed, and are to be afterwards provided with necessaries at the expense of their friends. The Committee will undertake to procure them in those cases where the friends of the pupils find it more convenient.

From the first of April, to the first of October, the Pupils are required to be at the School, from 6 in the morning, until 6 in the evening; from 8 to 9 being allowed for breakfast, and from 12 to 1 for dinner.

From the first of October, to the first of April, they are required to attend at the School from 8 in the morning, one hour being allowed for dinner, and leave at half past 5 o'clock.

The female pupils leave the School at 5 in the evening, during the whole of the year.

The pupils assemble every morning and evening to join in public prayer; the names of those who are absent, are noted in a book kept for that purpose.

The pupils regularly attend both parts of the Sunday, at some place of public worship. Those who belong to the establishment, assemble at the School every morning and afternoon, a quarter of an hour before service time, and accompany the Superintendent and Matron to church.

The pupils who do not belong to the establishment are required to bring certificates of their regular attendance at their respective places of worship, from the ministers who officiate at them.

The pupils attend at the School on a Sunday evening, in order to join in public prayer, and to be examined in the catechism.

Strangers who visit the School are requested to observe, that neither the Superintendent, Matron, nor any of the pupils are permitted, on pain of Expulsion, to receive Money, or any other Gratuity. The Superintendent is authorised to receive Benefactions and Annual Subscriptions; and Boxes are provided for the reception of occasional Donations.

Instances of Irregularity which take place in the conduct of the pupils, are represented to the visitors or committee, who adopt whatever measures they may think necessary to prevent their recurrence. In those few cases where practices have been detected, of a nature which it was apprehended might prove injurious to the morals of the rest, the committee have thought it proper to return the parties offending to their friends.

CLOTHING

FOR MEN AND BOYS.

Top Coat,
Suit of Clothes and Hat for
    Sundays,
Do. or Jacket and Trousers,
    and Hat to work in,
Four Shirts,
Four Pairs of Stockings,
Two Pairs of Shoes,
White Cravat,
Two coloured Cravats,
Three Pocket Handkerchiefs,
Two Night Caps

FOR WOMEN AND GIRLS.

A Cloak or a Top Coat,
A Gown, Two Bedgowns,
Two Skirts or Upper Coats,
Two Flannel Under Coats,
Four Shifts,
Four Pairs of Stockings,
Six Caps,
Two Shawls,
Three Pocket Handkerchiefs,
Two Bonnets,
Two Pairs of Shoes,
Two Night Caps.

A LIST of THE NUMBER OF PUPILS ADMITTED into the SCHOOL FOR THE BLIND

From its Commencement, January 10, 1791 to December 31, 1810

With a statement of the circumstances under which they appear to have been totally or partially deprived of sight.

N.B. the partially Blind had lost their Sight to all useful purposes.

BLIND	TOTALLY,	PARTIALLY,	TOTAL
From their birth	5	24	19
In consequence of small pox	78	12	90
inflammation	56	21	77
cataracts	9	24	33
external injury	12	7	19
gutta serena	18	9	27
imperfect organization	1	4	5
Lost their sight at sea	8	1	9
by gradual decay	3	0	3
after fever	3	0	3
measles	0	2	2
hooping cough	1	0	1
convulsions	1	2	3
from causes not mentioned, or imperfectly described in the certificates,	5	10	15
	214	97	311

Of which, only 71 have belonged to the Parish of Liverpool, and 240 to other parts of the United Kingdom.

From its Commencement, January 10, 1791 to December 31, 1846:

BLIND	TOTALLY,	PARTIALLY,	TOTAL
From their birth	61	40	101
In consequence of small pox	188	44	232
inflammation	238	155	393
cataracts	44	90	134
external injury	80	39	119

defect in optic nerve	68	58	126
amaurosis	6	4	10
imperfect organization	3	10	13
Lost their sight at sea	8	1	9
by gradual decay	5	1	6
after fever	10	2	12
measles	6	5	11
convulsions	2	3	5
from causes not mentioned, or imperfectly described in the certificates,	16	13	29
	735	465	1200

Of which, 194 have belonged to the Parish of Liverpool, 259 to other Parishes in the County of Lancaster, and 747 to other parts of the United Kingdom.

Note: The above statistics have been taken from the Annual Reports of 1811 and 1847, and are reprinted in their original format.

Appendix 10
ODE TO SAMUEL GOODACRE AND OTHERS

The *Ode to Samuel Goodacre* was written in reply to the events taking place at the School and in the Committee Room during 1869 (see chapter Seven). It was printed in *The Porcupine*, a Liverpool satirical newspaper of the later nineteenth century. Below is the full extract as it appeared on 31 July 1869 (Vol. II, 1869-70, p. 168). Names in capitals were committee men (except Twining).

BRAVO GOODACRE!

Proper Undertaker
To bury old abuses,
And to its proper uses
See applied the money paid by Christians, good and kind,
To lighten the dark sorrows of the blind.
That small gross estimate has proved a poser
The gross mismanagers admit the *grocer*
(in accents somewhat snivelling and nervous)
Has used his eyes to do the *blind* good service.
The "Giant-killing Jack" did some bean-stalking;
You – like him – o'er "one Bean" have been walking,
And single-handed, fighting for the right
Against the odds of wrathful *Albion's* might.
Within those meshes, thinking you were caught,
Crippled and helpless, chivalrous McNAUGHT
(A query here crops up, and that is, ought he
In future for this deed be called McNAUGHTY?)
Moved, sticking to you like a home-made blister
(Most kindly seconded by Mister LISTER).
That, not that he bore the slightest animosity,
Still for a crime of such extreme atrocity
As finding out abuses, and then trying
To let the public know them, thus defying
The power of the committee (better men sure
The world could not produce),
DESERVED A "VOTE OF CENSURE."
                As (here's a chance for simile bucolic)
When in the clovered fields the gay sheep frolic
Where'er the largest mutton choose to lead,
The smaller follow him with reckless speed.
So the committee – as like sheep they ought -
Followed their battering-ram, the great McNaught.

Combined in numbers 'gainst the single man,
The great M.D. had brought beneath his ban!
The blushing books disgraced, the vote received,
And truth's detractors felt themselves relieved,
As criminals must on finding they're reprieved.
Too soon they had worse cause to feel aggrieved.
For you were not alone, sir, oh! dear, no!
That sturdy friend of truth and humbug's bitter foe,*
Arm'd with the poison that all evil kills,
Brave printer's ink! imbued his daring quills,
      Came boldly out,
      Declaring he'd no doubt
You were correct in all you said and did,
And more than hinted, "those who wish things hid
From public view are slightly injudicious,
Concealment being at the least suspicious."
How patiently you put up with the snubs
Of prating MINSHULL, BOWEN, DALE – the scrubs!
The Treasurer – too, self thought first of sages,
Searcher of baskets, inspector of cabages –
Slippery CRUTTENDEN, and LISTER dull,
JONES (CHARLTON), RICKARBY, AND F.S. HULL;
And MILLS, in language neat, well set and smooth,
Who undertook to prove truth is not truth;
"Dundreary" FISHER, full of grand pretence,
Mistaking naturally sound for sense,
So strongly armed in honesty, a laugh
Was all they got in answer to their chaff!
On all sides telling you that you were bowl'd out,
And, 'stead of selling them, were fairly sold out.
But truthful figures granted you their aid –
Mainsprings of commerce, life of honest trade.
No sophist with *their* truth can ever tamper –
No books "concocted" can their power hamper.
They proved what should have been the honest price
Of raisins, currants, sugar, starch, and rice;
Proved that a manager was scarcely thrifty
Who *sixty shillings* paid instead of *fifty*!
Or doubling forty – yes, and rather more–
'Stead of those figures chalks up eighty-four!
'Twould put even COURTENAY in no small fix
To prove that *thirty-five's* not less than *sixty-six*.
That adding *twenty-five* to *twenty-one*
Is strictly honest – yet this has been done;
Aye, and much more: blind leaders of the blind!
You great committee men! good, bland, and kind
Each to the other, through this wretched jobbery,
(Another word *would* rhyme) – princes of snobbery!

275

Proposing votes of thanks one to the other,
After your vain endeavours first to smother
The publication of the "cooked" accounts,
The awful difference in the paid amounts
By which the charity's fair funds have dwindled,
And the poor blind been honourably swindled!
Is that word strong? a tramp called a thief,
Last week, for stealing *one poor pound of beef.***
Can we a *crime of retail* robbery make,
But when *wholesale is't only a mistake*?
We rather think it must be pretty clear,
Loss upon loss has followed year by year,
And looming in the future we discern
Some strange distrust attached to a concern
So vilely managed. Therefore most painstaking
Of past or present chairmen, Mr. AIKEN,
Up to all dodges, known for putting down
All whose opinions are not quite your own;
When will you lend the injured blind your aid?
Pray, when commence mendicity's crusade?
When not on head, but held in hand your hat,
You'll start a begging sir? pray, answer that.
You had (not from presentiment, let's kindly hope)
A strange antipathy to soap and rope,
For one who boasts he does things with clean hands
You surely cannot fear Manilla strands
May, like the doctors, most unseemly vote
Stop yours: as that was hoped, GOODACRE'S – throat?
LISTER, THOU NOBLE AUDITOR,
By thine own circle ever hail'd with Laudator,
Because up fortune's ladder you're a mounter,
Should *counters* be despised by a *discounter*?
Do those who stand behind such, in a bank –
Say "BARNED'S", or the "ROYAL", take first rank
As worthy citizens and honest men?
Whence all this "buncombe" coming from you, then
About a GROCER, whence this dolorous whining?
Did you ne'er hear, pray, tell us, sir, of TWINING? #
He, like GOODACRE, was a grocer bold,
He dealt, like him, in teas – like you, in gold,
With this great difference – throughout the land
The *grocer*, as the *banker*, could command
In either *trade*, for both are *trades* – don't wince!
Respect alike from peasant, peer, and prince!
Just take this hint, remember, sir, from hence,
An honest, erring man may give offence.
He's not the first who, having do so, sends
A friendly PARRATT offering amends,

In *private* whispered, by another's tongue,
As fit atonement for a *public* wrong.
   TO ALL CONCERNED, -
  Gents, don't you think it best,
Now that GOODACRE'S right, must be confessed
To do him tardy justice? To be brief,
To tear from out your books that spiteful leaf,
Which bears a censure, not on him, but you!
In every heart, that's manly, just, and true?
We give this hint in genuine sincerity –
Bethink you something's due, friends, to posterity?
It won't be pleasant if, in future ages,
Some bookworm deeply pouring o'er its pages,
Should cry "Good Lord! in those degenerate times!
Plain honesty was held the worst of crimes.
For dealing with it what a piteous case!
A whole committee doomed to deep disgrace.
One of their members who, as here I find,
Ruined himself to benefit the blind!"
N.B. – He was not ruined, but we've no doubt history
Will add that fiction to enhance the mystery.
One question more we'll ask of MISTER LISTER,
(In cricket parlance, one he'll find a twister,)
As Auditor, now will you, if you can, sir,
To this plain question give as plain an answer,
Through twenty years – a most stupendous Innings –
WHO PAID THE LOSSES, AND WHO KEEPS THE WINNINGS?

* *The Porcupine*
** CON. What was the difference in the kitchen department of the Manchester and the
Liverpool Blind Schools?
   ANS. In Manchester the meat was boned outside. In Liverpool it was boned in.
\# When the great run on the London banks was made almost universally, that of Twining,
the grocer and banker, was one among the few that met all claims.

The following admirable skit upon the aristocratic failures, who had hitherto looked
down upon Twining as a grocer as well as banker, was, at the time, universally read and
believed in:-

   "Be it known to all present throughout the broad land,
   That names well with callings agree;
       So *Twining*, the *banker*, who thrives in the Strand,
   Would be whining, if not for his T."

Appendix 11
SIGHTLESS SCHOLARS

The following article is taken from *The Liverpool Review* of 6 May 1887, and reveals a visitor's impression of the Hardman Street School.

"The 'Blind School', as it is popularly called, if not as old as Liverpool itself, is a good deal older than what may be described as modern Liverpool, that is to say the part of the city which has been built within the last three quarters of a century. It dates, in fact, from 1791, though it was not incorporated by Act of Parliament until 1829.

On entering the school building from Hardman Street, I found myself in a sort of bazaar, for the sale of fancy work such as mats, baskets, etc. Leaving this under the guidance of Captain Pearson, the obliging Superintendent, we crossed a circular hall lighted by stained glass oriel windows of scriptural subjects, and entered a room containing an organ, and arranged with seats for concerts which take place on the second and fourth Tuesday in each month, the performers being the pupils of the institution. They were practicing when we entered, seated opposite to each other in rows three or four deep on a platform before the organ, and from their appearance evidently found much pleasure in their occupation.

Leaving the concert room and crossing the hall again we entered the practicing rooms, a couple of small rooms with two pianos in each. In one of these a boy was seated at one of the instruments who appeared to be in his musical novitiate. Before him was a folding screen with notes and scales upon it in relief so that their shape could be felt by passing the hand over them. He looked, I thought, rather a melancholy figure in his solitude, an impression which his very subdued manner was certainly calculated to strengthen. On this point it may be remarked that blind people always give one the idea of being much more depressed in manner than deaf and dumb people for instance.

This was still more noticeable in the boys' schoolroom, where I was handed over to the care of Mr George Terry, the Schoolmaster. The boys here, who ranged in age, I should think, from about nine to fourteen, were in rather striking contrast to those of an ordinary school. There was no whispering, or pushing, or pinching, but a general apathetic listlessness both of manner and expression, as if the poor little fellows felt that they had no interest in life and didn't want to have any. That this was a misleading first impression, however, was shown by the way their faces brightened up when they were spoken to and invited to display their accomplishment.

'Do you find much difficulty in the work of teaching?' I asked Mr. Terry, who is a shrewd looking middle aged gentleman, with a prompt decisive manner and tone, yet withal very kindly in his way of speaking to and dealing with his pupils.

'It's just the same as with boys who have their sight,' he said. 'A matter of native intelligence. Some are brighter than others, and it requires a very brief observation to find out which are the dull and which the smart ones. That boy, for instance, has only been here a couple of months, but I'm afraid it will be impossible to make much of him.'

Here he pointed to a little fellow siting by himself whose vacuous expression, even without the monotonous movement of his head from side to side, was sufficient to show that he was not naturally by any means a bright subject. The fact was presently demonstrated by putting this boy and another of the same age to read from a book in raised type.

Both lads had been in the Institution the same time, two months, but while one could spell out words, the other was not yet even within sight of this rudimentary stage.

'Is all your teaching done with raised letters?'

'No; that is only for beginners. For more advanced pupils we use the Braille system, a French invention introduced about 14 years ago. Under this, each letter of the alphabet and certain grammalogues are represented by dots; 'a', by one dot, 'b', by two dots one under the other, 'c', by two dots in a line, 'd', by three dots in a right angle, and so on.'

Here Mr Terry handed to one of the pupils a peculiar sort of small drawing board, a number of which were lying about, and of which this is a rough sketch; (see illustration)

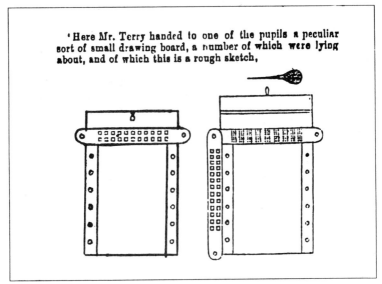

'Here Mr. Terry handed to one of the pupils a peculiar sort of small drawing board, a number of which were lying about, and of which this is a rough sketch,

A modified form of this early Braille writer is still sold today by the R.N.I.B.

one representing the board shut and ready for use and the second open. The double flap at the top which shuts down with a catch is to hold the paper to be written upon – or rather punched. The brass bar at the top is slightly perforated with a double row of dots, 25 squares containing six dots in each row! This is covered by the paper and over the paper is laid and fastened down another brass bar perforated with square holes, each of these being over one of the groups of six dots. The boy took the prepared board, and with a small punch began from right to left – the reverse way of ordinary writing but quite as rapidly – produced the sentence – 'Honour thy father and thy mother, that thy days may be long in the land which the Lord thy God giveth thee'. That is to say by punching from right to left through the square holes, he produced, in proper order on the reverse side of the paper, to be read by touch from left to right, the series of dots, which represented the above sentence, and in the same way he afterwards produced the alphabet, and grammalogues used in its construction.

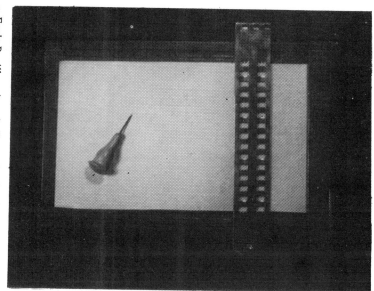

a. Early Braille writer similar to the sketch of 1887, held in the School Archive.

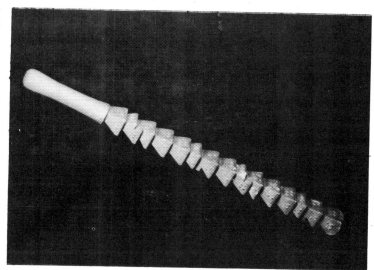

b. Early Braille music notation modulator held in the School Archive invented by Dr A.G. Purchas of New Zealand.

'The great difference between the raised letters and the Braille system is,' said Mr. Terry, 'that the latter may be written as well as read as you have seen. Here for instance, is a collection of volumes, copies of standard authors, which have all been written by the pupils on the Braille system, and thus you see they are able to provide themselves with intellectual recreation.'

Here he indicated a pretty large cupboard containing a collection of volumes, in folio form. Among these were Scott's *'Lady of the Lake'*, *'Lord of the Isles'*, and *'Marmion'*; Aesops *'Fables'*, in three volumes; two volumes of miscellaneos English poetry and two volumes of prose; three volumes of arithmetic; *'Robinson Crusoe'*, in five volumes; a selection from *'Hymns Ancient and Modern'*; *'Dates in English History'*, two volumes; and Biographical miscellanies.

'The boys seem fond of Scott,' I observed.

'Yes, he is quite a favourite. I introduced his work to them when I came about nine years ago, and his popularity has never waned.'

At this point two of the boys at his request read alternately from *'Marmion'* and I followed them in the printed edition without detecting the slightest slip or omission, though I had reason to admire the appreciation they showed of the meaning of the author, which was quite different from the usual schoolboy sing song. A reading of another little fellow 12 years of age from the tenth chapter of St. Luke was equally successful, both as to correctness and accuracy of emphasis.

Taking down one of the volumes from the School library Mr Terry said, 'This is an exception to the general choice of subjects by the boys. What do you think it is?' On expressing my inability to guess he said, 'Euclid – or at least the beginning of it. That was begun by a boy named Alexander Anderson at 15 years of age, but he unfortunately died at 17 before he had got very far with it. An extraordinary boy he was. Always would puzzle everything out for himself without asking anybody, even if he had to lie awake all night thinking it out.'

'An extraordinary boy indeed to grapple with Euclid when blind. The *pons asinorum* is too much for many boys who have their sight. How do you teach arithmetic?'

Here Mr Terry produced a flat zinc tray with raised sides about the size of an ordinary school slate. This was covered with a zinc plate perforated with octagonal holes in regular rows. The small space at the top was filled with type of a peculiar construction, bearing not a figure or a letter, but simply two dots. Placed in the hole so that the dots were on one side of the octagon they represented the figure 1, in another 2, in another 3, and so on. One of the boys placed the types in the holes to represent the numerals from 1 to 0 quite as rapidly as I could have written them. This was scarcely surprising, however, when I was told this boy was doing sums in interest.(*)

'What becomes of the children when they have passed through the School?' I asked.

'Most of them, return to their native places; only a small proportion of them belong to Liverpool. Some of them stay and learn a trade in our workshops, mat or basket making, or chair re-caning and then return with something like a trade in their fingers.'

'They are supported by their friends while here, I suppose?'

'Something has to be paid for them either by their friends or by the parish to which they belong, but not enough to support them. In the workshops for instance, they pay, or have paid for them, four shillings and sixpence per week for lodging and food, but that would scarcely keep them outside.'

'Do you think the Royal Commissioners who visited the Institution last year are likely to give favourable report of it?'

'They seemed very well satisfied with what they saw, and I am not at all afraid that we shall suffer by comparison.'

On afterward visiting the workshops, crossing to do so an asphalted courtyard where an awkward squad were giong through a sort of manual exercise with what looked like broom staves, I found both the basket and mat making industries in full activity. While the former occupation, however, seemed to be conducive to taciturnity, the latter made the workers much more talkative, and occasionally jocose.

The men employed in these two departments were mostly of full age, some of them having lost their sight by accident. In the mat making department their first occupation is to plait a fibrous material into bindings for doormats. Their next step is to be place alongside a more advanced worker at the same articles and follow his mode of manipulation by touch until able to imitate it and work independently.

Some were slow and some were quick at learning said the overseer of the room, but the average time taken was about two years. They did not employ the men after they had taught them a trade. They had to find work elsewhere. Some of them, he believed, were engaged at the Workshops for the Outdoor Blind in Cornwallis Street, and a good many more worked at home. He couldn't say what their average earnings were, but thought it was generally enough to live upon.

In conclusion it may be noted that the musical department of the School is in a very satisfactory condition. I find by the last annual report that during the year twelve musical pupils entered an open examination held by the Society of Professional Musicians. Of these ten entered for theoretical examination eight taking honours, one passed and seven being examined in practical (vocal) music, five obtained honours and one passed satisfactorily, Alexander C. McKenzie Mus. Doc. has also visited the School and expressed himself in terms of high commendation of its management and results under Mr. W. D. Hall and Miss Bishop.

(*) This apparatus was originally designed in 1720 by Nicholas Saunderson, the blind Professor of Mathematics at Cambridge University. It was featured in Diderot's *Essay on Blindness*, an original translation of which is in the School Archive (c. 1770).

Appendix 12
EXPERIENCES OF THE BLIND UPON THE RECOVERY OF SIGHT

The following unedited extract is an appendix taken from a short publication entitled *'Blindness: or, Some Thoughts for Sighted People (A Sermon Preached in the Chapel of the School for the Blind,* Liverpool, February 20th, 1887 with Appendices) by the Chaplain T.W.M. Lund'.

"The operation* by which Louisa Newson, a pupil in our Liverpool School for the Blind, received sight for the first time consciously, after nearly 20 years of blindness, was made in April 1884, by Mr. George Walker, Hon. Surgeon to the Institution.

The girl had never seen, having contracted in birth an ulceration of the cornea, which had resulted in such an adhesion of the iris as to render both eyes useless.

The left eye, however, gave some small promise of improvement under skilful treatment, and Mr. Walker proposed to make the attempt to give that eye sight enough to enable the girl to move about in the house without falling over pieces of furniture. At first, both Louisa and her Father absolutely refused to consent to the operation. She had been taught that her defect was the will of heaven, and not due to ignorance or defect or neglect in her earliest infancy, and she had come regard it as part of her religion to acquiesce in her deprivation. 'When I die, and go to the world above,' she said, 'where everything is beautiful, I shall be able to see there just the same as anyone else, so I don't care about seeing now.' At length, however, the reluctance of both Father and daughter was overcome, and the less desperate of her eyes was systematically attacked in a series of delicate and interesting operations, which ended in a gift of sight, sufficient to enable the patient to take her place with the rest of the sighted world.

A sympathetic friend in St. Paul's Eye and Ear Hospital, where the operations were made, wrote down Louisa's account of her own sensations at this critical time, and from this manuscript I am able to quote.

Her first feeling after the admission of light into the eye, was one of profound horror. She says, that when she became conscious of sight she was terror stricken by the sense of space, and felt 'as if she would fall down somewhere, but she did not know where.' At a later period, after more experience of the world, she described her feelings as that of 'one who looks over a precipice, and fears that she will be impelled to throw herself down.' She bitterly regretted having consented to the operation, and went through some agonies of emotion, over which it is perhaps better to draw a veil. It was at first almost feared that she would lose her reason. It will be enough to say in her own words that the world appeared so different from any conception she had formed of it, that *the twenty years she had lived suddenly became a void, and she began life afresh.*

At first, the appearance of every object gave her alarm, and she would deprecate its approach by putting out her hands to ward it off. Only when she had felt it with her hands, and ascertained its form and character through touch, as she had been used to do in the past, were her apprehensions allayed. Even after she had learnt to read, she would speak of a letter different in form from her old Moon Type, as 'what you call A or Z.'

Some of her earliest ideas of the objects she saw, are very interesting and entertaining.

A canary hopping about in its cage inspired her with intense fear. She compared it to a 'jumping lemon'. A man was described as 'a couple of sticks with a bundle on the top', while another with fair whiskers appeared, at a later period of her experience, 'to have his face wrapped in a sponge'.

She took the Woodside ferry-boat for 'a live creature, with two things dressed in red, sticking up in the middle, and all moving about together'.

A flat in full sail was, 'something like a church moving about in soapy water'.

The number of people she saw in the streets was a huge surprise, and she wondered 'where they all came from, and what they all found to do'.

As the sight grew stronger and she became more familiar with the novel world in which she found herself, the longing for her old experience waned, and she not only became reconciled to her new state, but found increasing satisfaction with all around her, which proved far better than her most sanguine hopes had dreamt of.

One of the St. Paul's Hospital Staff bore the highest testimony possible to the marvellous fidelity of the representation of the phenomenon of the birth of sight in 'King Rene's Daughter', by exclaiming in undisguised astonishment: 'Why, that's just like Louie,' meaning the patient described above.

In the Tatler of Aug. 16, 1709, an interesting account is given of the gift of sight to a young man of twenty years of age, who had never seen. The following extracts may well be compared with what is written above.

When the patient first received the dawn of light, there appeared such an ecstasy in his action, that he seemed ready to swoon away in the surprise of joy and wonder. The surgeon stood before him with his instruments in his hands. The young man observed him from head to foot; and after which he surveyed himself as carefully, and seemed to compare him to himself; and, observing both their hands, seemed to think they were exactly alike, except the instruments, which he took to be part of his hands... 'Where is Tom, who used to lead me? But I could now, methinks, go anywhere without him.' He offered to move, but, seemed afraid of everything around him ...Mr C. asked him what sort of thing he took Tom to be before he had seen him? He answered, 'he believed there was not so much of him as himself; but he fancied him the same sort of creature' ...As he saw the crowd thickening, he desired Mr C. to tell him how many there were all to be seen... With much reluctance he was prevailed upon to have his eyes bound; in which condition they kept him in a dark room, till it was proper to let the organ receive its objects without further precaution. During the time of his darkness, he bewailed himself in the most distressing manner, complaining that some incantation had been used upon him, and some strange magic used to deceive him into an opinion that he had enjoyed *what they called sight*. He added that the impressions then let in upon his soul *would certainly distract him*, if he were not so at present. At another time he would strive to name the persons he had seen in the crowd... and would pretend to speak, in perplexed terms of his own making, of what he in that short time observed."

---

* The details of the operation appeared in *The Lancet*, 6 June 1885.

Appendix 13
DAVID FRANCIS (1865-1929)

On 14 May 1985, an opening ceremony took place at a small cottage at Llechwedd Slate Mines in Blaenau Ffestiniog, Gwynedd in Wales. A single-storey cottage with a roof loft, its age was unknown, but its construction out of rounded boulders, gathered off the mountain-side, were evidence of its erection before Blaenau Ffestiniog became a slate producing area in the late eighteenth century.

It was here that David Francis was born on 25 July 1865. He was destined to earn fame as "Y Telynor Dall o Feirion" – his Welsh bardic name meaning the Blind Harpist of Meirionnydd.

While accompanying his mother, Sarah, and his grandmother to the office at the Slate Mine where his grandmother worked as a cleaner, young David fell while carrying a bottle of ink. He badly injured an eye, but infection soon spread to the other and he became blind. He was only four years old.

When David was ten, Marianne Greaves, the young bride of John Earnest Greaves, arrived at Plas Weunydd, the large house still standing at the entrance to Llechwedd. John Greaves had taken over the running of the mines following the retirement of his father five years earlier. Within a month of Marianne's arrival she had written to the Liverpool School for the Indigent Blind, then at Hardman Street, seeking a place for David Francis.

Her application was successful and David was enrolled on 5 October 1875, with six years tuition arranged and supported by her husband. Although hampered by understanding only a few words of English, David showed an early aptitude for the piano and greatly benefited from the musical atmosphere of the Liverpool School, where he joined the choir and took part in the weekly concerts.

On 10 November 1877, the School performed a concert at the adjacent Philharmonic Hall, accompanied by the band of the Liverpool Rifle Brigade and conducted by the School Music Master, William D. Hall. David took part and it proved to be one of the highlights of his years in Liverpool.

David Francis (1865-1929) (Ivor Wynne Jones).

While at home in Blaenau Ffestiniog during the School holidays, David was encouraged to take up the harp by Dr. Robert Roberts of Isallt, a harpist and composer, who was impressed with the boy's natural ability. Subsequently, on leaving the Liverpool School, the Greaves family paid for an initial course of lessons with a Professor of the harp at 19 Oxford Street in Liverpool.

Still only 17 when he returned home, he began to earn his living making mats, a trade he had learned while at School. His first love, however, was music and in 1886 he began playing concerts at the Belle Vue Hotel in the new Spa of Trefriw, to those who had come for the "cure". This lasted up to the First World War by which time he had become one of the best known harpists in Wales, earning his bardic title (noted above) at the romantic Garddwest Geirionnydd, the annual counter-eisteddfod which dated from 1863, held on the shores of Geirionnydd Lake above the Conwy Valley.

His services as an accompanist were frequently sought by choirs, including Cor Telyn Barlwyd when invited to give a concert during Welsh week at the great Wembley Exhibition of 1924.

His cottage had now become a well known musical academy to which a stream of pupils had made their way over many years, among them Eleanor Dwyryd, later to earn fame in her own right as a harpist. In 1927 the people of Blaenau opened a fund to buy David Francis a new harp in gratitude for his services to the local community. On a memorable evening in the local Assembly Rooms in January 1928 a handsome Spiral Gothic Harp was presented to David at the *"cyngerdd telyn Dafydd"* (the concert of David's harp).

Sadly, he did not have long to enjoy his new instrument as he died in September 1929, in the same bed in which he was born in his Llechwedd cottage. The funeral was the biggest ever seen at Blaenau Ffestiniog, the Gothic Harp being paraded in an open waggon before the coffin as the procession wound its way to Bethesda cemetery.

The cottage remained the family home until 1944 but by 1972 it had become derelict and was on the point of demolition. However, in that same year the abandoned Victorian sections of the mine were opened as a tourist attraction, the success of which prompted the restoration of David

Francis's cottage with the interior returned to its appearance when he lived there. It was opened to the public in 1985 in the same year that J.W. Greaves & Sons discovered that the company were still paying an annual subscription to the Liverpool School for the Blind for £1.05 (the old guinea), which was begun by John Greaves in 1875. The company promptly upgraded the figure, to continue one of the longest periods of unbroken support to the Liverpool School.

Sources:
Royal School for the Blind, Liverpool, Archive.
Ivor Wynne Jones, *Minstrels and Miners – The Life and Times of David Francis*, Gwynedd (1986).
LLechwedd Slate Caverns – 'Opening of David Francis's home to the public', press release, 14 May 1985.

PRESIDENTS

1791/94	John Sparling	1831	Lord Lilford
1795	John Bolton	1832	Lord Bradford
1796	George Venables	1833	Sir Henry Philip Hoghton
1797	William Roe	1834	The Earl of Burlington
1798	William Roscoe	1835	The 13th Earl of Derby
1799	Revd. John Smyth B.D.	1836	Lord Sandon
1800	William Rathbone (IV)	1837	Earl of Dartmouth
1801	Peter Leicester	1838	Lord Stanley, M.P.
1802	John Blackburne	1839	Wilbraham Egerton of
1803	Thomas Hinde		Tatton
1804	William Harper	1840	Lord Bishop of Chester
1805	The 12th Earl of Derby	1841	Cresswell Cresswell
1806	The Earl of Wilton	1842	Sir Thomas Bernard Birch
1807	The Earl of Sefton	1843	Sir Howard Douglas, M.P.
1808	The Earl of Stamford &	1844	Lord Skelmersdale
	Warrington	1845	Pudsey Dawson
1809	The Earl of Grosvenor	1846	The Earl of Sefton
1810	Lord Stanley	1847/61	William Brown, M.P.
1811	Edward Wilbraham Bootle	1862	Lt. Col. William Brown
1812	James Gerard, M.D.	1863	Sir William Brown
1813	George Naylor	1864	Sir William Brown (until
1814	Sir Thomas Dalrymple		March)
	Hesketh Bart.		The Earl of Sefton
1815	Peter Patten Bold	1865/68	The Earl of Sefton
1816	William Barton	1869	John A. Drinkwater
1817	John Wright		Revd. A. Campbell
1818-19	The Revd. Lord Bishop of	1870	Revd. A. Campbell
	Chester	1871/78	James Aikin
1820	The Earl of Stamford &	1879/80	Thomas Fisher
	Warrington	1881/82	Thomas Mills
1821	Sir John Tobin	1883/85	Joseph Richardson
1822	The Most Reverend and	1886/88	Col. C. E. Crosbie
	Right Honourable, The	1889/90	Horace Walker
	Lord Archbishop of York	1891/97	J. F. Collier
1823	The Earl of Wilton	1898/99	W. J. Lockett
1824	The Lord Bishop of Sodor	1900/11	Henry Wade Deacon
	and Man	1912/27	A. Isaacson
1825	The Revd. Lord Bishop of	1927/33	Sir Henry Wade Deacon
	Chester	1933/39	W. J. Smith
1826	Joseph Ridgway	1939/45	Edwin Green
1827	H. Blundell Hollinshead	1945/51	Harold Smyth
1828	John Bolton	1951/55	George R. Stubbs
1829/30	Lord Skelmersdale	1955/91	John C. Smyth

SUPERINTENDENTS

1791-1793 Revd. Henry Dannett	1885-1886 John Wyllie
1793-1799 John Graystock	1886-1890 Capt. Charles Christie
1799-1804 John Smith	Pearson
1805-1815 Joseph Brand	1890-1909 Thomas Taylor
1815-1847 John Lucy	1910-1913 Walter Littlewood
1847-1849 William Watts	1913-1945 Samuel Stevens
1849-1869 Henry Addenbrook	1945-1969 Edward Keates
1869-1884 Frederick E. Brunton	1969-1991 Thomas C. Milburn

HEADTEACHERS (WAVERTREE)

1898-1910 Walter Littlewood	1917-1927 School directly under
1910-1913 Archibald A. Cowan	Superintendent
1914-1916 E. Gledhill	1927-1953 C.V.H. Egerton-Jones
1917 T. Gillespie (Temporary	1953-1960 Miss M.A. MacLennan
Appointment)	1965-1990 H.S.D. Marks O.B.E.
1917 Lloyd M. Davies ('Assistant	
Schoolmaster')	

CHAPLAINS OF ST. MARY'S, CHAPEL OF THE SCHOOL FOR THE BLIND

1801-1820 Revd. William Blundell	1913-1918 Revd. Charles Forster
(School Chaplain only)	Gunton
1819-1867 Revd. Edward Hull (first	1918-1919 Revd. Harold Davies Littler
minister of Chapel)	(Temporary Acting
1867-1882 Revd. Alexander Whishaw	Chaplain)
1882-1884 Revd. Clement E.E.	1919-1927 Revd. C.F.H. Soulby
Appleyard	(Temporary Acting
1884-1913 Revd. Thomas William May	Chaplain)
Lund	

CHRONOLOGY

1601	Poor Law Act specifically mentions relief to be given to the destitute blind.
1687	John Locke, *Essay on Human Understanding* published.
1709	Dr Berkeley, *Theory of Vision* published.
1728	Nicholas Saunderson invents Mathematical Board.
1728	Cheselden, *Account of observations* published.
1749	Diderot's *Essay on Blindness* published in France.
1749	Liverpool Infirmary opened
1752	Liverpool Seamen's Hospital opened
1756	13 November, Edward Rushton born
1772	Liverpool Workhouse (3rd) opened on Brownlow Hill
1774	'Education of the Blind' by 'Demodocus' published in *Edinburgh Magazine and Review.*
1778	Liverpool Dispensary opened in North John Street.
1783	Thomas Blacklock's article on 'The Blind' appears in *Encyclopedia Britannica.*
1785	Valentin Haüy opens the National Institution for the Young Blind in Paris
1786	Valentin Haüy, *Essay on the Education of the Blind* published in France.
1790	Edward Rushton's philosophical society discuss idea for the relief and education of the blind.
1790	October, Meetings held at the house of Revd. Henry Dannett to formulate plans for a blind school.
1790	22 November, Plans published in local press.
1791	3 January, Announcement regarding the opening of the new school appears in local press.
1791	10 January Liverpool School of Instruction for the Indigent Blind opened in two rented houses at 6 Commutation Row.
1791	Valentin Haüy's School is closed
1793	Henry Dannett resigns and subscribers to the Charity elect a Management Committee, with John Sparling as its first President, to run the affairs of the Asylum.
	Edinburgh Asylum for the Industrious Blind opened.
	Bristol School for the Blind opened.
1800	1 March, New purpose built school building is opened in London Road, Liverpool (site is occupied today by the Odeon

	Cinema complex) – designed by John Foster.
1806	18 September, Prince of Wales (later George IV) and the Duke of Clarence (later William IV) visit the School. Prince becomes Patron and donates 100 guineas.
1809	Medical Committee formed at the School consisting of the Towns's most learned doctors and surgeons. New programme begun to examine and treat all pupils.
1809	March Electrical Machine presented to the School by Mr Brandreth, Surgeon to the Infirmary. Probably used to stimulate eye muscles or optic nerve.
1811	Death of John Christie, co-founder of the School.
1812	30 December, New extension building on the rear of the London Road School completed. Designed by John Foster.
1814	22 November, Death of Edward Rushton, co-founder of the School
1818	6 October, Chapel foundation stone laid amid great ceremony. Designed by John Foster.
1819	6 October, St. Mary's, the Chapel of the School for the Indigent Blind.opened.
1820	June, Liverpool Institute for Curing Diseases of the Eye opened at 30 Basnett Street.
	August, Liverpool Ophthalmic Infirmary opened at 29 Slater Street.
1828	Louis Braille invents his embossed 'Domino Six' alphabet.
	13 April, Act of Incorporation passed in Parliament, which regulated the government of the School and Chapel.
1832	Edinburgh Society of Arts offer prize for the best type to enable the Blind to read.
1838	Liverpool Dispensary for the Diseases of the Eye opened.
1838	James Frere introduces his reading method into the Liverpool School.
1841	Liverpool Catholic Blind Asylum opened (St. Vincent's).
1849	August, Plans to extend Lime Street Station and demolish School finalised.
1851	25 May, Chapel, which has been removed from its former site to the corner of Hardman Street and Hope Street, is consecrated.
	11 July, New Hardman Street School is opened.
1852	Death of Louis Braille
1859	Liverpool Home Teaching Society founded. Later became the

	Liverpool Workshops for the Blind.
1868	British and Foreign Blind Association founded by Dr T.R. Armitage in London.
1870	Elementary Education Act
1871	St. Paul's Eye Hospital founded by George Edward Walker in three rooms at 6 St. Paul's Square.
1873	First International Conference held on the Education of the Blind – Vienna
1874	Liverpool Home for Blind Children established at Miller Street, Toxteth. (The first home for blind babies; in 1891 it moved to Devonshire Road, Toxteth, before closing in 1912.)
1889	July, Report of the Royal Commission on the Blind, Deaf & Dumb published.
1893	Elementary Education (Blind and Deaf Children) Act – compulsory education of blind and deaf children from 5-16.
1899	12 January, Wavertree School opened to educate children aged between 5-16 in compliance with the terms of the 1893 Act.
1901	First Tutor of Braille Music Notation in any language published. It had been compiled by Edward Watson, Director of Music at the Liverpool School for the Blind.
1902	Secondary Education Act
1914	British and Foreign Blind Association becomes the National Institute for the Blind at Great Portland Street London
1918	Education Act – under this Act vocational training of the Blind became an obligation on the L.E.A.
1920	Blind Persons Act – made it the duty of local councils to provide for the welfare of the Blind.
1921	Education Act – all previous Education Acts consolidated into a single statute.
1930	March, Demolition of the Chapel commenced.
1932	31 October Opening of the New Extension on the site of the Chapel.
1939	1-2 September, Evacuation of Wavertree and Hardman Street to the former North Wales School for Blind Children, Rhyl.
1944	Education Act.
1945	21 February, Conference with Ministry of Education held to discuss regional reorganisation. Wavertree becomes a Primary School for the North West. Henshaw's in Manchester becomes Secondary School for the Region.

1947	Hardman Street certified as the Technical School for the North West.
1957	31 July, Hardman Street Technical School closed.
1960	1 October, Appointment of Mr. H.S.D. Marks as Headmaster of Wavertree.
1962	Perkins Braillers introduced at Wavertree.
1964	Language Laboratory introduced at Wavertree.
1966	By the Liverpool Corporation (General Powers) Act the Institution was renamed The School for the Blind, Liverpool. In July, by Royal Assent, the title became The Royal School for the Blind, Liverpool. Abbeyholme School, adjacent to the Wavertree School purchased.
1970	Vernon Report published (Report on the Education of the Visually Handicapped).
1972	Clifton House, a property at the rear of the School on Prince Alfred Road purchased.
1976	Education Act
1978	Warnock Report published (Special Educational Needs; Report of the Committee of Inquiry into the Education of Handicapped Children and Young Persons). Approval given for the provision at Wavertree of a Secondary Age Unit for children with additional handicaps.
1981	Education Act
1982-3	National & regional conferences take place to discuss the future of education of the visually handicapped. Wavertree's role becomes "the education and training of visually handicapped children with severe learning difficulties and additional handicaps between the ages of 3 and 18".
1986-89	Redevelopment scheme at Wavertree to provide necessary facilities to cater for the new role.
1990	Derek Marks awarded O.B.E. Ronald Wright, pupil at the School 1935-44 awarded B.E.M. 13 November, Bicentennial Appeal targeted at £2.5 million officially launched.
1991	22 March, Visit to The Royal School for the Blind, Liverpool, by Her Majesty The Queen, the Patron of the School.

NOTES

Abbreviations

A.R.   Annual Reports of the School
Lp.R.O.   Liverpool Record Office
M.C.M.B.   Management Committee Minute Books of the School
P.R.O.   Public Record Office
S.A.   Archive of The Royal School for the Blind, Liverpool
T.H.S.L.C. Transactions of the Historic Society of Lancashire and
            Cheshire.

Chapter 1

1. Ramsay Muir, *A History of Liverpool*, Liverpool University Press (1907), p. 180.
2. Ibid, p. 182.
3. Liverpool merchants had participated in the slave trade earlier than 1747, although on a much lesser scale. An excellent summary of recent research on this topic can be found in the *Transactions of the Historical Society of Lancashire and Cheshire*, Occasional Series Vol. 2 (1976), Revised 1989.
4. Anon. The Blind, *National Review*, No.XIX, January 1860, p. 5.
5. H.J.Wagg & M.G.Thomas, *A Chronological Survey of Work for the Blind*, London (1932), p. 1.
6. Ibid.
7. Ibid, p. 2.
8. Ibid.
9. Ibid, p. 3.
10. M. Anagnos, *Education of the Blind; An Historical Sketch of its Origin, Rise and Progress*, Boston (1882), p. 5.
11. Lennard Bickel, *Triumph Over Darkness, the Life of Louis Braille*, London (1988), p. 5.
12. Anagnos, op. cit., p. 6.
13. Cheseldens report is also contained in Diderot's *Essay on Blindness* (1749) from which this quotation is taken (p. 114).
14. Diderot, p. 39.
15. Translated and published in English in 1773 as *Essay on Blindness*.
16. Ibid, p. 4.
17. Ibid.
18. Ibid, pp. 4-5.
19. Ibid, p. 13.
20. Biographer of Saunderson – *The Life and Character of Dr Nicholas Saunderson, Late Lucasian Professor of the Mathematics in the University*

of Cambridge, by his Disciple and Friend, William Inchclif Esq., Dublin (1747).

21. Diderot, op. cit., pp. 68-9.
22. Spence, *An Account of the Life, Character and Poems of Mr Blacklock*, Edinburgh (1754).
23. Anagnos, op. cit., p. 33.
24. Such an educational system did not of course necessarily include afflicted persons, but it is important to appreciate attitudes towards education generally.
25. Valentin Haüy, 'An Historical Summary of the Rise, the Progress, and the Actual State of the Institution of the Blind Children' contained within his *Essay On The Education of The Blind,* Paris (1786) (translated by Blacklock, Edinburgh (1793)), p. 31.
26. Ibid.
27. Ibid.
28. Ibid, p. 32.
29. Ibid, p. 33.
30. Thomas Blacklock, 'The Blind': the complete extract under that heading in the *Encyclopedia Britannica*, Edinburgh (1783), Revised 1817.
31. Ibid
32. Liverpool Vestry Books 1682, Vol. 1, fol.5v, Liverpool Public Record Office.
33. Muir, op. cit., p. 243. (Sir Thomas Erskine was a jurist, M.P. and briefly Lord Chancellor in 1806. He was famous for his defence of several English radicals, especially Thomas Paine, who were charged with sedition and libel during the French Revolution.)
34. Muir, op. cit., pp. 270-1.
35. *Liverpool and Its Environs*, A Liverpool Guide Book (1795).
36. Muir, op. cit., p. 288.
37. W. Roscoe, *Mount Pleasant* (1772).
38. J.A. Picton, *Memorials of Liverpool*, Vol. 1, Liverpool (1875), p. 225.
39. St. Johns stood on the site of St. Johns Gardens, St.Georges Hall.
40. B. Whittingham-Jones, 'Liverpool's Political Clubs, 1812-1830' *T.H.S.L.C.*, Vol. 111 (1959), pp. 133-4.

Chapter 2

1. Malignant Ophthalmia causes the eyelids to become red and swollen, and from between them issues a dangerous discharge which causes the lids to stick together and imprisons the malignant fluid. This, in the course of a few days, works irreparable damage to the eyes.
2. When William Cobbett, the famous antagonist of Paine, returned to England from America in 1819, he arrived in Liverpool bringing with him Paine's bones which had been disinterred from the grave on the dead man's farm. He also brought back a fragment of the gravestone which had been

destroyed by his enemies. Cobbett gave this fragment to Edward Rushton
Jnr. who had become an intimate acquaintance. The extent of the inscription read (brackets indicate what was missing from the fragment):

THOM(as)
AUTHOR OF COMMON (sense)
DIED JUNE 8TH (1809)
AGED 74 YEARS

A full account of this can be found in W. L. Rushton, *Letters of a Templar 1820-50*, London (1903), pp. 60-2. (The letters belonged to his father
Edward Rushton jnr.)

3. Shepherd later wrote Rushtons' biography included in Edward Rushton,
    Poems and Other Writings London.1824.
4. This may be the *Liverpool and Lancaster Weekly Herald*, first published in
    June 1788, becoming the *Liverpool and Lancashire Weekly Herald* in No-
    vember 1789. No trace of the '*Liverpool Herald*' can be found (as stated by
    Shepherd, op. cit.).
5. E. Rushton, *Will Clewline*, London (1806).
6. His son Edward, born on 22 September 1795, became a prominent figure in
    Liverpool politics, was called to the Bar on 18 November 1831 and ap-
    pointed Stipendary Magistrate of Liverpool on 17 May 1839.
7. B. Whittingham-Jones, op. cit., p. 134.
8. Taken from a lengthy account written in 1804 by Rushton at his home in
    Paradise St. It was later sent by his son Edward jnr. to the *Liverpool Mer-
    cury* for publication to settle a dispute regarding the founding of the school.
    It was printed in full in the newspaper on 31 October 1817.
9. Ibid.
10. Ibid.
11. Ibid.
12. Ibid.
13. Ibid.
14. Ibid. (Lowe was a Professor of Music of 44 Duke Street.)
15. Ibid.
16. Ibid.
17. Ibid.
18. Owners of local newspapers.
19. Rushton (1804 & 1817) op.cit
20. Ibid.
21. Ibid.
22. Ibid.
23. Ibid.
24. Ibid.

25. Management Committee Minute Book (1793-1803) – (hereafter MCMB) SA – MCMB/1, p. 1.
26. Rushton (1804 & 1817), op. cit.
27. MCMB/2 (1804-1815) – 4 October 1805.
28. A notable exception being J.A. Picton, *Memorials*, op. cit., pp. 191-4 (v.II)
29. H. Smithers, *Liverpool – its Commerce, Statistics & Institutions*, London (1825), pp. 239-40.
30. Wallace, pp. 166-7.

Chapter 3

1. Shaw's Brow is known today as William Brown Street and is the site of the Walker Art Gallery, City Museum and Museum of Labour History.
2. H. Dannett. *'Report of the State of the Liverpool Asylum for the Indigent Blind'*, January 1793, School published pamphlet, SA AR/1/4.
3. Ibid.
4. Ibid.
5. Ibid.
6. H. Dannett, *'Some Particulars Relative to a Plan for Affording Relief for the Indigent Blind'*, p. 3, School published pamphlet, 1 December 1790 (2nd ed. Jan 1792), SA AR/1/2.
7. Dannett, Report (1793), op. cit.
8. John Sparling, *Decisions made at the first meeting of the Friends of the Institution for the Indigent Blind, Golden Lion, Liverpool. 1 March 1791*, School published pamphlet notice, SA AR/1/5.
9. M.M. Schofield, 'The Virginia Trade of the Firm of Sparling and Bolden of Liverpool 1788-99', *T.H.S.L.C.*, Vol. 116 (1964), pp. 117-65 and E.F.Cunliffe, *Pages from the life of John Sparling of Petton*, Edinburgh (1904), Lp.R.O.
10. So named as the previous owner, George Campbell, had made his fortune when one of his ships captured a rich vessel from the island of St. Domingo, West Indies.
11. Cunliffe. op.cit., taken from R. Syers, *History of Everton* (1830).
12. Committee Fund-raising Circular, 6 August 1793. Liverpool – SA AR/1/8.
13. 'Liverpool Asylum for the Indigent Blind, Report of the General Meeting of 16th March 1793', Liverpool – Pamphlet Notice, SA AR/1/6.
14. 'Report of the State of the Liverpool Asylum for the Indigent Blind for 1793' (hereafter Annual Reports) – 14 January 1794, Liverpool – SA AR/1/9.

Chapter 4

1. William Moss, *The Liverpool Guide*, Liverpool (1796), p. 2.
2. Muir, op. cit., p. 272.
3. Moss, op. cit., p. 83.

4. W.A.R. Thomson, *Black's Medical Dictionary*, A & C Black, London, p. 940.

5. Committee Fund-raising Circular addressed to local clergy by George Venables President of Blind Asylum, on behalf of the Committee, Liverpool, 13 December 1796, SA AR/1/15.

6. Annual Report for 1 Jan to 31 December 1795 – Liverpool January 1796 SA AR/1/14.

7. Fund raising circular, op. cit.

8. MCMB/1, p. 138-9, 2 February 1796.

9. Ibid, p. 140, 9 February 1796.

10. Ibid, p. 175, 16 August 1796.

11. Picton, op. cit., Vol. II, p. 171.

12. MCMB/1, p. 185, 10 June 1797.

13. Annual Report for 1797, January 1798, SA AR/1/18.

14. MCMB/1, p. 203, 1 May 1798.

15. Today the site of Abercromby Square and the University Buildings.

16. MCMB/1, p. 206, 2 October 1798.

17. Ibid, p. 207, 6 November 1798.

18. Ibid, p. 206, 2 October 1798. This form of punishment was common for certain religious misdemeanours by parishioners, especially after a Bishop's Visitations to the locality, to whom they would be reported. Offenders usually had to stand on a stool at the front of the congregation, sometimes in a white cloak, and pray for forgiveness after publicly confessing their sins. This would be repeated for several consecutive Sundays, depending on the severity of the offence.

19. Ibid, p. 226, 16 August 1799.

20. Ibid, p. 238, 3 December 1799.

21. Ibid, p. 240, 17 December 1799.

22. Ibid, p. 247, 4 February 1800.

23. Ibid, p. 252, 18 Mar 1800.

24. Ibid, p. 219, 2 Apr 1799.

25. Ibid, p. 221, 7 May 1799. William Livesley, who was responsible for the invention, was later presented with a silver watch by a grateful Committee, with the engraving: *'The gift of the Trustees of the School for the Blind at Liverpool to William Livesley for his successful assistance in making the Willow Plantation at Formby'*.

26. 50 Geo III, c. 109, 18 April 1810.

27. A full and graphic account of the duel can be consulted in Stonehouse, *Recollections of Old Liverpool by a Nonagenarian*, Liverpool (1863), pp. 84-91. Other accounts in F.H. Taylor, *Liverpool and the Athenaeum*, Liverpool (1965), pp. 16-18 (which also includes the Letter sent to Sparling); Picton, op. cit., Vol. II, pp. 372-3; *Liverpool Review*, 28 June 1890.

28. Muir, op. cit., p. 234.

29. Stonehouse, op. cit., pp. 93-98 (again a graphic, detailed account). Full ac-

counts can be consulted in Picton, op. cit., Vol. II, p. 234; G.W. Mathews, 'John Bolton, a Liverpool Merchant 1756-1837', *T.H.S.L.C.*, Vol. 93 (1941), pp. 102-3; *Liverpool Review*, 12 July 1890, p. 12.

30. Billinge's *Liverpool Advertiser*, 23 December 1805.
31. MCMB/2, 3 October 1806.
32. An Address in favour of the School for the Blind in Liverpool, Liverpool (1804 – later editions, 1808 & 1811). This was a small booklet detailing the affairs of the School since its inception, and the aims for the future, which included copies of Fosters plans of the School and the extensions. It was primarily intended as printed appeal for support for the Charity and Building Fund.

Chapter 5

1. MCMB/3, 12 July 1815. As a consequence, masters and pupils were banned two weeks later from smoking, drinking and patronising public houses.
2. MCMB/1, 10 January 1800.
3. MCMB/1, 9 October 1801.
4. MCMB/1, 1 July 1803
5. MCMB/2, 25 January 1805
6. AR/1/30, 10 January 1806
7. MCMB/2, 25 January 1805
8. MCMB/2, 26 March 1811
9. MCMB/2, 6 October 1809
10. MCMB/1, 8 April 1801
11. AR/1/26, 26 February 1802. Successful operations to restore sight were not new. An interesting account of a 20 year old man receiving sight for the first time and his subsequent reactions is given in the *Tatler* of 16 August 1709 (see appendix 12).
12. MCMB/2, 25 September 1810.
13. MCMB/2, 27 February 1812.
14. The best work regarding Liverpool's medical past is T.H. Bickerton, *A Medical History of Liverpool*, Liverpool (1936). Also, by the same author 'A Medical Sketch of Liverpool 1551-1840' in W.T. Pike, *Liverpool and Birkenhead in the 20th Century*, Brighton (1911), pp. 80-96 and 'A Historical Sketch of Dr. John Rutter' in *Liverpool Medico-Chirurgical Journal*, Liverpool (1910). (Rutter was a first cousin of William Rathbone IV.) Mr. Bickerton was Opthalmic Surgeon to the Liverpool Royal Infirmary, and President of the Liverpool Medical Institution. He was Hon. Ophthalmic Surgeon to the School between 1920-32.
15. Committee member and an upholsterer by trade, he is more widely known as the antiquarian who compiled and published the Portfolio of Fragments in 1817, containing documents and accounts regarding early Liverpool history. His collection of papers was combined with those of John Holt, an

eighteenth century Liverpool schoolmaster, and the Holt-Gregson Papers as they are known are now held by the Liverpool Record Office.

16. MCMB/2, 9 November 1812.
17. Ibid.
18. MCMB/2, 19 November 1912.
19. MCMB/2, 3 June 1814.
20. Ibid.
21. MCMB/3, 6 August 1818
22. This was William Rathbone the fifth, 1787-1868 (son of William 1757-1809, the abolitionist friend of Roscoe, and Chairman of the School in 1800). Mayor of Liverpool in 1837-8, he was an active reformer and Liverpool M.P. His statue stands in Sefton Park.
23. T.H. Bickerton, op. cit., p. 121.
24. Picton, op. cit., Vol. II, p. 310.
25. Mayor William Barton – he was also the current Chairman of the School
26. MCMB/3, 23 April 1816.
27. MCMB/1, 25 January 1803.
28. Gibson contributed an article to the Edinburgh Medical and Surgical Journal in 1807 on infantile ophthalmia, which arguably shows him far in advance of his contemporaries. An account of the operation on Rushton can be consulted in; Gibson, B., *Practical Observations on the Formation of an Artificial Pupil*, Cadell & Davies, London (1811).

Chapter 6

1. MCMB/3, 8 June 1818.
2. Ibid, 8 April 1817.
3. Ibid, 3 July 1818.
4. Ibid, 4 August 1818.
5. *Gore's General Advertiser*, Liverpool, 8 October 1818 (School Archive).
6. St. Peters once stood in Church Street near Church Alley. Today, a brass cross laid into a paving stone near Burton's Store marks its former site.
7. *Gore's*, ibid, 8 October 1818.
8. Ibid.
9. Ibid.
10. Anon., *Imperial Magazine*, Vol. 1 (1819), pp. 773/4, Lp.R.O.
11. H. Smithers, op. cit., p. 32.
12. Austin S., *Views and Illustrations in Lancashire*, London (1831), p. 95. (Mr Sylvester was a member of the Committee.)
13. Stranger in Liverpool, visitors guide book, 10th edition (1831), p. 207.

Chapter 7

1. MCMB/5, 7 July 1846 & 13 July 1846.
2. Ibid, 1 December 1846.
3. Ibid, 6 April 1847.

4. Picton, op. cit. II, p. 194.
5. Revd. D. Thom, 'Liverpool Churches and Chapels; their Destruction, Removal or Alteration', *T.H.S.L.C.*, Liverpool, Vol. 4 (1852), pp. 153/4.
6. Arthur Holme had previously designed the Mechanics Institute in 1837 (later the Liverpool Institute) and the re-design of St. Mary's in Walton in 1841. Both Samuel and James were to serve as Mayor during the 1850s and James was also to be elected to the School Committee.
7. Anon. 'Sketches of Eminent Clergymen in Lancashire' *The Hermes; a Literary, Moral and Scientific Journal*, Liverpool, 16 November 1822, Vol. I, No.3, p. 1.
8. *The Porcupine*, Liverpool, 12 January 1867, pp. 486-7.
9. Revd. Edward Hull, *A Sermon in Commemoration of the Fortieth Anniversary of the opening of the Chapel of St. Mary*, Liverpool, published by the School, (1859), p. 11 contained in Annual Report of the School for the Blind, Liverpool 1856-61, S A ref. AR/12.
10. Ibid, p. 13.
11. *The Porcupine*, op. cit., p. 487.
12. *The Porcupine*, Liverpool, 15 May 1869, Vol. II, 1869-70, p. 56 Lp.R.O.
13. '*Report of the Sub-Committee to Special Meeting of Board, June 8 1869*', S.A. ref. Box 3/doc 14.
14. *The Porcupine*, 31 July 1869, Vol. II, 1869-70, p. 168 (see appendix 10).

Chapter 8

1. This system achieved contemporary notoriety. Barbier and his two pupils were invited to the Paris Institution by Professors de la Cépéde and Andre Marie Ampère (the genius of electrical science who gave his name to "Amp") to test the system. Barbier, who claimed his invention to be the ultimate answer to the problems of the blind was awarded the sizeable sum of a thousand francs to complete his work.
2. Abbé C. Carton (Director of the Deaf, Dumb and Blind Institute of Bruges), *The Establishments for The Blind in England: A Report to The Minister of the Interior and of Foreign Affairs*, Bruges (1838), p. 83.
3. Ibid, pp. 42-3.
4. J.M. Richie, *Concerning the Blind*, Oliver & Boyd, London (1930), p. 43. (Dr. Richie was Chairman of the Association of Workshops for the Blind.)
5. James Gall, *An Account of the Recent Discoveries which have been made for the Facilitating the Education of the Blind*, Edinburgh, (1837); John Alston, *Statements of the Education, Employments, and Internal Arrangements adopted at the Asylum for the Blind*, Glasgow, Glasgow (1842).
6. Charles Baker, 'On the Education of the Deaf and Dumb and of the Blind' *Contributions to the Society for the Diffusion of Useful Knowledge and the Central Society of Education*, privately published (1842). Much of this work appeared in the English (or 'Penny') Cyclopedia (1859).
7. In 1812 Brougham had fought a famous Parliamentary election in Liver-

pool for the Whigs against the Tory candidate, George Canning. He was an abolitionist, staunchly supported by Roscoe throughout his campaign. He also played a major role in the founding of the Yorkshire School for the Blind in 1835. In 1858, then Lord Brougham, he founded and chaired the Social Science Côngress held at St. George's Hall under the Presidency of Lord John Russell. The Society, with many other distinguished men present, including the Earl of Shaftesbury, the Earl of Carlisle and Sir James Stephen, visited the Liverpool School for the Blind as part of their Conference activities in October 1858.

8. Hansard, Vol. xx, 142.

9. MCMB/6 (1856-1880), 17 January 1862.

10. AR/13 1862

11. A request was also received at the School from Mr. Gladstone in a letter to the Committee recommending 'that a room be set apart for teaching the Pupils reading, writing, history, geography, etc.'. The letter was referred to the Chaplain but no further mention was made. (MCMB/5, 4 July 1848). It is not clear either as to which Mr Gladstone it was. Both the future Premier, William Ewart, and his brother Robertson, who was Mayor in 1843, were active in Liverpool politics at this time.

12. In April 1816, a Miss Casson donated a Panagram (a reading/writing apparatus, the exact form of which is unknown) which had cost her ten guineas. She may have been closely related to John Casson).

13. MCMB/3, 6 September 1816.

14. MCMB/3, 3 December 1822.

15. The School had received other literary donations during the first half of the nineteenth century; In 1802, Mrs Blacklock of Edinburgh donated 48 copies of the poetical works of her late husband Doctor Blacklock to be "sold for the benefit of the institution". In 1835 a copy of St. Mark's Gospel in embossed letters was received from the Pennsylvanian Institution for the Instruction of the Blind (founded 1833). This was quite a handsome copy and had cause to be mentioned in Charles Baker's article (p. 55). Also from America a Book of Psalms "adapted for the use of the Blind" was received from a Boston donor in 1838. Sadly, no trace of any of the above books can now be found.

16. Turner, M.& Harris, W. A, *Guide to Institutions and Charities for the Blind*, London (1871). This work was the result of the surveys made by these two gentlemen of the Leicester Institution during the 1860s while attempting to encourage a plan for the regulation of all institutions. They visited the Liverpool School in March 1866 as part of their researches.

17. Report of the Royal Commission on the Blind, The Deaf and Dumb, etc., H.M.S.O. (1889), intro., p. b3.

18. The Saxon System was named after a scheme developed in Dresden, whereby pupils who had returned home after learning a trade were supplied with initial tools and materials at cost price by their institution, who would

also assist in sale of wares and sometimes buy completed goods if trade was slack.

19.   Report of Royal Commission, op. cit., para. 243, 247.
20.   Richie, op. cit., p. 98.

Chapter 9

1.   Original recorded source unknown, but probably written as an obituary. This quote taken from Annual Report of 1957/58, p.29.
2.   J.A. Maw, 'The History of Wavertree' (unpublished) (1974), p. 14.
3.   Ibid. The Wavertree Hall of the Church Road site should not be confused with that of the Wavertree Hall which formerly stood on land which is now Wavertree Park, adjacent to Littlewoods Pools Building and the Technology Park. That Hall was also known as Plumbe's Hall after John Plumbe, the well known Liverpool attorney, who built the Hall in 1719. It was later occupied by Charles Lawrence, the first Chairman of the Liverpool and Manchester Railway Company.
4.   *Liverpool Daily Post*, 11 January 1899.
5.   *Liverpool Daily Post*, 12 January 1899. The disease referred to was Opthalmia Neonatorum which became a compulsorily notifiable disease in England and Wales in 1914. This act had immediate effect in the reduction of blind infants.
6.   The School cited a paper written by Mr H.W.P. Pine, (Superintendent and Secretary of the Midland Institution for the Blind), as suitable terms of reference on which to base their own scheme (from *The Blind* No.5, London). The following extract was specifically referred to.

"When the Director of the Institution considers that a pupil is sufficiently master of his trade to be able to support himself, he looks out for some suitable opening for him in his own locality, and unless there are any special reasons why he should not go home, he returns there. If his home surroundings are unsuitable then some other place is found for him. The Director visits the locality where the pupil is to settle, and arranges for some leading person in the district to act as his guardian or foster parent so to speak. This is usually the clergyman, doctor, mayor, or some other benevolent practical person of influence. His duties are to advise the blind man in his business whenever necessary, introduce him to customers, keep an interested an watchful eye upon him, and to keep the Director informed as to his circumstances and conduct.

The pupil is also expected to write to the Institution at stated times, saying how he is getting on and giving full particulars about himself. The pupil is started with an outfit of tools and materials, or whatever is suitable for his particular business, supplied with materials at cost price where required, and is assisted if necessary when suffering from sickness, or accident, or whenever any extra outlay is needed which is beyond his power to defray. The Institution will further assist him by selling the goods which he himself is unable to dispose of. The Director visits the former pupil from time to time, and also in case the Guardian requires advice or help." (AR/27 1905.)

7.   Richie, op. cit., p. 127.
8.   AR/28 1912, 24 January 1913.
9.   AR/28 1915, 28 January 1916
10.   AR/28 1913, 23 January 1914.
11.   AR/28 1917, 21 May 1918.
12.   Richie, op. cit., p. 123.
13.   Letter from Mr A. Isaacson (President of the School) to Henry Stainsby, Secretary-General of the N.I.B. 27 September 1920 – S.A. Box 7 Doc 69.
14.   *Liverpool Daily Post*, 1930.
15.   *The Architect & Building News*, London, October 7 1932, pp. 8-10.

Chapter 10

1.   R. Padley & M. Cole, *Evacuation Survey* (1940), pp. 46-7.
2.   Report of the Evacuation – Samuel Stevens. AR/32 1939/40 (June 1940).
3.   'A Diary of the Evacuation to Rhyl 1939-1941', compiled by the Staff and Senior Girls of Hardman Street, School Archive. Despite attempts to trace the person who made most of the entries in the Diary (which appears to have been a collective contribution) efforts have proved fruitless. It is most likely that they were made by Mrs S.T. Williams, a technical teacher from the Hardman Street School, who left Rhyl in 1941 – the same time the handwriting changes briefly, before ending completely.
4.   Splash Point lies at the end of Rhyl Promenade near the bottom of Russell Road and was a favourite place of the pupils during their walks.
5.   I believe that this adds credence to the theory that Mrs Williams made the entries in the diary!
6.   Annual Report 1945-56 (June 1946), AR/32.

Chapter 11

1.   Dr Pritchard was Head of the Sub-Department of Special Education at the University of Liverpool when he was appointed to the School Management Committee in December 1971. Regrettably, he did not see a full year on the Committee as he took up an appointment at the University of Swansea in July 1971. He was well versed on the background and history of the School as he made extensive use of the Archive for his Book from which the quote was taken.
2.   Act of Parliament 7 & 8 George VI, Ch. 31, Section 33 (Education Act, 1944).
3.   Blind, Deaf, Educationally Sub-normal, epileptic, physically handicapped, diabetic, delicate, maladjustment, handicapped speech, partially sighted, partially deaf. (Replacing the five categories of the Blind, Deaf, epileptic, and physically and mentally defective.)
4.   J.S. Hurt, *Outside the Mainstream; A History of Special Education*, London (1988), Batsford, p. 174.
5.   Butler's Education Act: (1) raised the school leaving age to 15 (eventually

to be 16); (2) provided for secondary education for all children according to ability, and aptitude in Secondary Grammar, Technical or Modern Schools; (3) provided for the eventual establishment of County Colleges for compulsory part-time education to 18; (4) abolished school fees in schools assisted by local authority grants; (5) established a Ministry of Education.

6. H.M.I. J. Lumsden – Visit to Russell Road, Rhyl, 16 June 1944. H.M.I. Internal Ministry Report, Ministry of Education Reports and Correspondence relating to the Liverpool School for the Blind, Public Record Office (Kew), Ref E.D. 32/953/XC154907 Doc. 28816/58.

7. Temporarily at Whitfield Hall, Hexham due to damage caused by enemy action. Southport was not reopened until 1953.

8. H.M.I. Internal Ministry Report, 25 September 1951, P.R.O. Ref. ED 32/2297/XC154907 Doc. 28816/103.

9. Mr Egerton-Jones was to run a guest house in Prestatyn on his retirement.

10. H.M.I. Internal Ministry Report, 14 January 1953, P.R.O. Ref. ED 32/2298/XC154907 Doc. M492/7023/110

Chapter 12

1. Under-Secretary of State for the D.E.S. – House of Commons debate, 13 July 1970 on the Education (Handicapped Children) Bill July 1970.

2. Annual Report, 1967/68. S.A. AR/35.

3. The Report of the Board of Education on Partially Sighted Children (1934).

4. DES, *Report on the Education of the Visually Handicapped* (Vernon Report), HMSO, London 1972.

5. DES Statistics of Education, Vol I, 'Schools' (1977), p. 48, in this case cited in J.S. Hurt, op. cit., p. 175.

6. DES, *Special Educational Needs: Report of the Committee of Enquiry into the Education of Handicapped Children and Young Persons* (Warnock Report), Cmnd 7212, HMSO, London (1978).

7. Ibid, p. 100.

8. The Pack has an extensive history of its own which space, sadly, does not allow to be reprinted here. An unpublished account has been written, however, and a copy is held in the School Archive. (Brooksbank A & L, 'A History of the 21st Picton Cub Scout Pack (Royal School for the Blind) 1909-1988'.)

BIBLIOGRAPHY
(arranged in chronological order)

ARCHIVE OF THE ROYAL SCHOOL FOR THE BLIND, LIVERPOOL (a selection only)

Dannett, Revd. Henry, *'Some Particulars Relative to a Plan for Affording Relief for the Indigent Blind'*, School published pamphlet, 1 December 1790 (2nd edition January 1792), SA AR/1/2.

Sparling, John, *Decisions made at the first meeting of the Friends of the Institution for the Indigent Blind, Golden Lion, Liverpool, 1 March 1791*, School published pamphlet notice, SA AR/1/5.

Dannett, Revd. Henry, *'Report of the State of the Liverpool Asylum for the Indigent Blind'*, January 1793 (School published pamphlet) SA AR/1/4.

Sparling, John, *'Liverpool Asylum for the Indigent Blind, Report of the General Meeting of 16th March 1793'*, Pamphlet Notice, SA AR/1/6.

Committee Fund-raising Circular, 6 August 1793, SA AR/1/8.

Annual Reports of School and Management Committee, 1793-1990.

Management Committee Minute Books, 1793-1991.

Treasurers Books, 1794-present

Committee Fund-raising Circular (addressed to local clergy by George Venables President of Blind Asylum, on behalf of the Committee), Liverpool, 13 December 1796, SA AR/1/15.

An Address in favour of the School for the Blind in Liverpool, Liverpool, 1804 (later editions, 1808 & 1811).

Chapel Books and Documents, 1804-1927.

Management Committee Waste Minute Books, 1823-1958.

Visitors Report Books, 1827-1899

Hull, Revd. Edward, *A Sermon in Commemoration of the Fortieth Anniversary of the opening of the Chapel of St. Mary, Liverpool*, published by the School for the Blind, 1859.

'Report of the Sub-Committee to Special Meeting of Board, June 8 1869' (S.A. ref. Box 3/doc. 14).

Medical Officer Report Books, 1897-1927.

'A Diary of the Evacuation to Rhyl 1939-1941', compiled by the Staff and Senior Girls of Hardman Street (unpublished), 1941.

Brooksbank, A. & L., 'A History of the 21st Picton Cub Scout Pack (Royal School for the Blind, Liverpool) 1909-1988' (unpublished), 1988.

EDUCATION & CARE OF THE BLIND

Inchclif, W., *The Life and Character of Dr. Nicholas Saunderson, Late Lucasian Professor of the Mathematics in the University of Cambridge, by his Disciple and Friend, William Inchclif Esq.*, Dublin, 1747.

Diderot, D., *Essay on Blindness*, 1749.

Spence, *An Account of the Life, Character and Poems of Mr Blacklock*, Edinburgh, 1754.

'Demodocus', 'A Letter on the Education of the Blind', *Edinburgh Magazine and Review*, September 1774.

Blacklock, Thomas, 'The Blind', *Encyclopedia Britannica*, Edinburgh, 1783 (revised 1817).

Haüy, Valentin, *Essay On The Education of The Blind*, Paris, 1786 (translated by Blacklock Edinburgh 1793).

Lettsom, Dr. John Coakley, *The Blind – Hints Designed to Promote Beneficence, Temperance and Medical Science, with an account of the Asylum for the Blind at Liverpool*, by Thomas Bernard, London, 1801.

Alston, John, *Statements of the Education, Employments, and Internal Arrangements adopted at the Asylum for the Blind, Glasgow*, Glasgow, 1842.

Gall, James, *A Historical Sketch of the Origin and Progress of Literature for the Blind*, Edinburgh, 1834.

Anderson, Thomas, *Observations on the Employment, Education, and Habits of The Blind*, London, 1837.

Anderson, Thomas, *An Account of the Recent Discoveries which have been made for the Facilitating the Education of the Blind*, Edinburgh, 1837.

Carton, Abbé C., *The Establishments for The Blind in England: A Report to The Minister of the Interior and of Foreign Affairs*, Bruges, 1838.

Frere, J.H., *Type for the Blind*, 1840.

Baker, Charles, 'On the Education of the Deaf and Dumb and of the Blind', Contributions to the Society for the Diffusion of Useful Knowledge and the Central Society of Education (privately published), 1859. Much of this work appeared in the *English* (or 'Penny') *Cyclopedia*.

Anon., 'The Blind', *National Review*, No.XIX January 1860.

Knie, J.G., *A Guide to the Proper Management and Education of Blind Children*, London (translated by Taylor, W.), 1861.

Armitage, T.R., *The Education and Employment of the Blind*, London, 1871.

Harris, W., & Turner, M., *A Guide to Institutions and Charities for the Blind*, London, 1871.

Anagnos, M., *Education of the Blind; An Historical Sketch of its Origin, Rise and Progress*, Boston, 1882.

Fuchs, E., *Causes and Prevention of Blindness*, 1885.

Wilson, H., *Information with Regard to Institutions, Societies, and Classes for the Blind in England and Wales*, London, 1887.

Illingworth, W.H., *History of the Education of the Blind*, London, 1910.

Scott, E.R., *History of the Education of the Blind prior to 1830*, London, c.1916.

Richie, J.M., *Concerning the Blind*, Oliver & Boyd, London, 1930.

Thomas, M.G. & Wagg, H.J., *A Chronological Survey of Work for the Blind*, London, 1932 (a supplement to this work, by Mary Thomas was published in 1953).

Joint Committee of the College of Teachers of the Blind and the National Institute for the Blind, *The Education of the Blind, A Survey*, London, 1936.

308

Birmingham Royal Institution for the Blind, *The Story of the Birmingham Royal Institution for the Blind, 1847-1947*, 1948.

M.G. Thomas, *Edward Rushton, R.N.I.B.*, London, 1949.

R.N.I.B., *The History of Blind Welfare in England and Wales*, London, 1955.

M.G. Thomas, *The Royal National Institute for the Blind 1868-1956*, Brighton, 1957.

Barnard, H.C., *A History of English Education from 1760*, University of London, 2nd edition, 1961.

Pritchard, D.G., *Education and the Handicapped 1760-1960*, Routledge, London, 1963.

Rose, J., *Changing Focus: the Development of Blind Welfare in Britain*, London, 1971.

Bickel, Lennard, *Triumph Over Darkness, the Life of Louis Braille*, London, 1988.

Hurt, J.S., *Outside the Mainstream; A History of Special Education*, Batsford, London, 1988.

CONFERENCE REPORTS (selection)

Buckle, A., *Report on the International Congress for the Amelioration of the Condition of the Blind, Paris*, York, 1879.

Report of the Conference of Managers, Teachers, and Friends of the Blind, York, Yorkshire School for the Blind, 1889.

Report of the International Conference on the Blind, Edinburgh, Glasgow, 1905.

JOURNALS

The Beacon.
The Blind.
The New Beacon.
Teacher of the Blind.

ACTS OF PARLIAMENT

Poor Law Act 1601.
School for the Indigent Blind at Liverpool, Incorporation Act 1829.
Poor Law Amendment Act 1834.
Elementary Education Act 1873.
Elementary Education (Blind & Deaf Children) Act 1893.
Education Act 1918.
Blind Persons Act 1920.
Education Act 1921.
Liverpool Corporation Act 1927.
Blind Persons Act 1938.
Disabled Persons Employment Act 1944.
Education Act 1944.
National Health Act 1946.

National Insurance Act 1946.
National Assistance Act 1948.
Liverpool Corporation (General Powers) Act 1966.
July Education (Handicapped Children) Bill 1970.
Education Act 1976.
Education Act 1981.

GOVERNMENT REPORTS

Report of the Royal Commission on the Blind, The Deaf and Dumb, etc. H.M.S.O. 1889.

H.M.I. Internal Ministry Report, Ministry of Education Reports and Correspondence relating to the Liverpool School for the Blind, Public Record Office (Kew), Ref E.D. 32/953/XC154907 Doc.28816/58, 1932-56.

Board of Education, The Report of the Committee of Inquiry into Problems Relating to Partially Sighted Children, 1934.

Ministry of Education, Education of the Handicapped Pupil 1945-1955, Pamphlet No. 30, London, 1946.

Ministry of Labour and National Service, Report of the Working Party on the Employment of Blind Persons, 1950.

DES, Report on the Education of the Visually Handicapped (Vernon Report), HMSO, London, 1972.

DES, Special Educational Needs: Report of the Committee of Enquiry into the Education of Handicapped Children and Young Persons (Warnock Report). Cmnd 7212 HMSO London, 1978.

ASPECTS OF LIVERPOOL

Liverpool Vestry Books, vol.1 fol.5v, 1682.
Rushton, Edward: numerous writings, 1782-1806, notably:
> *The Dismembered Empire* (1782).
> *West Indian Eclogues* (1787).
> *Will Clewline*, London (1806).

Liverpool and Its Environs: A Liverpool Guide Book, 1795.
Wallace, James, *A History of the Ancient and Present State of Liverpool*, 1795.
Moss, William, *The Liverpool Guide*, Liverpool, 1796.
Stranger in Liverpool, visitor's guide book, several editions, 1800-1840.
Britton, J., *Topographical and Historical Description of the County of Lancaster*, Vol. 1 & 2, 1807.
Troughton, T., *History of Liverpool*, 1810.
Gregson, M., *Portfolio of Fragments: Holt-Gregson Papers*, 1817.
Moss, William, *Poems and Other Writings*, London, 1824.
Smithers, H., *Liverpool – its Commerce, Statistics & Institutions*, London, 1825.
Austin, S., *Views and Illustrations in Lancashire*, London, 1831.
Herdman, W.G., *Pictorial Relics of Ancient Liverpool*, 1847.
Aspinall, Revd. James, *'Liverpool a Few Years Since' by An Old Stager*, Liverpool, 1852.

Thom, Revd. D., 'Liverpool Churches and Chapels; their Destruction, Removal or Alteration', *T.H.S.L.C.*, Liverpool, Vol. 4, 1852.

Brooke, R., *Liverpool During the Last Quarter of the Eighteenth Century*, 1853.

Frazer, *Guide to Liverpool and Birkenhead*, Liverpool, c.1855.

Stonehouse, *Recollections of Old Liverpool by a Nonagenarian*, Liverpool, 1863.

Picton, Sir J.A., *Memorials of Liverpool*, Vol. I & II, 1875.

Hume, A., *Ecclesiastical History of Liverpool*, Liverpool, 1881.

Peet, H., *Two Centuries' Records of Liverpool Parish: Our Poor Law History*, Liverpool, 1898.

Hope, E.W., editor, *City of Liverpool: Handbook compiled for the Congress of the Royal Institute of Public Health 1903*, Liverpool, 1903.

Rushton, Edward jnr.(ed. by his son, W.L. Rushton), *Letters of a Templar 1820-50*, London, 1903.

Cunliffe, E.F., *Pages from the life of John Sparling of Petton*, Edinburgh, 1904.

Rathbone, E.F., *William Rathbone: A Memoir*, MacMillan, 1905.

Muir, Ramsay, *A History of Liverpool*, Liverpool University Press, 1907.

Blease, W.L., 'The Poor Law in Liverpool', *T.H.S.L.C.*, Vol. 61, 1908.

Bickerton, T.H., 'A Historical Sketch of Dr. John Rutter' in *Liverpool Medico-Chirurgical Journal*, Liverpool, 1910.

Pike, W.T., *Liverpool and Birkenhead in the Twentieth Century*, Brighton, 1911.

Murray, R.W., *Edward Alanson and His Times*, Liverpool, 1914.

Bickerton, T.H., *A Medical History of Liverpool*, Liverpool, 1936.

Mathews, G.W., 'John Bolton, a Liverpool Merchant 1756-1837, *T.H.S.L.C.*, Vol. 93, 1941.

Simey, M.B., *Charitable Effort in Liverpool in the Nineteenth Century*, Liverpool, 1951.

Chandler, G., *William Roscoe of Liverpool*, 1953.

Chandler, G., *Liverpool*, Batsford, London, 1957.

Whittingham-Jones, B., 'Liverpool's Political Clubs, 1812-1830', *T.H.S.L.C.*, Vol.111, 1959.

Murphy, James, 'The Rise of Public Elementary Education in Liverpool: Part One 1784-1818', *T.H.S.L.C.*, Vol. 116, 1964.

Schofield, M.M., 'The Virginia Trade of the Firm of Sparling and Bolden of Liverpool 1788-99', *T.H.S.L.C.*, Vol.116, 1964.

Taylor, F.H., *Liverpool and the Athenaeum*, Liverpool, 1965.

Sellers, I., 'William Roscoe, The Roscoe Circle, and Radical Politics in Liverpool, 1787-1807', *T.H.S.L.C.*, Vol. 120, 1968.

Channon, Howard, *Portrait of Liverpool*, Hale, London, 1970.

Maw, J.A., 'The History of Wavertree' (unpublished), 1974.

Liverpool Heritage Bureau, edited by, *Buildings of Liverpool*, Liverpool, 1978.

Waller, P.J., *Democracy & Sectarianism – A Political and Social History of Liverpool 1868-1939*, Liverpool University Press, 1981.

LIVERPOOL JOURNALS & PERIODICALS

Gore's General Advertiser.
The Hermes: a Literary, Moral and Scientific Journal.
Imperial Magazine.
Liverpolitan.
Liverpool Courier.
Liverpool Daily Post and Echo.
Liverpool Diocesan Review.
Liverpool Medico-Chirurgical Journal (1910).
Liverpool Mercury.
Liverpool Review.
The Porcupine.
Transactions of the Historical Society of Lancashire and Cheshire.
Williamsons Advertiser.

GENERAL

Locke, J. *An Essay Concerning Human Understanding, 1689,* Collins, Glasgow, 1689 (1984 edition).

Gibson, B., *Practical Observations on the Formation of an Artificial Pupil,* Cadell & Davies, London, 1811.

Brougham, Henry, *Observations on the Education of the People,* London, 1825.

Mill, James, Education, article in *Encyclopedia Britannica,* 1825.

Mill, J.S., *Utilitarianism,* 1853.

Mill, J.S., *On Liberty,* 1859.

Sutton, C.W., *Dictionary of National Biography,* 1885.

The Architect & Building News, London (October 7), 1932.

Cole M. & Padley, R., *Evacuation Survey,* 1940.

Dent, H.C., *The Education Act, 1944,* London, 1944.

Curtis, S.J., *History of Education in Great Britain,* London, 1950.

Berlin, I., *The Age of Enlightenment,* London, 1956.

Pollard, H.M., *Pioneers of Popular Education, 1760-1850,* 1956.

Walker, Kenneth, *The Story of Medicine,* London, 1959.

Hobsbawm, E.J., *The Age of Revolution,* Weidenfield & Nicholson, London, 1962.

LLechwedd Slate Caverns, 'Opening of David Francis's home to the public', press release 14 May, 1985.

Wynne Jones, Ivor, *Minstrels and Miners – The Life and Times of David Francis,* Gwynedd, 1986.

INDEX

317